C0-ATB-301

SOLOMON ZEITLIN: SCHOLAR LAUREATE

SOLOMON ZEITLIN: SCHOLAR LAUREATE

AN ANNOTATED BIBLIOGRAPHY, 1915 - 1970 WITH APPRECIATIONS OF HIS WRITINGS

by SIDNEY B. HOENIG

Yeshiva University

FOREWORD

by ZALMAN SHAZAR

President of the State of Israel

PUBLISHED BY

BITZARON, New York

Jointly With

DROPSIE UNIVERSITY

Alumni Association, Philadelphia

1971 — 5731

Library of Congress Catalog Card Number: 79-158450

First Edition 1971

This book is part of a series prepared under the General Editorship of Maurice E. Chernowitz.

Bitzaron, New York, N.Y. 10001

Distributed by Bloch Publishing Co.

Printed in the United States of America

תניא ר׳ ישמעאל ב״ר יוסי אומר: תלמידי חכמים כל זמן שמזקינין חכמה ניתוספת בהן, שנא׳ בישישים חכמה ואורך ימים תבונה.

(שבת קנב, א)

R. ISHMAEL, SON OF R. JOSE, SAID: *As scholars grow older, wisdom is added within them, for it is recorded* (JOB 12.12)—*'with the aged there is wisdom, and the long-lived possess understanding.'*

(SHABBAT 152A)

PREFACE

The world, in general, and Jewish communities, in particular, have experienced tremendous changes since 1914—a fateful year in modern history. Challenging philosophies—social, political, economic, and even spiritual—have erupted, necessitating new explanations and a reinterpretation of events, both ancient and modern. The destruction of six million Jews in Europe, the reestablishment of the State of Israel in its ancient homeland in the Near East, the desire for precise self-identification of the Jew in Israel and in the Diaspora, the attempt of the Vatican Council to remove the ancient accusation of Jewish responsibility for the Crucifixion (*deicide*), and the discovery of new Scrolls in the Judaean desert near the Dead Sea are only some of the major occurrences in the past five decades that have had a tremendous impact on intellectual activity, on research, and even on the perspectives for the relations between the Church and Synagogue. The impact of the new trends is evident to the man in the street as well as to the scholar in academic halls.

To understand the current aspects of the new world, recourse must naturally be had to the backgrounds and sources of the many perspectives, practices and philosophies that have operated throughout the centuries. These now call for better clarification and, as a result of the advances in academic research, even necessitate reevaluation.

"The scholar in his ivory tower" who has engaged in such reevaluation and who has contributed most to the understanding of the primary sources of Post-Biblical and Christian thought is Doctor Solomon Zeitlin, *Distiguished Professor of Post-Biblical Literature and Institutions* at Dropsie University in Philadelphia. Only now does the world begin to understand that the fountainhead, the deep well, and the flowing spring of the modern confrontation of Judaism and Christianity are to be found in the period of the Second Commonwealth—the age when the nature of Judaism was fixed, the time when Christianity emerged, the period of the parting of the ways, the era when rabbinic thought met the Graeco-Roman civilization. These combined elements formed the roots of the present-day world.

Professor Zeitlin has devoted more than a half-century, since 1914, to probing sources for these events. His essays are not merely academic, dry research or source-drilling. Aware of the modern problems affecting

Jew and non-Jew in this turbulent world, he has always probed with one distinct aim—to clarify and to correct, to explain and to guide—for a better understanding of the basic roots of the Judaeo-Christian civilization.

The present work in honor of Doctor Zeitlin is the result of admiration and esteem for a teacher who has influenced not only me, but numerous others who are now teaching in many universities and research institutes on several continents. His inspiring influence reaches back to my undergraduate days as his student in the Rabbi Isaac Elchanan Theological Seminary in New York City. After ordination, at the suggestion of the founder of Yeshiva College, the late Doctor Bernard Revel, who incidentally was the first graduate of Dropsie College, I, as a young student, sat at the feet of Professor Zeitlin in Philadelphia. It was under his guidance and sponsorship that I obtained my doctorate. In the many succeeding years I have always been very close to the master. The interchange of ideas, the examination of sources, and the close and friendly relationship of teacher and pupil (תלמיד-חבר) have continued to this very day.

It was felt that a volume such as this would bring the contributions of the scholar to the attention of the world. This book aims to provide a full comprehension of the original sources of Judaism and Christianity, and an interpretation of cognate facets. It may serve as a guide to the detailed analysis of Professor Zeitlin's many articles of research, which appeared in the *Jewish Quarterly Review* and in other journals. It will also aid pedagogically in displaying the advances in Jewish thought from the Haskalah period to the present day; for herein are not only Dr. Zeitlin's views, but also his incisive analyses of the opinions of his critics and opponents—of scholars, past and present, who disagree with him. Thus, we hope that this volume will serve as a basis for comparative investigation, giving the student the chance to weigh divergent perspectives. Dr. Zeitlin never says, "Accept my opinion" (קבלו דעתי). He only insists on serious research and scholarship that does not misinterpret or falsify the sources. Honesty, clarity, and basic proof are his incorruptible guidelines.

This volume is not merely bibliographical. The précis of each article, essay or book by Professor Zeitlin has been so designed as to give the reader an insight into the manifold problems of research and the conclusions that were reached. Yet, it is most important that the reader go back to the original article for all detailed proof and arguments. Only then can he make a definite comparison, if he wishes, with the deductions and conclusions of other scholars, and gain a deep insight into Professor Zeitlin's methodology and penetrating research. The attempt has been made to avoid repetition in the summaries. If in some of the articles Dr. Zeitlin repeated his views, it is only the newest idea (a *ḥiddush*), added by him later, that was included in a subsequent essay. The reason for the intensive expansion of the précis is due primarily to the desire to make this volume serve, not as a mere index to Dr. Zeitlin's writings, but rather as a reference work which students of the Second Commonwealth can use constantly as a direction for their own investigations and further studies. The Index of Subjects too, was planned purposely for student guidance. The numbers listed therein make reference to the many scholarly items elaborated upon in the original essay, which one can reread with benefit.

The bibliography, which constitutes the basis of this volume, was first prepared by Miss Miriam Stern who formerly served as secretary in the Library of the Dropsie College. The plan for its implementation was conceived by Mr. Maxwell Whiteman, the Librarian of the College, in 1965. A rearrangement of the bibliography was necessary, however, to bring it into chronological sequence. In 1948, in a review of a work containing a selected bibliography of the Jews in the Hellenistic world, Dr. Zeitlin stressed that a mere subject catalogue is insufficient. To assist students of the Hellenistic period, he held, it is important to make it more descriptive—i.e., to give some idea of its contents. It is this specific approach that is attempted in this compilation, and it is such a final, corrected, and full inventory that is published here.

The spelling of titles of the articles has not been changed despite apparent differences in renditions used in the summaries. At times, words such as synagogue, halakhah, scrolls, talmudic, amoraic, karaitic, etc., were introduced in capital letters to emphasize their importance in the given context. The reader will recognize their import.

Doctor Leo Landman, Secretary of the Faculty of Bernard Revel Graduate School of Yeshiva University and Doctors Jacob Reiner and Leon Stitskin, also members of its faculty, assisted in the summation of some articles and read some of the proofs. They, as myself, are disciples of Dr. Zeitlin. Miss Charlotte Eldot, my secretary, assisted in preparing the typescript. Mrs. Rochelle Leventhal helped arrange the Selected List of Hebrew Expressions. To all of them I am deeply grateful for their cooperation.

It is fitting that this volume open with a Hebrew message of congratulation from Zalman Shazar, President of the State of Israel, dealing with his reminiscences. He was Zeitlin's roommate and classmate in Baron David Günzburg's Academy in St. Petersburg in 1908. The words of greeting were originally intended to honor Professor Zeitlin in Jerusalem on the publication of his two volumes of history of the Second Commonwealth, and in response to the dedication of the book to the President. When I informed the President about the appearance of the present work, he sent his statement to be incorporated in these pages as our Foreword. I am most grateful to him. The affectionate friendship of the days of their youth continues with mutual feeling and attachment. The reunion of the two friends at *Bet ha-Nasi* in Jerusalem on November 1, 1970, when President Shazar was awarded an honorary degree from Dropsie University and received the doctoral hood from Professor Zeitlin, was most touching.

Dr. Philip Birnbaum and Dr. M. E. Chernowitz collaborated in the rendering of the Hebrew text into English, thus conveying the fond expressions of the President's message even to readers who may be unable to follow the beautiful classical Hebrew style of Zalman Shazar.

An essay by Dr. Abraham I. Katsh, the new President of Dropsie University, heads the section of "Recognitions." As a former student of Dr. Zeitlin, he expresses the respect and devotion that all of Dr. Zeitlin's disciples feel for their teacher. This is especially recorded in the Presidential Citation given him at a Convocation in Philadelphia in April, 1970. In like manner, the tribute of the Alumni Association of Dropsie University to its most illustrious member reveals the high praise every member has for Professor Zeitlin. The evaluation by Rabbi Joseph H. Lookstein, one of the first disciples of Dr. Zeitlin in the 1920's, demonstrates that the early inspiration has not lessened an iota.

The genius and the influence of Professor Zeitlin may be seen in the appreciations, concise and succinct, written by a number of his devoted students who have already become recognized as outstanding scholars in different disciplines: liturgy, Jewish history, rabbinics, Bible, law and historiography. I am deeply beholden to the authors for their participation in this tribute to their teacher, reflecting an earnest recognition of his exceptional learning. These words of appraisement are best summed up by the former Editor of the *Journal of Biblical Literature,* Professor Morton S. Enslin, who writes: "I am delighted to have a part in honoring a man whom I consider one of my choicest longtime friends." All their "papers" have helped considerably to make this volume in honor of Professor Zeitlin meaningful.

Thanks is especially due to Dr. Solomon Grayzel, Editor Emeritus of the Jewish Publication Society, who is currently a colleague of Dr. Zeitlin on the faculty of Dropsie University. Out of friendship and personal admiration for him, he read the manuscript and made stylistic suggestions.

The volume is dedicated to the memory of Senator Israel Stiefel of Pennsylvania who, in the years of his acquaintance with Dr. Zeitlin, became his ardent admirer and disciple, and who set aside funds for its publication. To his son, Mr. Jay Stiefel, thanks are expressed for carrying out his father's wish to promote scholarship.

In 1964, the Hebrew monthly *Bitzaron,* under the guidance of Dr. Maurice E. Chernowitz, first put out an issue dedicated to honor Dr. Zeitlin. The present work, too, summarizing the master's achievements, is being published under the friendly guidance of the Executive Editor of *Bitzaron.* The latter is responsible for the thorough Index of Subjects, which he carefully compiled and from a small nucleus brought up to its present size and fully serviceable content. Covering all the précis of the Annotated Bibliography, this detailed index will be found convenient by the scholar and the general reader alike, placing as it does at their instant command every topic and concept dealt with by Professor Zeitlin in a life span of scholarly writings—a welcome feature which should markedly enhance the reference value of the book. In addition, Doctor Chernowitz made significant revisions throughout the manuscript. A dedicated admirer and former student of Professor Zeitlin, ever ready with suggestions, he has been of indispensable assistance in his overall supervision of the painstaking operations and technical details involved in turning a rough draft into the finished book. For all this, I remain especially indebted to him.

Grants from the Alumni Association of Dropsie University, The Gustav Wurzweiler Foundation, Inc., The E. M. Black Foundation, The National Foundation For Jewish Culture, Mr. Emanuel Alexandre, and Mr. and Mrs. Joseph Liebowitz have made this book possible. Appreciation is expressed to all for facilitating the dissemination of a renowned scholar's teachings of more than a half century. Therewith the tradition of "cooperation of Issachar and Zebulun" (Gen. R. 72, 4) has again been greatly enhanced.

It is very becoming that this volume devoted to Professor Zeitlin's writings include as a Postscript his own most recent essay on scholarship and research. This is taken from the April 1970 (Vol. LXI, No. 4) issue of *JQR*, and is entitled "Eighty Years of the Jewish Quarterly Review," wherein Professor Zeitlin announced his retirement as Editor after full activity of thirty years, having assumed the editorship with Vol. XXXI, No. 1, in July 1940. He still continues as Chairman of the Editorial Board directing his student-colleagues in the furtherance of his work.

It is hoped that in the very near future, in a second edition of this volume, there will be an addendum of Dr. Zeitlin's most recent writings, for he is not laying aside his pen nor curbing the production of anticipated articles and books.

As now presented, this *Volume* is only a small token of our affection and reverence for the great teacher who has stimulated so much scholarly activity, raising many disciples to continue his labors. May the Almighty grant him many more years to guide, to teach, and to increase knowledge and fortify the truth.

SIDNEY B. HOENIG

Yeshiva University, New York City
Hanukkah 5731 — December 23, 1970

Contents

SOLOMON ZEITLIN: SCHOLAR LAUREATE

FOREWORD

By ZALMAN SHAZAR
President of the State of Israel

חסד נעורים

(אגרת ברכה לידיד נעורי ועתה זקן הפרופיסורים בדרופסי אוניברסיטה ומחבר „קורות בית שני", ד"ר שניאור זלמן צייטלין יצ"ו)

ידידי היקר והותיק, וחברי ללמודים, לפני כיובל שנים ויותר, בבית־המדרש הגבוה ללמודי היהדות של גדול מרכזי גולה בימים ההם, בקהלת ס. פטרסבורג, שאינה עוד זה כבר עשרות בשנים; אין יותר לא בית־המדרש ההוא ולא הקהילה ההיא, ואף המרכז היהודי הגדול עצמו התפורר, ונותק מגוף האומה בזרוע, והיה, חלילה, כלא היה. ואתה בינתים כבר לא אותו צעיר, סקרן צנוע ושוחר תורה, כאשר הכרתיך אז שם, כי אם נעשית מלומד יהודי מפורסם, בעל תריסין ובעל מוניטין, מורה המורים, העומד בראש במוסד מדעי גדול בלב המרכז של היהדות החדשה הזאת, שבכמותה מתמודדת עם יהדות רוסיה של אז ועלתה עליה, ואתה מרביץ שם תורה כבר עשרות בשנים, פוסק ופליג ומרעיש ארץ, וגידלת כבר תלמידים מובהקים, והנך עורך רבעון מדעי באנגלית לחכמת ישראל, ולא עוד אלא גם ממלא את המחברות של הרבעון בחדושי תורותיך, כמעין הנובע. כה תרבה וכה תוסיף!

האדע לספר לך איך השתאיתי וגם התגאיתי בלבי, כי את הכרך החדש של ספרך הגדול „קורות בית שני", שהוצאת השנה, בחרת להקדישו דוקא לי. אמנם בדברי ההקדשה שפרסמת בראש הספר תלית את הדבר באיצטלא שעטרתני בה כנסת מדינתנו, אבל לבי אומר לי כי לא רק זאת בלבד הניעתך לכך. הן לא הנשיא הראשון הנני למדינת ישראל. אין זאת כי בכבוד הזה חייב אני תודה לאותן השנים שישבנו בהן יחד על ספסל הלמודים ב„אקדמיה" ההיא, שרבנו הגדול דוד ב"ר הרץ גינצבורג ז"ל השכיל להקים בשלהי רוסיה הצארית, ואנחנו שנינו זכינו להיות בה — **בקומץ הראשון של תלמידיה**. מי פילל אז כי דוקא השנים ההן והשעורים ההם לא ימושו מזכרוננו כל השנים, וכי כעבור כששים שנה עוד ניועד שנינו כאן בבירת מדינת ישראל, ואתה את אוצרך המדעי תביא שי לחברך של אז?

ואכן. בעמוד 13 שבספרך אתה חוזר וכותב במפורש: „אני מקדיש ספר זה לידידי וחברי לכתה וכו׳. ויכוחינו בהיותנו תלמידי האקדמיה של הברון **גינצבורג בס. פטרסבורג רעננים עדיין בזכרוני. אני הייתי כבר אז מעונין**

בהיסטוריה של התלמוד ובמדה קטנה יותר בתולדות הבית השני, בעוד שהוא היה מעונין בתולדות התנועות המשיחיות. הוא היה כבר אז חסיד נלהב של תנועת העבודה הציונית אשר מטרתה הסופית — הקמת מדינה יהודית עצמאית בא״י וצדק לכל אדם״. אכן, לא טעיתי בהשערתי.

ואכן, יפה יפה זכורות לי עוד השנים ההן, הראשונות לחיי המבוגרים וכמעט האחרונות לכל יהדות רוסיה החפשית. אתה כבר היית אחד התלמידים המצויינים בקרב התלמודאים שבינינו. יחד אתך היו הראשונים לקבוצת התלמודאים, הסטודנט של האוניברסיטה בפטרסבורג, חוין, האחד מבינינו שהיה אח״כ לרב מטעם בהומל, ועם בוא הבולשביקים לוקח כבן ערובה ונהרג על קדוש השם, הי״ד; ולכל לראש ר׳ דוד כגן ילח״א, אז האברך הלמדן מראדין, ועכשיו המפורסם בינינו כהרה״ג הנזיר ר׳ דוד הכהן נ״י, ראש ישיבה במרכז הרב קוק זצ״ל, עורך „אורות הקודש״ שלו ועתה מחבר הספר המופלא „קול הנבואה״. כשהגיעו „האודיסאים״ (מי שהיו תלמידי „הישיבה הגדולה״ מיסודו של ה„רב־צעיר״), הופיעו ביניהם כתלמודאים מובהקים גם ידידי יהושע גוטמן ז״ל, שהיה צעיר ממך, ואתו חברנו יחזקאל קויפמן ז״ל, לאחר מכן חוקר התנ״ך, בעל „תולדות האמונה הישראלית״ ו„גולה ונכר״, שהיו פה שניהם פרופיסורים ידועים באוניברסיטה העברית בירושלים.

מדוע ועל מה ראה אלכסיי פבלוביץ׳ — האיש אשר הברון דוד גינצבורג מינהו על הבית, לזווג דוקא את שנינו לחדר אחד, רחב ידים, אשר ממול חדר ההרצאות, לא ידעתי. אבל בדיעבד שמחתי על שכנות זו ועל השיחות הארוכות ורבות הענין, שהתנהלו אז בין שתי המטות, זו שלצד מערב, שהיתה שלי, וזו שלצד צפון, שהיתה שלך. אינני זוכר כי אי־פעם רבנו אז בינינו גם כשהיינו מחולקים בדעות, וכי בכלל היו וכוחים סוערים בינינו, כאשר היו, למשל, ביני לבין חברינו צבי ווּיסלבסקי ויחזקאל קויפמן ז״ל, או אפילו עם הקרופניקים. אהבתי פשוט לשמוע לסיפוריך המרובים על הרבה ענינים יהודיים ולא יהודיים ועל ספרים שקראת בכל חדרי הספרות והעתונאות הרוסית.

זכורני כי הספרות העברית החדשה, שבה היינו אנחנו מעוגנים בראשנו וברובנו, וגם ספרות אידיש שאהבנו, ענינו אותך פחות. לעומת זאת ידעת יפה את הספרות הרוסית, העתיקה והחדשה. ובעיקר — לא היה דבר בתלמוד שלא ידעת אותו על בוריו. את המחקרים על התלמוד ידעת אז פחות והחשבת פחות, אבל את הש״ס הבבלי עצמו, ידעת „כמו שיודע אדם את סמטאות עירתו״. כך העידות אז על עצמך ללא שמץ של יוהרה. מתפלפל לא היית גם אז, ולא חיבבת את להטוטי „העלויים״ שבישיבות שביקרונו. זכורני, פעם אמרת לנו: „חכמי התלמוד הכותבים לועזית הם במחילת כבודם „עמי־הארצים״ גדולים, וחכמי התלמוד משלנו אינם מבינים כלום בתולדות התלמוד ובהיסטוריה של תקופת התלמוד״. ואכן, לא היה מה לקנא בת״ח רבני, שהיה בא ומגלה בפנינו איזה „כלל עיוני״ שחידש בדרכי הגמרא. אתה כאילו ישבת מן הצד ושמעת, אבל רק יצאנו אל המסדרון ובפיך שורה ארוכה של „הוכחות לסתור״, ממסכת זו וממסכת אחרת, המראות בעליל כי כל התיאוריה של המחדש בנויה על תוהו. לא היה אז בינינו כמוך „תנא ופליג״, וגם בין המתמידים לא נמנית אז. וכאילו

בלי כל יגע הציפו אותך מאליהן „ההוכחות לסתור", וללא כל כעס־רב, אלא מתוך איזה חיוך של לגלוג היית הורס את כל „ההכללות המלאכותיות" של המחדשים למיניהם.

נדמה היה לנו אז כי אתה „צנא דמלי סיפרי" (בבלי, מגילה כח, ב), אלא שאין בך כל צורך נפשי לקום ולהכניס סדר בכל הצנא הזה. ולפעמים נדמה היה לנו כי אין אתה גם בטוח ביותר, אם אמנם יש למצוא איזה סדר בכל „הצנא" הזה. ולשוא טורחים טרחיא. אכן, מעל לכל הפליא אותנו מאד כח הזכרון שלך. כל מה שקראת ושלמדת היה אצלך כאילו „מונח בקופסא", אלא לפעמים היה נדמה לנו, כי „הקופסא" היא לחוד, ואתה לחוד. ידיעתך את כל המונח בקופסא הפליאתנו מאד, אבל הזדהותך עם תוכן הקופסה לא היתה כה משכנעת. ולי היה אז נדמה לפעמים כי כח זכרונך הרב אינו אוהב גם לשים פדות בין דברים שראויים לזכירה ובין פרטים טפלים שלא כדאי כלל לזכרם. לוחות ופסלתם של לוחות היו מונחים כאחד באותה הקופסא — כעבור ימים רבים התאונן פעם בפני המנוח ר' נחום סוקולוב ז"ל, שהיה, כידוע, זכרן פנומנלי — כי לשוא משבחים אותו על סגולתו זאת, והוא, בעצם, רואה בכך מעין מגרעת, כי „*פשוט חסרה לי סגולת השכחה*". (בשפתו המיוחדת והציורית אמר לי זאת פעם, באחת ההפסקות בישיבות הועה"פ הציוני ששיעממו אותו מאד, לאמר: „יראה נא, אדוני, חושבני כי בשעה שכינס הקב"ה את הפמליא שלו להמלך בהם כיצד ליצרני, כמו שנאמר „נעשה אדם בצלמנו כדמותנו" — שכח כביכול להזמין להתיעצות זו את פורה שר השכחה, על כן נבצר מהשר פורה להביא גם את תרומתו ליצירה, כאשר זוכה לכך כל אדם, על כן יצאתי רחמנא ליצלן בעל מום, מעין בור סוד של ר' אליעזר בן הורקנוס, שאין זה כלל מעלה יתרה לגבי בעל הבור").

כאחד מבני השבט המיוחס ההוא של זכרנים גדולים ראיתיך אז, שנים רבות לפני שזימנה לי הציונות את הזכות להכיר את הנ"ס, אולי הגדול בקרב כל בעלי הזכרון שפגשתי.

ועל כן כה ברכתיך מאד על ספרך היסודי הזה „קורות הבית השני", שהקדשת בחברותך הנאה, ש' לי. כאן דוקא סגולת הבקיאות שלך צמצמה את עצמה, כדי לפנות מקום לאדריכלות של בנאות היסטורית, ויצא ההפסד בשכר רב. והבקיאות עצמה כידה הטובה עליך, גילתה רק את הברכה שבה לסייע למעשה של בנין מדעי רב ערך בהרצאת שלשלת של מאורעות התקופה המורכבה ההיא, ולא לפולמסנות של קטרוג, שכל כך הרבה שנים לא הרפתה ממך. אשריך, ידידי, שהתרוממת למפעל חייך זה, והלואי שתזכה להשלימו במלוא כחותיך ובכל צלילות הדעת שלך, בתנאים של שלום לארצנו ושגשוג לעמנו ובמזל של איזון הכחות והתעלות הרוח לכל התרבות האנושית, אמן.

לאחר הסתלקותו של רבנו הברון ד. גינצבורג ז"ל, בש' תר"ע, כשיצאנו עם ר' דוד הכהן (עתה הר"מ הנודע בשם „הנזיר") ועם המנוח שמואל שרירא (אח"כ בעל „המבוא לכתבי הקודש" ו„המבוא לתורה שבע"פ") לאוניברסיטה שבפרייבורג להשלים שם את למודינו, שמענו כי אתה יצאת לצרפת להכנס

לבית־המדרש לרבנים שבפאריס ולא שמעתי עליך ולא כלום, לא לפני מלחמת העולם ולא בכל שנות המלחמה. ימים הפרידונו וגם ימים סוערים מאד.

רק בסוף שנות העשרים כאשר התחלתי מזמן לזמן לבקר בארצות הברית כאורח נוטה לדון על עניני השעה שלנו, נודע לי שם כי אתה נעשית גברא רבא מאד בין המלומדים אשר בדרופסי וכי הנך שם פרופיסור לתורה שבע״פ. מאז עשינו לנו לחוק כי בכל ביקור שלי אשר כזה, היינו נועדים ליום אחד בניו־יורק לארוחת צהרים ומבלים יחד שעה ארוכה בשיחת רעים וברענון זכרונות נעורים, שהיו תמיד יקרים לשנינו.

אחרי הרבה שנים, כאשר קמה מדינת ישראל, ועל סף ימי התקומה עצמה קרה נס נוסף וידידנו המנוח, פרופיסור ל. סוקניק ז״ל — גם הוא חניך ומוכתר ד״ר של דרופסי בפילדלפיה ופרופיסור של האוניברסיטה העברית בירושלים — הצליח להשיג את כדי קומרן עם המגילות הגנוזות הראשונות, ואח״כ הלכו המגילות ורבו, ובנו, ידידי הפרופיסור יגאל ידין, מי שהיה הרמטכ״ל הראשון של צה״ל, התמחה יותר ויותר כארכיאולוג מצויין, ועשה גם פירסום לתגליות של אביו ושלו ושל חבריהם אתו, והרצה לפנינו כאן הרצאות מאליפות מאד עליהן — ופרץ הויכוח הגדול, נתפרסמת אתה כעומד בראש השוללים. לא התרעמתי כלל על עמידתך הביקורתית הזאת. גם אצלנו רבו המפקפקים בראשונה, ויש שהתמידו בהתנגדותם. וזכותם לכך אינה מוטלת בספק. ארצנו היא דמוקרטית ומחקרנו המדעי חפשי וגאותנו על כך. ומה גם שלפי עצם הענין עדיין רב הערפל מסביב לפרטי התגליות, ולא כל כך קל לקבוע מסמרות בכל הפרטים, אבל להט התנגדותך ושינוי הנימוקים־לסתור שלך חדשים לרבעונים החלו להזכיר לי במקצת את „התנא ופליג" של שנות נעורינו.

זכורני כי פעם, אחרי שטף „ראיותיך לסתור", שאלתיך בכל השקט, באין כל ציבור אתנו בשעת ארוחה בניו־יורק: נניח לרגע, לשם נוחות הברור, כי הצדק אינגו עם פרופי ידין, וכי כל היצירות שנתגלו במערות אינן שייכות לתקופת הבית השני, כדבריך, אבל הן תלמדנו אתה אימתי, לדעתך, נכתבו הן? ובאיזה פרק מפרקי תולדותינו צריך ההיסטוריון לשלבן? הלא לא בדה אותן פרופיסור סוקניק מליבו, והרי הן עתה לפנינו, לאיזה זמן אתה מציע ליחסן? ואני זוכר את חימת תשובתך החותכת: „אני אינני יודע. ואני אינני מחויב לדעת. אדרבא, יציעו זאת המוצאים הירושלמים. אני אינני היסטוריון של כל התקופות בישראל. אני היסטוריון של ימי בית שני, ותו לא! ואני אוכל לישבע לך בנקיטת חפץ, כי בכל מרחבי תקופת הבית השני, מגילות אלו לא היו ולא יכלו להיות".

מאליהן נסתתמו הטענות.

ועוד משהו לזכותך באותו הענין: בספר הגדול הזה שלפני, אין שמץ של טענה נגד חוקרי ירושלים בכל הענין הגדול הזה השנוי במחלוקת. ובפירוש הודעת בספר: „היה בדעתי לעסוק בכרך הזה במגילות ים המלח, כפי שהן נקראות, ברם מכיון וכו׳, חשבתי לנכון יותר לדחות את המסה אשר בה ידובר על הנושא הזה... לכרך הבא. אני מקוה להרצות שם על הסיבות שבגללן אין

המגילות יכולות לשמש כמקור לתולדות הבית השני". כלומר — כדין קדמונינו „הנותן מתנה לחברו בעין יפה נותן". וברוך טעמך, ידידי הותיק והיקר.

שא תודה וברכה, לאורך שנים בריאות וטובות. וצר מאד ללב, כי מכל רבותינו, שהיו ודאי שמחים על ההצלחה המדעית של תלמידם, אין כבר אף אחד אתנו בחיים, ואפילו מבין חברינו מאז לא נותרנו אלא מעט מן המעט... היה נא אתה לנו ברוך ומבורך. וכשם שזכית להסתכל בעיני רוחך במעלותיה ובמורדותיה של תקופת עצמאותנו השניה, כן תזכה נא לראות בעיני בשר, ומקרוב, את פלאי תקופת עצמאותנו השלישית, שעליה הובטח לנו, כי אין עמה חרבן עוד.

שלך, אסיר התקוה

זלמן שזר

FOREWORD

GREETINGS AND REMINISCENCES

By ZALMAN SHAZAR

President of the State of Israel

To my dear old friend and classmate of more than fifty years ago, Dr. Solomon Zeitlin, Distinguished Professor at Dropsie University and author of *The Rise and Fall of the Judaean State*:

We were both students at the Academy of Jewish Learning in the greatest center of the Diaspora in those days, namely the community of St. Petersburg. The Academy ceased to exist decades ago and even the great Russian Jewish center itself disintegrated, forcibly severed from the body of our people, as if well nigh vanished.

I remember you as that sprightly young man I knew then, inquisitive, unpretentious, a lover of learning. You have now become a famous Jewish scholar, a thinker of renown, a teacher of teachers, the most eminent member of a great institution of higher learning in the heart of the new Jewish center in America, which quantitatively has surpassed Russian Jewry of old. For decades you have been disseminating the knowledge of Torah, stimulating research, even disputing and causing great excitement in your studies. You have raised outstanding students, and all the while you have been serving as Editor of the scholarly *Jewish Quarterly Review,* which is devoted to primary Jewish learning. Furthermore, you grace each *Quarterly* issue with your ever-fresh notions, pouring forth with never-ending power like a veritable fountain-head, a bubbling spring. May you increase with verve and ever maintain this in the future!

Can I tell you how surprised and truly proud I was when you chose to dedicate to me the second volume of your great work, *The Rise and Fall of the Judaean State.* Recognizably, you based your dedication upon the position of honor which the Knesset had bestowed on me. Nevertheless, I am convinced that this fact alone was not what really motivated you. After all, I am not the first President of the State of Israel.

For your bestowal of this honor upon me I am more likely indebted rather to our student years together at the Academy, founded by our great teacher, Baron David Günzburg, son of Horace, toward the end of the Czarist regime. The two of us were then privileged to be among the first students. Who would have thought at that time that those years and those courses would never be blotted out from our memory, and that about sixty years later the two of us would meet again in Jerusalem, the capital city of the State of Israel, and that you personally would present your scholarly *opus magnum* to your colleague of old!

Indeed, in your Foreword to the book (page 13) you distinctly write as follows:

> Our discussions while students at the academy of Baron Günzburg in St. Petersburg are still vivid in my memory. I was already then interested in the history of the Talmud and, to a lesser degree, in the history of the Second Jewish Commonwealth, while he was interested in the history of the messianic movements, especially that of Sabbatai Zevi. Labor Zionism had already enlisted his enthusiastic support, the ultimate goals being the establishment of an independent Jewish State in the land of Israel, and justice for all people.

I dare say I was not too far from the truth in my projections.

I well remember those years, the first of my adult life and almost the last of a free Russian Jewry. Already then you were one of the foremost students among the talmudists in our midst. Together with you, in first rank, was Havin, a student at the University of St. Petersburg, who afterward became a crown rabbi in the community of Homel; with the advent of the Bolsheviks he was taken hostage and mercilessly killed. Also with you was David Kagan, outstanding then as the young Talmudic scholar of Radin and now famous as the eminent Rabbi David ha-Kohen, the *nazir,* Dean of the Merkaz ha-Rav Kook. He is editor of Rabbi Kook's *Orot ha-Kodesh* and now the author of that extraordinary work *Kol ha-Nevuah* (The Voice of Prophecy). Following this first class, there arrived the Odessa men. These were former students of the *Yeshiva Gedolah* of Rav Tzair (Chaim Tchernowitz). Among the recognized Talmudic students was Joshua Guttmann and along with him our mutual colleague, Yehezkel Kaufmann, both of blessed memory. The latter emerged as the Bible scholar, author of *Toledoth ha-Emunah ha-Yisraelit* (History of Jewish Faith) and of *Golah ve-Nekhar.* Both of these scholars served as prominent professors at Hebrew University in Jerusalem.

I still do not know why the steward of the Academy, Alexei Pavlovich, chose to pair us, to occupy one spacious room, facing the lecture hall. But, as it turned out, I was pleased with this proximity, which invited the weighty conversations that used to last through the night, carried on from the two beds, mine facing west and yours, you will recall, to the north. I cannot remember whether we ever actually quarrelled, even though we often held opposite views. Generally speaking, debates of a stormy nature, the kind of disputes that flared up, for example, between me and our colleagues Zvi Woyslavski and Yehezkel Kaufmann or even with the Krupniks, I believe, never occurred. I simply loved to listen to your detailed expositions on a variety of Jewish and non-Jewish subjects and about books you had read in all areas of Russian literature and journalism.

I remember that we were deeply involved in the new Hebrew literature, as well as the Yiddish literature which we loved, but these interested you less. On the other hand, you knew Russian literature well, both old and new. Above all, there was not a thing in the Talmud that you did not know to perfection. However, you paid slight attention to works about the Talmud, at that time. The Babylonian Talmud itself, as you had studied it in your home-town and in the many years thereafter, you knew "as one might know the paths and by-paths of his own quarter." You demonstrated this eminence without any conceit even then. You were not a quibbler; you were not fond of the jugglery of the yeshivah "boy wonders," the so-called *iluyim,* who joined us. I remember that you once remarked: " Many 'experts' who write on the Talmud in their own vernacular are big *am-haratsim,* while our own *talmidei hakhamim* do not understand at all the development of the Talmud and the history of the Talmudic era." Indeed, a rabbinic student was not at all to be envied when he revealed and expounded to us some "theoretic principle" he had innovated in the analysis of the Gemara. You used to sit on the side and listen, but no sooner had we emerged into the corridor than you gave expression to a long chain of "contradictory proofs," drawn from one Tractate or another, showing clearly that the entire theory of the innovator was based purely on nought—on thin air. Among us, there was no one like you, to be acknowledged as "an authority with the right to disagree." In fact, you were then not counted among the assiduous and indefatigable students known as *masmidim.* To the contrary, from your keen intellect the "contradictory proofs" would suddenly emerge without, as it were, any apparent effort on your part and without even much fury. It seemed to me as if only with the same sort of scornful look you demolished all those "artificial generalizations" of the different innovators.

To us then you were always a kind of "Talmudic storehouse," a veritable walking Talmudic encyclopedia, minus even the need to introduce some sort of order in this storehouse of knowledge. In vain were the efforts of those who tried. At times it occurred to us that you were not too sure yourself that some order could at all be found inside that "storehouse." But above everything else, your phenomenal memory amazed us. Whatever you read or studied was permanently deposited within you as in a kind of "filing cabinet." Occasionally, however, it seemed to us that you and that "filing cabinet" were two separate and distinct entities. On the one hand, your *knowledge* of the contents stored in the "cabinet" astonished us to the extreme; on the other hand, your personal *identification* with the contents was not always so convincing. To me it seemed at that time that occasionally your powerful memory even disdained to discriminate between matters worth remembering and insipid trivia that did not at all deserve recalling. As a result, not tablets alone but even the waste chips of tablets were faithfully stored in that filing cabinet of yours, equally, side by side.

I recall that many years later, the late Nahum Sokolow, known to possess a phenomenal mnemonic faculty, once complained to me that he was being extolled rather undeservedly for this capacity. He, to the contrary, regarded his memory essentially as a defect, exclaiming: "I simply lack the ability to forget." In his picturesque style, Sokolow told this to me when he felt bored, during an intermission at the sessions of the Zionist Executive. "Look here, my friend," he said, "I think that when the Creator assembled His retinue of heavenly angels to consult them how to fashion me (as it is written, 'Let us make man in our own likeness, to resemble us'), the Omniscient One, to my great distress, forgot to invite Pura, the celestial angel of forgetfulness, to participate in that consultation. Hence Pura was not in a position to make his contribution to my creation, as in the case of other privileged human beings. I therefore emerged a cripple, as it were, something like the cemented cistern which loses not a drop, a characterization applied to Rabbi Eliezer ben Hyrcanus. This is not at all an advantage so far as the owner of the cistern is concerned."

I already envisaged you in those early years as one of those belonging to that noble tribe of great mnemonists. This was many years before Zionism afforded me the privilege of meeting Nahum Sokolow, perhaps the most remarkable of men with a prodigious memory that I have ever encountered.

I again congratulate you most heartily upon the appearance of a work of fundamental importance on the history of the Second Commonwealth, which, prompted by our comradeship, you so kindly dedicated to me. It is apparent that despite the vast knowledge at your command, you restricted yourself to this specific period so as to be able to attend to the architectonic organization of historical structure. The loss has been offset by a great gain. Your extraordinary erudition with which you are especially blessed has succeeded in constructing in this history a valuable scientific edifice, displaying the chain of events during that complex period, without resorting to polemics, a characteristic of yours for so many years. You should consider yourself fortunate, my friend, that you are achieving your life work. May you be privileged to complete it with fullness of vigor and clear-mindedness, under conditions of peace for our country and flourishing progress for our people, and under the banner of strength and spiritual elevation, with universal salvation for all mankind.

Following the death of our teacher, Baron David Günzburg, of blessed memory, in the year 1910, I left, together with Rabbi David ha-Kohen (now the *nazir*) and the late Samuel Sherira (the author of *An Introduction to the Holy Scriptures* and *An Introduction to the Oral Law*), to enter the University of Freiburg, in order to complete our education. News then reached us that you had departed to enter the École Rabbinique in Paris. Since then I heard nothing about you, neither before the First World War nor through the years of its duration. Indeed, a period of very stormy days separated us.

It was only toward the end of the twenties, when I began to visit the United States, from time to time, to discuss cogent matters of Zionism, that I discovered that you had become illustrious among the scholars at Dropsie College and that you served there as Professor of Talmud. We since made it a rule to meet during each of my visits to New York. We would meet by appointment for lunch in New York, spending the hour or two together in most friendly conversation, always refreshing the youthful memories, so dear to both of us.

After many years, when the State of Israel emerged, an additional miracle occurred as our late mutual friend, Professor L. Sukenik—also a graduate of Dropsie College and later Professor at Hebrew University of

Jerusalem—succeeded in obtaining the Qumran jars with the first hidden Scrolls. These finds increased in number, and his son, my good friend, Professor Yigael Yadin, who had been the first Chief of Staff of the Israel Army, now specialized ever more therein as an excellent archeologist, and publicized the discoveries of his father as well as his own findings and those of his colleagues, lecturing constantly and informatively about them. The *great controversy* then burst forth. You soon became famous as the chief opponent. I did not at all resent this critical attitude of yours.

As we know, in this phase of the Scroll discoveries there were many skeptics at the outset, here in Israel too. Some have persisted in their opposition; their right to do so is not questioned. Our country is democratic and our academic research is free. We are proud of it, all the more so, in view of the fact that the very subject of the Scrolls is still basically beclouded as to the details surrounding their discovery. It is not an easy matter to nail down hard and fast conclusions in precise detail. The fervor of your opposition and your on-going arguments, aiming at refutation, as they freshly appeared in each of the *Jewish Quarterly Review* issues, began to remind me of the temperament of that "disagreeing authority" of our youthful years.

I recall that once, after you had disseminated an uninterrupted flow of proofs to the contrary, I quietly asked you, during a meal in New York, with no other person present: "Let's assume for a moment, for the sake of argument and clarification, that Professor Yadin is not right and that all the Scrolls discovered in the caves do not, as you maintain, belong to the period of the Second Temple, in that case please inform us precisely *when*, in your opinion, were the Scrolls written? To what period of our history should the historians relegate them? Surely, Professor Sukenik has not made these up in his own head. Here we are with the Scrolls before us. Now, just to what period would you say they belong?"

I well remember your intense, determined reply: "*I do not know, and I am not obliged to know.* To the contrary, let the Israeli discoverers propose it. *I am not a historian of 'all' the periods of Jewish history. I am a historian of the period of the Second Commonwealth,* and no more! I could swear to you, solemnly, that these Scrolls were not of any part of the entire time span of the Second Commonwealth and they could not be." Whereupon, my questions were automatically silenced.

There is one more thing to be mentioned to your credit. In your volume, now before me, which you have presented to me as a gift, there appears not a single item of argument against the Jerusalem scholars touching on this battle of the Scrolls. You have explicitly declared in your Foreword:

> It was my intention to deal with the so-called Dead Sea Scrolls in this volume. Since, however, some protagonists of the antiquity of the scrolls have actually identified their authors with the Zealots-Sicarii [sic] and the early Christians, it seemed to me to be more appropriate to postpone to the next volume the excursus in which this subject, including these groups, will be treated. I hope there to set forth the reasons why the scrolls cannot be used as sources for the history of the Second Jewish Commonwealth or for the beginnings of Christianity .

Verily, in accordance with the rule set down by our ancient Sages, "When a person presents a gift to his colleague, he should do so in a generous spirit." Blessed be your courteous approach, my dear old friend.

Accept my thanks, greetings, and blessings for long years of health and happiness. It is to be deeply regretted that none of our old teachers, who certainly would have been most happy over the scholarly success of their student, is alive to be with us today. Even from among our former colleagues, few have survived.

Be benignly blessed for us, and by us, my friend. Just as you have been privileged to probe spiritually the duration of the *Second Jewish Commonwealth,* may you also be favored to perceive physically, and at close range, the wonders of the era of our *Third Commonwealth*—the State of Israel, concerning which, we have been promised, "no ruin shall befall it."

With affectionate ties of hope,

ZALMAN SHAZAR

Translation: M. E. Chernowitz and P. Birnbaum

PORTRAITS

Dr. Zeitlin presenting his latest book to President Shazar
at **Bet ha-Nasi**, Jerusalem.

Zalman Shazar receiving an honorary degree from Dropsie University. From left to right, Prof. Zeitlin placing the doctoral hood on President Shazar in the presence of Dr. Katsh, President of Dropsie University.

RECOGNITIONS

A SCHOLARS' SCHOLAR

By ABRAHAM I. KATSH

Dropsie University

Scholars are the lifeblood of the academic world. They are preservers of knowledge, men who light the way to broader intellectual horizons, the links of wisdom between the generations. Indeed, the true measure of the greatness of an institution of higher learning is not its size or its wealth, but rather the caliber of its scholars.

The man whom this volume honors is one of those rare individuals who is a scholars' scholar. Dr. Solomon Zeitlin has been an integral part of Dropsie University's family of scholars for more than five decades as student, alumnus, and professor. He has been an unfailing inspiration to his students and colleagues in the pursuit of original and genuine scholarship. He has authored books, articles and reviews at a pace equal to that of an entire staff of departments of History and Rabbinics. If it is true that the academic world is ruled by the maxim "publish or perish," then Professor Zeitlin is virtually immortal!

Zeitlin epitomizes all the attributes enumerated by each of the disciples of Rabban Johanan ben Zakkai who, when asked which are the best qualities for a man to possess, replied: a good eye, a good colleague, a good neighbor, foresight, and a good heart. A man of true vision, a seeker after truth in the tradition of the ancient Hebraic scholars, Dr. Zeitlin's wisdom is revered throughout the world. His reputation as the leading authority on the Second Commonwealth derives from a lifetime of research, and from numerous essays and brilliant volumes, spanning more than a half-century.

His style is lucid; his insights into Talmudic sources are profound. As a scholar, he is a phenomenon—full of depth and originality; as a teacher, he is effervescent with challenge and with humanity; as a friend, he is sincerely devoted with all his heart.

His writings—essays, books, articles—are always enlightening; in them one discovers new ideas, brilliant thought dealing with sources that have eluded others. One learns better to appreciate the continuity of Jewish history that emerges from the pages he has produced.

Dr. Zeitlin's disciples are legion and are to be found all over the globe. He keeps in touch with them regularly, always the mentor, the guide, the advisor, the friend.

His two recent volumes bear testimony to his genius, to his originality in interpretation and investigation, and to his penetrating mind. With the skill of an architect he reconstructs the history of the Second Commonwealth based on original sources. He casts aside interpretations drawn by other historians who had relied on secondary sources. The result is a work that gives a truer understanding of Jewish life in a vital period of Jewish history. He is the kind of person who is fearless in his scholarship and believes that "in scholarship majority does not rule."

I have known Dr. Zeitlin as a teacher, colleague, and a valued friend. From the perspective of my long association with this institution, and my more recent post as President, I can attest to the strength and greatness that Dropsie University has derived from him as a scholar and as a man. Solomon Zeitlin has indeed enriched Jewish learning and learning generally as well. It was a great honor to bestow upon him at the Sixtieth Anniversary celebration of Dropsie University, the first Presidential Citation:

April 14, 1970

> When you began teaching at The Dropsie University in 1925, you were already a loyal alumnus with the degree of Doctor of Philosophy, Class of 1917.
>
> In the historic development of The Dropsie University as the foremost academy of higher Jewish learning in America and as Editor of the *Jewish Quarterly Review,* and Editor-in-Chief of the Jewish Apocryphal Literature, your vision and extraordinary erudition have been a great moral force. Your recent volumes are definitive studies on the history of the Second Commonwealth.
>
> Many attributes grace your accomplishments and kindness of character: scholar of scholars, teacher of teachers, humble sage full of vision, depth and imagination, you have remained the true mentor, the challenging guide, the creative advisor and the loyal and faithful friend.
>
> In quality of mind, heart, and character you are the true incarnation of the classic period of the great Talmudists who have inspired students with zeal for original research and the pursuit of knowledge. You lighted their path for study and kindled their excitement for the fountain of learning.

> The Dropsie University has already shown its appreciation by bestowing upon you in 1957 the degree of Doctor of Laws, *honoris causa.* Other institutions of higher learning have done likewise.
>
> Mine is a special privilege to award my teacher in affectionate esteem the first *Presidential Citation of The Dropsie University.*

The present volume bespeaks the admiration of Dr. Zeitlin's colleagues, disciples, and friends. Dr. Sidney B. Hoenig, its author, deserves our thanks for his labor of love—a tribute of a devoted student to his master.

TRIBUTE

By ELAZAR GOELMAN

President of the Alumni Association of Dropsie University

It is with a deep sense of pride and with much pleasure that the Alumni Association of Dropsie University joins *Bitzaron* in publishing the Bibliography of its most illustrious member, Professor Solomon Zeitlin.

If anyone has lived up to the advice of the Men of the Great Assembly to "raise many students," it was Dr. Zeitlin. For over five decades of teaching he succeeded in raising and developing several generations of Jewish scholars. Concurrently, by his unremitting insistence upon direct and personal contact with the sources, he advanced the cause of "Jüdische Wissenschaft" in its highest sense.

A prolific writer with intimate rabbinic versatility and keen historical insight, he enriched our scholarly literature to an unprecedented degree. In his fearless pursuit of truth, Dr. Zeitlin displayed utter disregard for unfounded newspaper headlines and unsubstantiated sensational claims. His simple, uncomplicated and unmatched dedication to eternal verities won him formidable adversaries and devoted disciples and admirers. It is no wonder that those who really know him are high in their praise for his personal integrity as well as his democratic spirit and genuine friendliness.

Because Dr. Zeitlin was adamant in refusing personal ephemeral honors, the members of the Alumni Association of Dropsie University who were privileged to benefit from their great teacher's תורה שבעל פה, decided to make his written contributions available to the wider community of scholars. In the spirit of great merit, מגלגלין זכות ע"י זכאי, it is most appropriate that this labor of love was done by a prominent member of the Dropsie Alumni, Dr. Sidney B. Hoenig, a loyal disciple of the wise Professor Solomon Zeitlin. We are grateful to him for his devoted task.

"LET YOUR EYES BEHOLD YOUR TEACHER"

By JOSEPH H. LOOKSTEIN

Yeshiva University

The quotation from Isaiah 30:20 which provides the title for this essay is not complete. The verse is preceded by another statement which is extremely significant. It is: *"Velo yikonef od morecho,"*—"Your teacher shall not be removed into a corner . . ."

This prophetic assertion is in a sense a characterization of my esteemed teacher, Professor Solomon Zeitlin. It could never be said of him that he was "removed in a corner." Great scholar that he is, he never allowed himself to become cloistered or isolated from the teeming life about him.

In this respect he followed an ancient tradition associated with the prophets of old. When Saul went in search of Samuel, he and his company inquired, "Is the seer here?" He and his companions were told, ". . . As soon as you come into the city, you will immediately find him."

The seer of former days is replaced by the scholar of today. The scholar would prefer solitude and seclusion in order to pursue his study and research. This, however, is a luxury that our turbulent days can hardly afford. The study of the modern scholar dare not be a sanctuary hermetically sealed off from the world and its challenges, its problems and perplexities. In the language of Scripture, ". . . As soon as you come into the city, you will immediately find him."

Such a scholar is Professor Zeitlin. The Jewish world is his classroom; the Jewish people are his students; and Jewish national anxieties are his scholarly concern.

When Reconstructionism expounded its philosophy of Judaism, Professor Zeitlin countered with a profound article entitled "Judaism as a Religion." When Toynbee questioned the historic rights of the Jewish people to Palestine, Professor Zeitlin, marshalling irrefutable historic evidence, proved Toynbee guilty of malicious error. When the vexing issue of "Who Is A Jew?" arose, Professor Zeitlin did not remain silent and spoke his mind with the authority of the concerned Jew and the consummate historian.

When the Ecumenical Council sought to correct a millenial wrong, it was Professor Zeitlin who criticized those who rejoiced in the thought that the Messiah of Brotherhood had finally arrived. He proved that there was still a long and difficult road ahead before the errors of history would be righted. His volume, *Who Crucified Jesus?,* is the learned documentary support for his scholarly position.

Then came the battle of the Dead Sea Scrolls. Here Professor Zeitlin proved himself an intrepid warrior, a scholarly gladiator. He was and remains *unus contra multos.* The arsenal of scholarly weapons that he used was evidence of his wide and extensive learning and simultaneously of his fearlessness even of scholarly opponents. Above all it was a further demonstration that here was a historian preoccupied with the past but alert to the problems of the present. His field of specialization may be the ancient world of the Second Jewish Commonwealth, but he remains equally concerned with the throbbing problems of the contemporary world.

This worldliness of Professor Zeitlin manifests itself in a more personal way. He is an aesthete. He loves culture in all of its forms. He is a lover of the opera and of music in general. He is a connoisseur of art and somehow finds time to visit museums and expositions the world over. He is a confirmed and inveterate traveler. If one were to classify him geographically he would have to say that Professor Zeitlin, for all his years in America, remained continental in his bearing, gracious in his conduct, and a gentleman to the manner born.

I was a student in the first class that he taught at the Rabbi Isaac Elchanan Theological Seminary long before Yeshiva University came into being. The school building was a small and modest structure on Montgomery Street on the old East Side of Manhattan. I recall how the young, slight and slim Solomon Zeitlin walked into our study room. It was the first lecture in Jewish history that many of us heard. Our curriculum was heavily weighted in the direction of Talmud which was almost the sole subject that occupied our time and attention. The course in Bible given by Doctor Moshe Seidel and the course in Jewish history by Doctor Zeitlin were the only two non-Talmudic courses to which we were exposed.

That first lecture and the many that followed over the years gave us a new insight into the up-to-then obscure world of the Talmud. We all loved our *Gemara* and it rarely left our hands or our sight. But some of us, in our imagination, saw the sages of the Talmud, from Hillel the Elder to Rav Ashi, seated on either side of an endlessly long table engaged in continuous dispute on a variety of involved subjects that had no immediate relevance to us. Their words were, of course, holy to us, but they themselves were dim images, sacred images to be sure, but dim none the less.

Doctor Zeitlin transformed those images into personalities, into living and vital presences. He placed them for us into proper perspective and made their opinions important for us as they were significant for their own day. Indeed, he taught us how to take our first strokes in the vast "sea of the Talmud." Strange, how a historian should so successfully supplement the work of a Rosh Yeshiva!

In time, other distinguished scholars of non-Talmudic disciplines joined the faculty of the Rabbi Isaac Elchanan Theological Seminary. Professor Isaac Husik came weekly to lecture on Jewish Philosophy. Doctor Pincus Churgin, of blessed memory, became the permanent head of the Teachers Institute and taught regular courses in Jewish history and Hebrew Literature at Yeshiva proper. Professor Nahum Slousch was invited as a visiting lecturer in his chosen field. Eventually the renowned Binyamin Menashe Levine was engaged to teach Geonic Literature.

But Professor Zeitlin was the pioneer and trail blazer who paved the way for all these distinguished scholars. What an illustrious company this was! They made possible the ultimate development of a Yeshiva into a great and comprehensive Yeshiva University. Only a Professor Zeitlin, essentially a *yeshiva bochur* himself, could serve as a forerunner to such eminent followers.

In time Professor Zeitlin became to all of us not alone a teacher but a friend. If a personal memoir is in order, I would not hesitate to express pride in the knowledge that I enjoyed my beloved teacher's friendship. He held me by the hand, as it were, as I took my first steps on the path of rabbinic scholarship, and taught me the fundamentals of scientific research. I found a *rav* and a *chaver* in one person, a teacher and a friend in a single personality. I retain profound reverence for the teacher and I cherish everlasting gratitude to the friend.

On June 15, 1965 I had the high privilege of presenting Professor Solomon Zeitlin to President Samuel Belkin of Yeshiva University so that he may confer upon him the honorary degree of Doctor of Humane Letters. On that occasion I delivered the Citation which follows:

Mr. President:

During the Second Jewish Commonwealth, normative Judaism, which is the substance and spirit of our faith, achieved its definitive character. One must comprehend that golden era of our history in order to understand the spirit of our eternal culture.

Before you is an acknowledged and respected authority of that period. He had done everything concerning the Second Jewish Commonwealth—except to restore it. He is the keen and resourceful historian, Professor Solomon Zeitlin.

He was educated in the traditional schools of his native Vitebsk in Russia, continued at the University of Paris and later at the École Rabbinique, from which he received Rabbinic Ordination and a Doctorate in Theology. In 1915 he came to this land and two years later received his Ph.D. from Dropsie College in Philadelphia.

Then began a glorious career as teacher and researcher. His first post was in the Rabbi Isaac Elchanan Theological Seminary which eventually blossomed into the Yeshiva University of today. Simultaneously he was appointed Professor of Rabbinic Law and Lore at Dropsie College and has served there for nigh forty years.

He is a brilliant teacher; exciting, stimulating, exacting, yet loving and beloved. Many disciples sat at his feet, drank of his scholarly waters and took their first plunge in the trackless sea of research under the watchful and encouraging eye of their master.

His *magnum opus* is the *Rise and Fall of the Judaean State.* But thirteen other works of equal importance came from his prolific mind and pen. Some three hundred of his articles, written in Hebrew, English, French and Russian appeared in scholarly journals the world over.

Those of us who are privileged to regard him as our teacher, salute him this day and rejoice to see him at the high altar of this sanctuary about to receive the academic benediction that his ministrations have earned.

I have the honor, sir, to present Solomon Zeitlin for the degree of Doctor of Humane Letters, *honoris causa.*

This condensed evaluation of my esteemed teacher continues to be my heartfelt tribute to him.

DOCTOR SOLOMON ZEITLIN: SCHOLAR LAUREATE

By SIDNEY B. HOENIG

Yeshiva University

Professor Zeitlin's pupils know him as a stimulating teacher; the scholarly world characterizes him as a stubborn controversialist; everyone agrees that he is one of our most learned, productive, and penetrating scholars. Mildness, modesty and helpfulness endear him to his friends and students; but where he believes that truth is involved, he fights, without fear or favor, even those for whom he has respect and, verily, affection. His numerous books and articles offer ample proof both of his ability to clarify a problem and his readiness to defend his viewpoint.

A. *Student and Teacher*

Solomon Zeitlin was born in Russia, Erev Shabuot 1892, into a family noted for its devotion to scholarship. Joel Zeitlin, his father, was a devout ḥasid and he named his son Shneur-Zalman, after the founder of the ḤaBaD movement. To this day, Professor Zeitlin has remained close to the Lubavitch viewpoint.

His earliest studies were of the traditional kind. He still recalls vividly his "reden in lernen," his discussion in Talmud with R. Joseph Rozin (the Rogochover) and R. Meir Simḥa of Dvinsk. His early rabbinic "lomdes" taught him not only to absorb the text, but also to penetrate deeply into its meaning. Before long he became interested in the application of modern methods to the old texts. At the age of seventeen Zeitlin made his way to St. Petersburg where, in 1908, Baron David Günzburg had opened, in his palatial home, an Academy for courses in Oriental Studies. Zeitlin enrolled in this institute and roomed with Zalman (Rubashov) Shazar, destined to become the third President of Israel. The teachers in the institute, in addition to its founder, were Simon Dubnow, Judah Loeb Katzenelson (Buki ben Yogli), Mark Wischnitzer, and Isaac Dov Ber Markon. Here again, as in his early Talmudic studies, the emphasis was on breadth of knowledge and penetrating insight. He also spent hours in learned discussions with Daniel Chwolson in that city.

From St. Petersburg, Zeitlin went to Paris, where he enrolled, in 1912, at the École Rabbinique. Among his teachers in Paris were Israel Lévi and the Reinach brothers, Théodore and Salomon. At the same time, he took courses at the Sorbonne where his fellow students were Jean Juster, already working on his *Les Juifs dans l'empire romain,* and Isaac Halevi Herzog, later to become Chief Rabbi of Israel. Zeitlin left Paris in the summer of 1914 and went to Berlin, where he made contact with Professors Ismar Elbogen, Hermann Cohen, Eugen Mittwoch, Eugen Täubler, Julius Guttmann, and Rabbi Leo Baeck. With the outbreak of World War I, his stay in Berlin became difficult. Within the year, he made his way to Denmark and thence to the United States.

He soon enrolled in the Dropsie College for Hebrew and Cognate Learning, in Philadelphia, the only nonrabbinic school for higher Jewish learning in the United States. Dr. Cyrus Adler was then president of the College, and among its small faculty were Professors Henry Malter and Max L. Margolis. The former was the man under whose guidance Zeitlin earned his doctorate in 1917. At Dropsie, too, he met Dr. Bernard Revel, the first graduate of the College, who soon became the Rosh Yeshiva of the Rabbi Isaac Elchanan Theological Seminary. As the Yeshiva was taking the first steps toward broadening its curriculum, Dr. Revel invited Zeitlin to join his faculty as Professor of History. Zeitlin occupied this chair for a good many years, until Dr. Adler invited him to take the chair left vacant at Dropsie College by the death of Professor Malter. For some years, Dr. Zeitlin taught at both institutions; after 1935 he limited himself to Dropsie College.

Above all, Zeitlin sought to encourage research and formulate standards in Jewish scholarship. This desire prompted him to join the coterie of scholars in 1919 to found the American Academy of Jewish Research together with Professors Louis Ginzberg, Israel Davidson, Israel Friedlander, Alexander Marx of the Jewish Theological Seminary, Jacob Lauterbach and David Neumark of the Hebrew Union College, and Henry Malter of Dropsie College. He was very active in the first years of the Academy's existence.

B. *The Creative Mind*

All this time, a steady flow of monographs—books and articles—came from Dr. Zeitlin's pen. His first article was written back in his Paris days, though the war interfered with its publication so that it did not appear in the *Revue des Études Juives* till 1917. Called "Les Dix-huit mesures," (The Eighteen Enactments), it foreshadowed his abiding interest in Talmudic legislation and in the contacts between Jews and non-Jews during the early centuries of the Common Era. His doctoral dissertation at Dropsie College was on *Megillat Taanit,* which dealt with the same period. The primary area of Zeitlin's scholarly productivity has remained the period of the Second Commonwealth, especially its latter half. A major part of his scholarly activity continued to be the effort to clarify the historical background of Talmudic discussion and legislation. To prepare himself for its legal aspects, he took courses at Columbia University with Dean Harlan F. Stone (late Chief Justice of the Supreme Court) who encouraged him in his research. The resultant article, "Intention as a Legal Principle," was dedicated to his teacher, Professor Israel Lévi, on the occasion of his election as Grand Rabbin de France. In the article Zeitlin points out that many have striven to discuss Talmudic law, but their discussions lacked consideration of historical development and a recognition of the dividing line between tannaitic and amoraic jurisprudence. It thus combined various aspects of Talmudic and general-jurisprudence research.

It should be noted that this study was expounded while Dr. Zeitlin was teaching at the Rabbinical College, now Yeshiva University. Soon he extended his work into closely allied fields, such as the literature of the Inter-Testamental period and the beginnings of Christianity, in both of which areas he produced a considerable number of articles. His very important book, *Who Crucified Jesus?* which appeared in 1941, represents a new and epoch-making approach to that important discussion.

Zeitlin's method of research and analysis is far from being one of dry scholarship. In the first place, he is very much interested in the human approach to the past; history is the story of people. To achieve historical knowledge one must recreate the life of the past, not merely study its documents. A critical edition of a literary work, for example, is hardly enough. It is necessary to go beyond textual accuracy into the spirit of the work. Sometimes internal evidence may even discredit a presumably well-established reading. Textual scholarship should not be mechanical, but creative.

This insistence on the broadest possible knowledge of background accounts for Zeitlin's fresh approach to the study of the origins of Christianity. He has consistently maintained that a thorough knowledge of the early tannaitic literature is indispensable for a proper grasp of the

Gospels and the early Church. Scholars, whether Jews or Christians, cannot otherwise properly understand "the Parting of the Ways, Josephus and Philo scarcely being enough. By the same token, he recognizes that one must know world history to understand Jewish history. It is therefore not surprising that his knowledge of Greek and Latin sources is wide indeed.

Appealing to the sources—to which any one of Professor Zeitlin's pupils will testify—is the chief characteristic of his method of teaching. Accuracy ahead of originality—to the edification of his pupils, he weighs the work of scholars by their use or misuse of source material. Naturally, he insists on the historical approach to, and clear distinctions among, tannaitic, amoraic, and geonic material.

Hasty evaluation of material is for him a cardinal sin. This is the reason for his vehement and persistent criticism of the widespread and unquestioning acceptance of the authenticity of the Dead Sea Scrolls. On an earlier occasion, Zeitlin had for years insisted that the Christ passage in Josephus was an interpolation. He stuck to this attitude despite the opposition of many great scholars, and he was eventually proven right.

No doubt Dr. Zeitlin loves to do battle; this is evident in any number of his articles on a great variety of subjects. But his arguments have always been *l'shem Shammayim,* for the sake of Heaven, in the search of truth.

C. *The Uses of History*

History has had for Zeitlin an element of eternity. The past never dies; it must live in the historian as it lives in the events and in the institutions of the present. He maintains that the purpose of writing history is not to show what Jews contributed to the world. Rather, it should be demonstrated what Judaism is and how its history developed. It is the historian's duty to search for the past for the sake of clarifying and stimulating the present. Dr. Zeitlin's fascination with the continuity in Jewish history has led him to investigate eras later than the Second Commonwealth, which has nevertheless remained his central subject of research.

Thus, his biography of Rashi and his book, *Maimonides,* appear as natural continuations of his research on earlier Jewish thought. For the same reason it is not surprising to find him maintain that Hasidism was the greatest religious movement in Judaism since the destruction of the

Second Temple, and to see him bolster this contention with his vast knowledge of how Judaism manifested itself throughout the ages. It is not surprising that, when David Ben-Gurion asked the question, "What is a Jew?" Zeitlin sought the answer in Jewish history.

But he always returns to the period of the Second Commonwealth. Scores of articles have come from his pen on various aspects of the development of the Oral Law, the rise of Pharisees and Sadducees, the calendar, the rules of hermeneutics; the Synagogue and prayer; and many more. Each of these articles has a *ḥiddush,* a new insight, a new turn to material often discussed before by others.

It is not surprising, therefore, that two major volumes should have climaxed these studies. His important work, *Who Crucified Jesus?* has already been mentioned. The second is an ambitious project which is to serve as a summary of a lifetime of research and writing. It aims at nothing less than a structured history of the Second Commonwealth—its political, cultural, religious, as well as its economic development. The first volume, under the title, *The Rise and Fall of the Judaean State* (JPS), appeared in 1962, and the second was published early in 1967, two more volumes still being scheduled. Here it is not a question of dull antiquarianism, but of the valid presentation of the vibrant problems of a living people.

D. *Editor and Critic*

Since 1940, Dr. Zeitlin has served, along with Dr. Abraham A. Neuman, as editor of the *Jewish Quarterly Review.* Until that year the editorship of this scholarly periodical was in the capable hands of Dr. Cyrus Adler, at whose demise the life of the *Quarterly* was also threatened. Drs. Neuman and Zeitlin thereupon undertook the difficult task of raising the necessary funds to keep the *Quarterly* alive, as well as by even more arduous efforts, to maintain the magazine on its former high level of scholarship. In time the subscription list grew and the scholarly contributions did not diminish. This aspect of Dr. Zeitlin's activity represented a heavy burden which he has borne cheerfully.

A publication of this nature is to be judged, not only by the monographs it published, but also by the cogency and helpfulness of its reviews. There has been hardly an issue which did not carry one or more essays by Dr. Zeitlin himself. He has never taken the easy way of making friends by blinking at faults, and his criticisms have rarely been confined to generalizations. He expects authors to make thorough use of the sources on which their monographs are based, so that when he takes issue with a statement or a conclusion he does so with exemplary thoroughness and directness. No doubt some authors have been hurt, but in the end the book thus scrutinized has been the more useful to its readers for having been subjected to such close examination that the reader has been able to evaluate the documented criticisms for himself. At times, he himself, in typical dedication to accuracy and truth, has not hesitated to make corrective modifications of his own articles (see, for instance, nos. 101, 104).

E. *The Challenger*

Possessing a fine memory, a keen intellect, and exceptional love of the Jewish people, Dr. Zeitlin, without leaving the "four ells of Halakhah" and his academic cloister, has constantly battled for Jewish dignity against those who malign it in scholarship. His attitude was first displayed in his *Who Crucified Jesus?* and one can also perceive it in his later battle with Professor Arnold Toynbee. In answer to the English Professor's "Jewish Rights in Palestine," Zeitlin wrote his essay, "Jewish Rights in Eretz Israel." This professorial controversy was not a matter of emotion; it was primarily concerned with the sources of Jewish history, revealing Toynbee's ignorance in that area.

Toynbee maintained that the human rights of the inhabitants of a country override the historical claims of the descendants of a people who inhabited the same country a long time ago. Hence, Toynbee argues that Arab refugees have not forfeited their rights.

Zeitlin, on the other hand, showed that there never ceased to be a number of Jews in Palestine. Jews never abandoned title to the country. They fought, prayed, and hoped for the establishment of a Jewish State. Judaism is the only religion, and Jews are the only people who, from earliest times till the modern day, are religiously, historically, and legally identified with Palestine. To reach these conclusions, Zeitlin carefully reviewed all the sources in Jewish, Christian, and Islamic literature, making clear that his arguments were not offered out of Jewish bias. Such is his unswerving "search for truth." His essays on anti-Semitism and its development, likewise, aim to uncover factually the perennial wrongs in the calumny and deed against the Jewish people.

It was only a few months ago that Dr. Zeitlin decided to relinquish a part of his burden. He now serves as the Chairman of the Editorial Board of the *Jewish Quarterly Review,* to which have been appointed young men who have been close to him during the years. As he expresses it: "With the exception of two, the members of the Board are former students of mine. I am confident that they will continue the long tradition of the *Quarterly,* its high standard in scholarship and its integrity."

In addition to his editorial work on the *Quarterly,* Dr. Zeitlin also undertook a major task, in 1948, in connection with the series of volumes, *Jewish Apocryphal Literature,* to be published under the auspices of Dropsie University. Having organized a distinguished board of scholars, he sought to edit, in Greek and in English, the important branch of Jewish literary remains from the Second Commonwealth and the inter-Testamental period. Dr. Zeitlin, in direct charge of the work, supervised it and, in the case of several of the volumes published during the next few years, wrote additional notes and comments on the text. Six volumes have already appeared in the series, and more are to come.

F. *Gentleman and Friend*

Those who first meet Zeitlin are sometimes struck by an apparent exterior boldness, but in a few moments they learn that Zeitlin is possessed of an inner sensitivity and compassion that is immeasurable.

Zeitlin does not merely insist on sources, but actually goes to them. In preparation of his volume *The Rise and Fall of the Judaean State,* he went to Crete, Cyprus, Greece, and Turkey—the entire Hellenistic area—in order to gain afresh the spirit of the environment—to be able to write, not from secondary sources, but with full personal knowledge of places and fresh feeling for events—indeed, recapturing the past.

Dr. Zeitlin has aided students in different fields of study, such as in the publication of works on *Jacob Emden, Tanya, Rabbi Meir of Rothenburg, The Great Sanhedrin, Jewish Law in the Diaspora,* etc. Never has an honest and sincere student been told by Zeitlin that he is "too busy" for him.

To those who are close to Professor Zeitlin, it is known that he has always encouraged his students to challenge his views. Often his conclusions are crystallized and shaped in the classroom. The devotion and admiration his disciples show him, reaching the heights of a David-Jonathan affinity, of a combination of filial intimacy, rabbinic respect, and cordial companionship, have earned the envy of many contemporary teachers, aware of this exceptional student-teacher relationship. Those who read the *Jewish Quarterly Review,* not knowing him personally, may create in their minds an image of Zeitlin as a scholarly deviationist, but to his many colleagues—Jewish and non-Jewish—and to his pupils and personal friends, there cannot be a more charming personality. He combines the characteristics of Russian austerity, German punctuality, French suavity, with American democracy, Jewish universalism, and unwavering friendship—a combination that is rare in one personality, but is a fitting concomitant to his exceptional mind, background, intellectual training, scholastic discipline, broad travel, vast interests, and steadfast companionship. Never will he accept a favor from an individual, nor will he make a personal request. The opera, an interest in current events, in political manifestations, and a volume on classical literature, and good fiction are not ignored or neglected despite the many hours he puts in daily in his academic research in the privacy of his rooms.

Many personalities in the wide world with different realms of activities are close to him. Since 1925 he has made many trips abroad to academic conferences, becoming acquainted with the scholarly worlds of many countries. Everywhere, be it Oxford, Moscow, Jerusalem, he has been well received, for he possesses an endearing human quality of sociability (מעורב עם הבריות). His students—submitting class papers, preparing their dissertations, writing articles for *JQR,* or simply asking questions—have at times felt his academic severity and apparent brashness. But they realize immediately that he cannot countenance generalities in questions or statements and that he has little patience for mediocrity in scholarship; his own incorruptible scholarship demands the use of basic sources only. Sitting with him at lunch, or taking a long walk, or conversing with him in the halls on a quick visit to a scholarly conference, always results in sparkling instruction for his fortunate companion.

A *Citation of Excellence,* bestowed upon him by the Board of Rabbis of Philadelphia, read by Dr. Leo Landman, well elucidates upon his traits:

> How is this man different? How is he distinguished, A man may possess great abilities, even genius, but these are not honored if they stand alone. What matters most of all is the quality of the character of the man so endowed. It is here that Solomon Zeitlin is distinguished. I have studied under Dr. Zeitlin and I know of his great efforts to encourage his students to make their contributions to scholarship—how he inspires them to continued research

and how concerned he is not only with their scholastic achievements but, like a father, worries about their personal welfare as well. By means of this attachment—bonds of long lasting friendship have been cemented.

A most interesting description of Dr. Zeitlin may be found in his personal relationship to the late, esteemed Professor Louis Ginzberg, [as told by Eli Ginzberg in his *Keeper of the Law* (pp. 274-275)]:

> Solomon Zeitlin of Dropsie College came often and became a close friend. My father early developed a great personal liking for Zeitlin and helped him get settled academically. And Zeitlin always treated my father with a deference that he showed no one else. They talked shop for hours on end, weekly or fortnightly, from the time Zeitlin first settled in the United States during World War I. My father was very indulgent about Zeitlin's theories and his altercations with other scholars, although I am sure that he was more than once astonished by them. As is so often the case, sympathy is the key to understanding which in turn is the key to acceptance.

G. *Faith and Influence*

More than 400 articles and books have been written by Professor Zeitlin in the course of the past fifty-six years. Interesting and thought provoking as they are, their writer himself is even more stimulating. A dedicated Jew, his hopes for Jewish life in America are high, but not unmixed with misgivings. He sees Torah, in the broadest sense of the term, as the quintessence of Judaism: "Judaism without knowledge is a body without a soul." Philanthropy and the defense against anti-Semitism will not by themselves nourish Judaism.

But the situation is not as bad as superficial signs appear to indicate. Jewish learning has been on the increase in the United States. The growing number of *yeshivot* is encouraging, and the narrowness which now characterizes many of them must, in time, rub off. Dr. Zeitlin's own pupils have done much to emulate his industry and dedication to scholarship. His influence is not at an end.

The list of his essays and books will, one must hope, grow in the coming years: לא כהתה עינו ולא נס לחה—For his eye has not dimmed nor has his intellectual vigor abated (Deut. 34:7).

APPRECIATIONS

RECONSTRUCTING THE PAST

By SOLOMON GRAYZEL

Dropsie University

The old argument, whether history is a science or an art, though occasionally joined, sounds a bit hollow now. History is neither, and it is both. There is no doubt, however, that its methods should be scientific. The sound historian bases himself on proven facts and on reliable sources. His greatest sin is to fail to probe the available source material and thus fall into the trap of wishful thinking. At this point, the personality—indeed, the character—of the historian comes into play. Can he control his wish that things had been different? No wonder that prophecy, theology, patriotism, and any fixed interpretation of the historical process make for bad history.

By this standard, Professor Zeitlin ranks high as a historian. Especially in his essays, but also in his more extensive historical works, wherever source material was available, he has consistently gone back to it. He disdains to buttress his conclusions with other people's views. When he takes issue with other scholars and challenges their conclusions, he invariably goes back to the sources. He has to see matters with his own eye, interpret the sources with his own mind and draw conclusions which he himself considers justified. This is not stubbornness or rigidity, it is scholarly integrity; it is the only scientific approach to history.

Incidentally, given this veneration for the recognized sources, it stands to reason that Professor Zeitlin would be exceedingly circumspect about admitting new material to that exalted status. He would want such material subjected to meticulous tests—paleographic, epigraphic, linguistic and, not least, the test of its harmonious fitting into the body of source material already so classified. His quarrel with the proponents of the authenticity of the Dead Sea Scrolls is a case in point. The very uniqueness of the Scrolls makes them, from his point of view, open to suspicion. He does not reject; he challenges. It is characteristic of Zeitlin's historical approach that he is not awed by the near unanimity of those who differ with him. Truth is not subject to the democratic process.

Sometimes, to be sure, sources are elusive; one has to dig the historical material out of them. To do this successfully, the would-be user of such material must know how to accept it on its own terms: recognize its allusions, appreciate its subtleties. This is especially true of rabbinic material. The ancient rabbis were not historians, yet they were very careful to build upon the past. Only a most profound knowledge of rabbinics—such as Professor Zeitlin possesses—and of the methods of argumentation and interpretation used by the rabbis enables the researcher to apprehend the nuances that often hide changes in meaning and application. Such knowledge and such skill are indispensable for tracing the history of Jewish religious institutions.

Sometimes, moreover, even well-established sources fail the historian. They simply do not yield sufficient information to see the past whole. The authors of the sources could not know what the modern historian would be interested in, what questions he would ask of them across the distance of the centuries. Authors in former days did not see the importance of the economic forces that operated in their midst; they took no specific note of the gradual changes in their institutions. Yet these and similar matters are of supreme importance to the modern researcher. Under such circumstances, the modern historian must fall back upon his creative imagination, accepting hints in lieu of facts, vague suggestions where he would have liked to hear clear recitals of causes and effects. Or he must consider the totality of the historical picture and decide what, under the circumstances that then prevailed, was possible or likely. Herein lies the art of the historian. It is based on vast knowledge, to be sure, but also on percipience and skill. Like an artist restoring a damaged painting, the historian must reconstruct the past persuasively on the basis of the known facts, so that the resulting picture of the age he deals with might have verisimilitude. It is, above all, at this point that the historian must free himself from prejudgments and preconceptions and refrain from reading into the past the ideas, be they ever so strong and widespread, that prevail in the present.

Consider, for example, what it is that makes Zeitlin's *Who Crucified Jesus?* so convincing. It is due, first of all, to his complete grasp of the social and political situation of the Jews of that day. Every facet of their life, culled from all available source material, was clear to him. He could consequently apprehend the relations between the upper-class Jews and the Roman government, between the Pharisee leaders and the Jewish masses, and sense the relationship between Jesus and his devoted followers. When he therefore recognized in the sources a clear distinction between the unofficial *synhedria* and the official *Beth Din,* when he appreciated the high priest's attitude toward the procurator and the latter's certain reaction to an uprising of the masses, the picture he drew became completely acceptable. Books by the thousand have been written on the Crucifixion, but none is as convincing as this, where everything falls into place.

After a continuous flow of argumentative essays over almost half a century, Professor Zeitlin embarked on the ambitious project of writing a narrative history of the Jews during the Graeco-Roman period. Whereas his essays were interesting because they offered open challenge to what was theretofore accepted knowledge, or because they revealed the source material in a new light, his narrative history claims interest as a synthesis. In one respect, this type of historical writing is more satisfying than the argumentative essay type, since it offers a continuous descriptive flow by fitting events into a chain of cause and effect. It can never be conclusive, however. Another historian will always come along and arrange the links in the chain differently and assign different causes for the events recorded. This is especially true of institutional history, where the gaps in the source material are usually the widest. Now, most of Professor Zeitlin's briefer studies have been devoted to this aspect of the Jewish past, his thorough command of the rabbinic sources having enabled him to make remarkable contributions to the understanding of the evolution of Judaism and its institutions. In these studies he laid the groundwork for his narrative history. One reads the two volumes of *The Rise and Fall of the Judaean State* which have thus far appeared and notes that their unique character derives in large measure from the attention they pay to the inner workings of the social and religious aspects of Jewish life.

It is one of Dr. Zeitlin's firmly held convictions that no one historian can write authoritatively on more than one period of Jewish history or on more than one aspect of it. The Jews have been affected by too many influences, lived in too many environments, undergone too many changes for a single historian to measure up to the challenges which their long and varied history presents. Whether or not this is so, it is obvious that breaks in the history of any people are never sudden or complete. The history of any period cannot be completely separated from the one that preceded or followed it. That Dr. Zeitlin recognizes this basic unity and continuity of Jewish history is evident from the fact that his first volume on the Second Commonwealth is prefaced by a long prologue describing the events and changes that occurred before the Alexandrian conquest of western Asia. He takes note in this chapter of the variety of forces and influences which were to mold the Jewish people when they emerged into the full light of history after the Alexandrian conquest, among them the sense in which the Judaean State became a theocracy; the appearance of parties, religious and political; the emergence of the Pentateuch as the constitution of the Second Commonwealth, and others. Each of the basic factors in Jewish life receives further treatment throughout the two volumes. Political history also is detailed with many startlingly new insights. In that respect, to be sure, Dr. Zeitlin's discussion is more or less paralleled in the works of other historians, who may agree or differ but do not change the basic facts; whereas in everything that touches on religious and institutional life his views are fresh, cogent, and convincing. Thus the second half of the second volume offers admirable descriptions of Jewish life as it was actually lived in the home and in society, at work, at worship, and at play.

Any attempt to summarize a historical period in narrative fashion involves a problem which reflects on history as a study and on the historian as a philosopher. It is the problem of the part which the element of chance plays in history, or (as it has been put), the "ifs" in history. Granted that things happened as they did, could they have happened otherwise? To say that the general historical forces play an ineluctable part in the historical process, and that in one way or another the results would have been much the same, is to bring history closer to being a science. But it is also to dehumanize it and to make statistics its ultimate resource. History would then, in fact, become what it is currently classified as being, a part of Social Studies. If, on the other hand, one assumes that the course of history is unpredictable, and if one sees it in human terms, he turns it—as Dr. Zeitlin does—into a thrilling study of human nature struggling against powerful odds in behalf of freedom to seek one's own ideal of life. If Ezra and Nehemiah, the Hasmoneans and Johanan ben Zakkai had not appeared at crucial moments in Jewish history, would there now have been a Judaism or a Jewish people?

Professor Zeitlin is fond of quoting the Ciceronian phrase, *Historia magistra vitae.* History should teach and inspire. Herein lies a further challenge to the historian, to his narrative ability, to his art of presenting life as a drama. Fortunately for the historian, especially for the Jewish historian, life usually is a struggle. Few peoples have long survived uninterrupted success. If power corrupts, success debilitates; it hardens the successful generation and softens the succeeding ones. This is why tragedy has proved more inspiring than comedy and defeat more instructive than triumph unrelieved by substantial doses of pain.

Had Jewish history come to an end at any given moment—say, with the fall of the Judaean State—it would not be difficult to speak of its past glory in terms of a Greek tragedy. But Jewish history did not stop there; and Professor Zeitlin is very much aware that it went on. Throughout these two volumes the reader senses his desire to continue describing those vital powers that would enable the Jewish people to rise above the destruction, and long outlive the destroyers of the State. For he recognizes the vitality of those institutions that gave it strength; he feels them: he can describe them and show how they helped the Jewish people bridge the nineteen centuries till the State would rise again.

May it be given him to complete his task.

THE MASORAH

By HARRY M. ORLINSKY

Hebrew Union College — Jewish Institute of Religion, New York

The same methodology and philosophy of history that have characterized the work and achievements of Professor Zeitlin in the field of rabbinics, history, institutions, halakhah—have stood him in good stead in his relatively few incursions in the area of biblical research. As I learned from the very first day that I became a student of this acute, learned, and compassionate scholar, in October 1931 at the Dropsie College, nothing was more important and sacred in scholarship than truth, and that the purpose of scientific learning was to determine why any given event happened at the time and place that it did. It was simply not enough to seek out and collect pertinent data that would reveal how that event happened—that is the work of a chronicler; rather, the data had to be put together in such manner that a clear pattern emerged, one that revealed the underlying causes of the event. In short, an event had to be accounted for, not merely described.

His considerable knowledge of the rabbinic texts, as well as the related literature of the Second Jewish Commonwealth, Josephus, and the Church Fathers, has enabled Professor Zeitlin to comprehend the nature of the Masorah historically. Thus his comments on the use of *matres lectionis* (medial alef, yod, waw, and final heh) in biblical texts before, during, and immediately after the tannaitic-amoraic-saboraic period (from about 200 B.C.E. to about 600 C.E.) not only have considerable validity, but are of the kind that the specialist in matters biblical must reckon with.

Thus Dr. Zeitlin took a biblical scholar to task, and proved him to be in error, for asserting that the Masorah was fixed prior to the time of Rabbi Akiba (first half of the second century C.E.) and that the biblical text had been fixed even earlier, before the destruction of the Second Temple. Indeed, it is one of Dr. Zeitlin's great merits that he has emphasized time and again the clear fact—for not many biblical scholars ever get to examine the sources directly—that the Hebrew text of the

Bible was not really fixed, that the Targums and the tannaitic literature have preserved genuine readings that differ from those that have come down to us in the traditional (masoretic) text.

Professor Zeitlin's essay, "Some Reflections on the Text of the Pentateuch," begins with this very matter in connection with the ten words in the Pentateuch specified in the Sifre as dotted: ". . . It is evident from the statement ascribed to Ezra that the sages were in doubt as to whether these ten places over which dots were placed belonged to the original text of the Pentateuch or came into the text by error. . . ." By analyzing closely both the statements in the Sifre and the biblical passages, Dr. Zeitlin is able to show that ובינה ("and between her"), rather than the received ובינך ("and between you") is the original term in Gen. 16:5; that the word אליו ("to him") in Gen. 18:9 is not original (note that the term אמר throughout the chapter is otherwise used absolutely, without the use of אל to indicate the person addressed. Or could it have been the final ו in ויאמרו—rather than אליו—that was suspect, since it is followed by ויאמר, the singular in v. 10); that it may well be the entire phrase את-צאן אביהם ("their father's flock") in Gen. 37:12, and not merely the particle את, that is unoriginal, leaving וילכו אחיו לרעות בשכם ("His brothers went to pasture at Shechem") as the original reading (cf., v. 13 הלוא אחיך רעים בשכם and v. 17 איפה הם רעים, both without צאן as an object); that the word אהרן is a gloss in Num. 3:39; and so on.

In the same article there are several additional acute observations on other words in the Pentateuch which arose through error. In Deut. 6:20, the Palestinian Talmud and the Sifre as well as the Septuagint are cited as evidence that it was by error that אתכם was preserved for אתנו; attention is drawn to the interesting fact that in Deut. 28:66 the original order was not received "night and day" (לילה ויומם) but rather (with Targum Jonathan and the Septuagint, and as is usual in the Bible) "day and night." A forceful argument is presented for the opinion that in Exod. 28:36, "You shall make a frontlet of pure gold and engrave on it the seal inscription: 'Holy to the Lord' 'קדש לה'," the word קדש was not included along with "*To* YHWH" in the inscription; rather, argues Dr. Zeitlin, discussing *inter alia* also the pertinent passages in Josephus and the Talmud, it is only the word YHWH that is inscribed (". . . and engrave upon it the engravings of a holy signet: YHWH . . ."). A pity in this connection that the precise force and implications of the terms YHWH and *Azazel* are unclear in Lev. 16:8.

One could readily continue in this vein, pointing out the numerous observations that Dr. Zeitlin has made on biblical terms and passages, e.g., his rejection of the translation "[So that] tribute [shall come] to him" offered in the new Jewish version of the Torah for עד כי-יבא שילה in Gen. 49:10. Or one could dwell on Dr. Zeitlin's reasons for rejecting the opinion that there were ever three Torah scrolls with variant readings in the Second Temple's Azarah. However, it is hoped that even in the brief space allotted, it has been possible to indicate to the reader the reverential approach that has characterized Professor Zeitlin's analysis of the biblical text, an approach that has little sympathy with the uncritical, but manifests much concern for the scientific. For it is only by the methodology practiced by Dr. Zeitlin that the authors and transmitters of the biblical text can receive their just due and appreciation in history.

BIBLICAL SCHOLARSHIP

By ROBERT GORDIS

Temple University and Jewish Theological Seminary

For nearly fifty years Doctor Solomon Zeitlin has served as Professor of Rabbinics at Dropsie University. For the last thirty years he has also stood at the helm of the *Jewish Quarterly Review* as its Editor. This latter period virtually coincides with the period that I have been privileged to call him "my Master." I have learned from him not only *Torah shebikhtabh,* through the medium of his many books and papers, but also *Torah shebe'al peh,* through personal contact, first at the Beth Midrash Lemorim of Yeshivat Rabbi Isaac Elchanan during my early teens, then at the Dropsie College during my graduate studies, and since then through our ever closer association and friendship.

It is a privilege to add my personal tribute through the medium of this all too brief description of one facet of his vast learning. The full range of Dr. Zeitlin's interests and the extent of his creative contribution to many areas of Jewish scholarship are revealed in the extraordinarily rich Bibliography presented in this volume. His primary field of research is, of course, the history of the Second Commonwealth and rabbinic literature.

The Bible, too, has been the subject of research by Dr. Zeitlin, both because of its intrinsic interest and its role as the foundation for the edifice of normative Judaism. He has expressed his views on such themes as "the Servant of the Lord" prophecy in Isaiah chap. 53, Koheleth and the Essenes, and the cryptic numbers in Daniel. One of his most important studies has dealt with the canonization of Scripture. Both biblical and rabbinic data are laid under contribution in his discussion of the changing concepts of proselytism in these two great eras of Jewish history. His mastery of biblical and rabbinic sources served also as the basis for his papers on the nature of Jewish peoplehood. Dr. Zeitlin's interest in the Masorah has prompted his comment on the orthography of רבשקה (II Kings 18:17 ff.; Isa. 36:2 ff.) and his theory regarding the origins of the so-called final letters מנצפ"ך.

Dr. Zeitlin's vigorous opposition to a Second Commonwealth provenance for the Dead Sea Scrolls is well known. In harmony with this standpoint is his low estimate of the value of the Isaiah scrolls found at Qumran and his denial of the relevance of the Dead Sea biblical scrolls and fragments for the pre-history of the Masorah. To provide additional support for his position he has called attention to Aramaic elements in the language of the Dead Sea Scrolls and analyzed the form and content of the Psalm Scroll, recently published by J. A. Sanders.

He has dealt frequently with the Apocrypha and the Pseudepigrapha, both in his *History* and in many papers, in addition to serving as Editor of the *Jewish Apocryphal Series* sponsored by Dropsie University.

In every area of scholarly concern, his views have been challenging and original. Even when scholars have differed with him, they have never failed to be stimulated and instructed by his work. Professor Zeitlin has inspired countless scholars and students to deeper and more vigorous research, including a re-examination of their own positions.

Genius is as rare in scholarship as everywhere else. Most competent scholars possess industry, diligence and knowledge of their particular specialty. They make useful contributions to our understanding of the past and are worthy of respect on that account. But a scholar of the calibre of Professor Solomon Zeitlin possesses in addition another constellation of qualities—originality of insight, independence of outlook and an unquenchable vitality of spirit. Solomon Zeitlin belongs to that rare group of scholars who are able to make learning exciting and the past come alive.

It is a privilege to add my gratitude to those of his countless students everywhere, and voice the hope that for many more years he may continue to magnify the Torah and keep it glorious.

THE LEGAL MIND AND TANNAITIC LAW

By EMANUEL RACKMAN

Yeshiva University

"The Greeks made law a philosophy, the Romans made it a science, the Jews made law their religion." Thus writes Professor Zeitlin in an essay introducing the reader to tannaitic jurisprudence. This thesis is central to one's understanding of Judaism and to Zeitlin's approach to Jewish history. As he reminds us, the Hebrew phrase for describing apostasy is to speak of one as having "changed his law," not his faith. Judaism is more a legal order than a religious fellowship or communion; and to understand Jewish history—to deal with the source materials and to evaluate the persons and the movements in the drama—one must be very knowledgeable in the field of law. In one of his book reviews, Zeitlin virtually suggests that the student of Jewish history must either know law or keep hands off the subject. Thus, to him, one who cannot swim easily in the sea of Talmud, so that he can understand not only the milieu of the codes and responsa but also their argument, should realize his limitations. If it is Jewish history in which such a one seeks to do research, then at least the span from the Second Commonwealth to the Enlightenment should be avoided. Without proficiency in law—Jewish law and perhaps also Roman law, Zeitlin insists—one will simply draw false conclusions from the literature with which he must deal.

Utilizing a legal definition, Zeitlin describes the Jewish state until the period of the Hasmoneans as a "theocracy," and the succeeding period as a "nomocracy." One might take issue with this. Indeed, the period of the Hasmoneans might be the only period in Jewish history when there was a theocracy, while during all the other periods after Moses the rule of law prevailed. If Zeitlin uses the term "theocracy" as it was defined by Josephus—the rule of God—then the legal order of Judaism always was, and still is, a theocracy, for its fundamental norm is still that God exists and that His will is law. If, however, he defines "theocracy" as we do today, as the system of government in which the religious hierarchy exercises, at one and the same time, temporal and spiritual power, then only during the period of the Hasmoneans was this the case in Jewish history. At all other times the temporal and spiritual authorities were separate and distinct from each other.

Moreover, while Jews were not especially committed to their legal heritage prior to the Second Commonwealth, it may be misleading to say that the nomocracy was established in the Second Commonwealth. The Second Commonwealth scribes simply fulfilled what was promulgated in the Pentateuch. The Law of Moses, which became continuously central in Jewish life after Ezra, was also accepted as normative in one period or another of the First Commonwealth. Thus the character of Jewish society as a nomocracy was ordained long before the Hasmoneans, even though it came to fruition only during the Second Commonwealth.

Accepting that law is basic in Judaism, it follows that just as one cannot study Jewish history without preoccupation with the law so, Professor Zeitlin insists, one cannot study Jewish law without an awareness of history. He distinguishes between the dogmatic study of Jewish law and the historical approach. Today jurists are more prone to describe the dogmatic approach as analytical. John Austin is the father of this school in Anglo-American circles; Hans Kelsen in Europe. It describes the analysis of the rules of law in any legal system as the data to be defined, classified, and related to each other. Historical, sociological, and teleological considerations are deemed irrelevant except to the legislator. For the judge, they are beyond the pale. Zeitlin propounds that, for the Jewish jurist, history is important not only because without a view of its historical evolution his understanding of the rule will be defective, but also because in Jewish circles most legislation is by the judge, the *Posek,* and he dare not remain oblivious of origins.

As an example, he praises Chief Rabbi Isaac Herzog's writings on Jewish law as a model of the dogmatic approach, whereas his own essays on Jewish law—what it is and what it ought to be—are in the realm of historical analysis. He stresses that Jewish law is marked by development. It changed from period to period, The Rabbis interpreted and reinterpreted it so that it was ever viable. Modern Rabbis who hesitate to do this—especially Rabbis in Israel—receive their due measure of censure from Zeitlin. When one reads his essay "Who Is A Jew?" one finds that he scores the rabbinical leaders for not reckoning with the past and coping with the special problems confronting them now, as a consequence first of the holocaust, and secondly of the immigration to Israel from behind the Iron Curtain.

Nonetheless it would be unfair to let it appear that only history, and not analysis, is Professor Zeitlin's forte. On the other hand, one of his greatest contributions to our understanding of tannaitic jurisprudence is the light he shed analytically on so many controversies between the schools of Shammai and Hillel. The difference is still a basic one for students of jurisprudence, and Zeitlin seeks to probe their fundamental principle.

To what extent does the law reckon only with objective acts and to what extent is intention—the subjective state of mind—a controlling factor affecting the decision to act? There are jurists who even distinguish between law and ethics by stating that law is concerned with deeds while ethics is concerned with will and intention. Without referring to, or challenging, the validity of this distinction, Zeitlin credits Hillel with the notion that intention is the operative factor in any legal situation. What is especially interesting—though not surprising—is that he spells out this thesis not only in civil law but also in the entire gamut of Jewish law, including the rules pertaining to holidays and other religious observances.

Moderns may not realize that this same controversy rages today. Shall parties to a contract, for example, be held to what they said—giving their words commonly accepted meanings—or shall they be held only to what they intended, assuming, of course, some reasonable basis for considering the subsequent declaration of intention to be honest? In modern law the pendulum has swung back and forth; while Holmes favored the former view, many contemporary jurists favor the latter view.

As far back as Shammai and Hillel, more than two thousand years ago, the controversy raged. It was Hillel who was responsible for the emphasis on intention, and for a theocentric jurisprudence this principle is, as it should be, most formidable. A jurisprudence strongly oriented in the direction of equity and righteousness cannot help but give maximum attention to man's will. If the law were property-oriented, rather than God-centered, acts might be more important than thoughts. But as the Rabbis always said, "God seeks the heart."

Many of Professor Zeitlin's writings, in essays and in rejoinders to critics, contain the exposition of his thesis about Hillel's contribution to Jewish law and his defense of it. This, to the probing student, is legal analysis—not history! That is how Zeitlin proves himself the master in both areas—in what he calls the dogmatic approach and, of course, in historical analysis.

His study on slavery according to Jewish law reveals, too, not only his skills as historian and jurist, but also his mastery of Roman law and Christian literature on the subject. That he should have chosen to make so intensive a study of an institution long dead in the West is understandable. Few legal topics lend themselves as well to an appreciation of how the humanitarianism of Judaism influenced and ultimately abolished one of the ugliest of social and economic institutions. It might even be added that the humanization of Roman law in this area was due more to Stoicism than to Christianity, which condoned slavery as punishment for sin (Augustine). Who knows how much Judaism may have influenced Stoicism, which was founded by a half-Semite!

In his essay on "Hefker" (*res nullius*) and *Ye'ush* (renunciation) he enters into fine legal distinctions of a comparative nature. He maintains that according to Roman law an owner could not relinquish title to movable goods by *Ye'ush* (renunciation) alone, whereas Jewish law upheld the notion. This unique concept of Jewish law he attributes to the fact that the Torah deems a man's forgetfulness of his piles of sheaves in the field as the equivalent of *Hefker, res nullius* (lack of ownership), because of renunciation. This may be so, but generally Jewish law was less preoccupied with the formal than was Roman law. In such a system of jurisprudence, which is less preoccupied with the formal, what difference is there between making property ownerless by removing it from your legal domain of possession with a declaration that anyone can take it, or making the property ownerless by revealing that you despaired of ever repossessing it again?

This appreciation would not be complete if one did not also refer to Professor Zeitlin's concern for his people in their contemporary existential situation. His essay on the rights of the Jewish people to the land (once called Palestine) is a masterpiece of both historical and legal analysis. It reveals him as the historian and jurist *par excellence,* though, basically, it was a retort to Professor Toynbee's arguments supporting Arab claims. With the passage of time and today, especially, Zeitlin's devastating rebuttal based on historico-legal premises has lost none of its significance or poignancy.

Moreover, one of the great problems of our day is to make intelligible, not so much to Christians and Muslims as to intellectuals generally, how a people whose constitutents claim nationality and citizenship in scores of countries throughout the world can also maintain with each other a continuing sense of kinship that transcends their own particular locations and is focused on a tiny tract of land to which they are bound by a hoary past and a prophetic vision. This Professor Zeitlin enunciates in a legal brief—factual and eloquent. The phenomenon is so unique—none except Jews respond to its argument existentially. Perhaps his keen documentation will help others to reconcile themselves to the fact of uniqueness, even if they cannot feel it.

Dr. Zeitlin makes it clear that "Palestine" has places that are holy to Christianity and to Islam, but it is only Judaism that considered the whole land as holy. Furthermore, "there was no period when there were no Jews in Palestine." And lastly—as only Zeitlin, the jurist, could demonstrate—the Romans never acquired title to Palestine; and their conquerors have no better title than the Romans had. The rights of the Romans, Arabs, and Turks were based on possession, not title, and title always remained vested in the Jews.

But if Zeitlin demonstrates, on the one hand, that he is concerned with the problems of the community and the world at large—a people's continuity—and that the answers to these can be found only in careful legal analysis, nonetheless his research has not neglected man's personal desire for perpetuation of his holdings. Zeitlin, therefore, studied the metamorphosis of "testamentary succession." He shows that the Bible does not contain laws of testaments and wills; real property in biblical days always reverted back to the original owner in the Jubilee Year. In the Second Commonwealth, however, the principle of bequest by will, called *diatheke,* was accepted. Yet if it should contradict any of the laws of inheritance recorded in the Pentateuch, such a will was invalid. Later it was ruled that a will to a potential heir was also valid; but if the will was the legal transmission of a gift of property to others than the family, the Rabbis did not consider such an act commendable. Only later was it accepted that a person may give even real property to a stranger by writing a will or bestowing it as a gift. These laws of testamentary succession were introduced to meet the needs of the changing social and economic life. Basically Dr. Zeitlin, as is his wont, demonstrates that in their legal interpretation the Rabbis were most cognizant of the needs of the day and were able, through their hermeneutics and legislation, to meet any demands, while still upholding, unwaveringly, the sanctity of the Torah. Harmonization was a distinct part of their legal process. And this method also applied to the law of personal status, as he illustrates in his insightful essay, "Who Is A Jew?"

In sum, it is in Professor Zeitlin's studies on law that we have the full measure of the man—historian, jurist, and champion of his people's cause.

NEW TESTAMENT STUDIES

By MORTON S. ENSLIN
Dropsie University

There are few into whose hands this volume of respectful—and for some of us, affectionate—homage to a prince of scholars is likely to come who do not know Solomon Zeitlin as the tireless and persistent combatant, ever ready to take on singlehanded anyone, scholar or publicist, who ventures to dispute historical values for the period of his special love and interest, the Second Commonwealth, and the Dead Sea Scrolls. Many more, both here and abroad, know him as a scholar unexcelled, perhaps unrivaled, in his profound knowledge of the rabbinic literature, where he has long walked as one who needs no guide. For many decades he has used his colossal knowledge to illumine the field of his chief concern, the history of what he loves to style "the Second Commonwealth," a period which saw the birth and adolescence of Christianity, and the eventual parting of the ways between mother and child. But this library of writings—tannaitic and amoraic alike—where he has long been at home, but which all too often is *terra incognita* to many who strive to know, is but a part of his kit of tools. The writings of the early Christians, both those styled canonical and the subsequent productions of the so-called Church Fathers, are to him of interest and concern, for he rightly feels that they are necessary for the scholar who would work in that field with understanding, be he Jew or Christian.

This is where Dr. Zeitlin has made his most telling contribution to New Testament scholarship. All too few Jews have seemingly been especially attracted to this phase of their history; too many Christians, for whom it may well be a period of almost greater concern than the perplexing 1970's, are hampered—I might almost say "fettered"—by their lack of familiarity, which can come only through firsthand knowledge, with the people of whom Jesus of Nazareth and Paul of Tarsus were proud and devoted sons. Much of the hostile criticism, each for the other, which blotted the pages of much of the writing, Christian and Jewish alike, of seventy years ago has lessened, in no small part due to the devoted work of men like Israel Abrahams and C. G. Montefiore, of George Foot Moore, and Travers Herford, to mention but one very influential quartet. There still remain sad gaps in our knowledge, even though unfortunate, often stupid, prejudices have been quietly but steadily removed.

In an article, "The Political Synedrion and the Religious Sanhedrin," which appeared in Volume 36 of the *Jewish Quarterly Review,* of which he has been for many years the distinguished editor and to which he has been a constant contributor of articles and lengthy reviews, Dr. Zeitlin wrote, in reply to critics of his volume, *Who Crucified Jesus?*:

> All the reviewers of my book, with few exceptions, impressed me as being open-minded on the question. However, many of them showed that their knowledge of the history of the Jews and Judaism of that period was very meager. They relied upon the literature written by German theologians. This may be the fault of the Jews themselves; since they have not yet produced an authoritative book on the history of the Jews of the Second Commonwealth. On the other hand the Jewish reviewers have not shown any familiary with the origin of Christianity or with the history of the Jews of that period (p. 138).

This criticism, severe and to some overly general, indicates the nature and aim of Dr. Zeitlin's chief contribution to New Testament studies. Many lengthy and incisive reviews of current scholarship have come from his never-capped pen and, regularly, his appraisal has included the stressing of points which, in his judgment, evidence the writer's failure or inability to use sources of knowledge which, if employed, would have led to different conclusions. Notable in this long list of article-length reviews—he rarely writes book notices!—is his almost thirty-page essay, "Studies in the Beginnings of Christianity," which appeared in 1923 in the *Jewish Quarterly Review.* Here he examines, with appreciation but with severe criticism, three works which had recently appeared: Eduard Meyer's *Ursprung und Anfänge des Christentums,* Foakes-Jackson and Lake's first volumes of the *Beginnings of Christianity,* and Joseph Klausner's *Jesus of Nazareth.* In this survey and critique, as in the many which have followed, his "review" is carefully limited to specific points which he feels were inadequately or uncritically handled. To some this sort of treatment has seemed somewhat remote from the standard sort of reviewing. Instead, it uses the work under survey as a point of departure—some might say "springboard"—for a somewhat independent study. But these excursions have been of great value to many critical readers, not infrequently leading them to question and to reexamine this point or that which had been too easily regarded as definitely settled.

His magnum opus, *The Rise and Fall of the Judaean State,* of which two volumes have already appeared, is very definitely of concern to the student of Christian beginnings. It is an important part of Dr. Zeitlin's contribution to New Testament studies, for herein are to be found not only a very detailed treatment of background themes and subjects which are essential for an understanding of the period which saw the emergence of the daughter religion, but also comparatively brief but illuminating studies of such topics as Jesus and his followers.

It is no adverse criticism of Dr. Zeitlin's contributions to New Testament study, contributions which are very real to me, to say that their principal value lies in his treatment of occasional problems which have assumed importance in his eyes. A notable example is to be found in his repeated treatment of Josephus and tightly related concerns, very important for the student of early Christianity. It is no exaggeration to say that here Dr. Zeitlin has made a monumental contribution. That he regards, as do most interpreters today, the oft-debated "Christ passages" as Christian interpolations is not surprising. But in his repeated discussion of this theme—for subjects he feels important he regularly discusses and rediscusses with never-failing verve in articles which might well be captioned "Once Again a Look at . . ."—he has constantly drawn attention to details easily bypassed. One of his constant concerns in all his studies is the choice and use of words and phrases. It is on this seemingly small detail, as is known to every student who has been concerned with the debate about the scrolls from Qumran, that he has repeatedly leaned in his insistence that an early date for any of these writings is impossible. So in the case of the famous interpolation in Josephus in which Christians are styled a "tribe" or "race" (*phulon*). Since it is Dr. Zeitlin's proclaimed contention, which he backs up by constant references to the phraseology of the early Fathers—in the original languages, of course, for Dr. Zeitlin notoriously scorns translations: secondhand scholarship is, he is sure, usually second-rate—that this designation is not to be found prior to Eusebius; the fact that it is found in Eusebius' citing of the passage leads him to the daring guess that Eusebius himself was the inventor of the paragraph and that it was never a part of the text until Eusebius inserted it in his transcription. While to some this may seem insecure and of no profound importance, they cannot overlook the fact that it is to Dr. Zeitlin that the credit must be given for the proper appraisal of the Slavonic Josephus. The earlier claims of Robert Eisler and his *pedisequi* that this writing was a transcript into Slavonic of a conjectured Aramaic version of the *War* which Josephus had written for Jews in Babylonia were shattered by Dr. Zeitlin's stormy blasts and convincing arguments following his trip to Russia to examine the manuscripts. They had nothing to do with any Semitic original and had not been translated by Khazars in the ninth century into Slavonic, but were rather a product of not earlier than the eleventh or twelfth century written in Old Russian (not Slavonic), and were full of interpolations by Christians.

Another problem of great concern to Dr. Zeitlin has to do with the crucifixion of Jesus; many are his studies in this connection. His volume, *Who Crucified Jesus?* now in a fourth edition, is a notable contribution, and of no small moment to students of the rise of early Christianity. Incidental to this particular problem is Zeitlin's well-known and frequently argued and reargued contention that, in the days of Jesus, there had been several courts: a Great Sanhedrin, lesser sanhedrins, and the political synedrion, which latter was called together by the high priest when the occasion seemed to him to warrant it. Thus the Bet Din at Jamnia was an actual continuum, as it believed itself to be, of the earlier "Religious Sanhedrin." In consequence, not only is the Mishnah tract, Sanhedrin, of more historical value than is often allowed, but the real Sanhedrin—and with it the Jewish people—had not been involved in the trial and condemnation of Jesus: it was the Romans and their "stooges," the chief priests, who had crucified him.

This is but an example of the many problems—some central, some peripheral—with which the student of the New Testament constantly lives, which demand Dr. Zeitlin's attention and elicited his pronouncements. This particular problem, with its many ramifications, provides a good example of the way that he puts his knowledge of rabbinic literature to good use. Some will feel that, occasionally, he reads later material too far back, even though he tries scrupulously to distinguish between early and later strands; at times I should be inclined to agree, but his treatment is uniformly both rewarding and enlightening.

These are but a few of the problems of major concern to the student of the New Testament, about which Dr. Zeitlin has written, either as a principal contention or incidentally. And regularly, although his New Testament colleagues may not always agree with his conclusions, they have found themselves forced to reexamine and to rethink matters they had been inclined to take for granted. For example, the origins of the synagogue and of proselyte-baptism—both commonly regarded as definitely established prior to the Christian beginnings—are both pronounced by this stormy petrel whom we regard so highly, as having been subsequent to the destruction of Jerusalem in 70 C.E.

Unfortunately, many of his New Testament colleagues do not know the literature in their own field which this amazingly productive scholar has produced. My shelves carry a large number of his studies, many of them with his scribbled word of presentation, and they have all been read, many of them again and again. But a glance at the assembled list in this volume shows how many I have yet to read. Many of my colleagues, into whose hands the *Jewish Quarterly Review* does not regularly come, might well do a bit of neglected research. It would not be without profit. Some might discover what those of us who know him more intimately, know full well that there are more than five stones, and not all of them smooth, in the shepherd's bag of this David—or was it Elḥanan?—set to slay the giant, this time from Qumran. Many of his contentions have been, and will continue to be, challenged. It is well to remember that we learn most from those whose opinions are not identical with our own. No one can work through the many studies of this tireless twentieth-century Wrede without finding that his own knowledge is greatly deepened, and that matters too easily sidestepped as "definitely established," and thus not to be questioned, demand fresh attention. In a word, here is a scholar who cannot be ignored. I, for one, would be the last to attempt to do so.

INTER-TESTAMENTAL HISTORIOGRAPHY

By ELLIS RIVKIN

Hebrew Union College, Cincinnati

Professor Solomon Zeitlin has spent close to half a century attempting to make the inter-Testamental period intelligible. Although he has clarified aspects of the Jewish history of other periods, and although his historical interests have roamed far and wide, Professor Zeitlin has always given priority to the history of the Second Commonwealth. And this is not surprising. His earliest writings already show a keen awareness of the crucial significance of this epoch. He recognized that this was one of the great watersheds of history whose value was insufficiently appreciated. He also was intrigued by the seemingly insuperable obstacles that stood in the way of intelligibility. He was struck by the inadequacy of the reconstructions of his predecessors, an inadequacy which he attributed either to an ignorance of tannaitic sources or a misuse of them. Equipped as he was with a truly staggering knowledge of the totality of rabbinic literature, and gifted as he was with a remarkable memory, Zeitlin entered the lists as the champion of a radical revision of the history of the Second Commonwealth. For this venture, he brought with him not only the *talmuda de'yankutha*, but also the scientific disciplines of the West and a thorough mastery of classical, Hellenistic, Roman, and Christian literatures. But most of all, though hardly aware of it himself, he brought a dynamic, viable, and fruitful concept of the nature of the historical continuum. Zeitlin's major contribution to the history of the Second Commonwealth is not his superior knowledge of the sources, but the method by which he constructs an intelligible past from them. Because he had certain notions about the dynamics of the historical process and certain concepts about the pattern of change, he was able to use his sources differently than his predecessors, and he was able to extract from these sources data whose significance had been overlooked. His conceptions permitted him to reevaluate the sources and to confront scholars with evidence that they were loath to accept, not because the sources were misread, but because they recoiled at the implications of this reading for their own conceptualization of the historical continuum.

Professor Zeitlin's commitment to a law-abiding past is perhaps nowhere more evident than in his approach to language. He insists that words reveal the times. A writer is not free to have any language that he wills, or any vocabulary that he chooses. His coinage of new words is severely circumscribed by the structure of the language, for though new words do emerge to express new concepts, or to name new things, they must conform to the syntactical patterns in use, otherwise communication is impossible. And though the structure of language does undergo change, it is a slow and ponderous process.

Professor Zeitlin's work clearly reveals that he adheres to this methodological principle, even if he does not always affirm it explicitly. He argues, for example, that the synagogue, *Bet ha-K'nesset,* must have had its origin in a secular activity, for the name carries with it no evidence of a religious function. Had its origin been as a house of prayer, it would have been called *Bet ha-Tefillah,* for when it subsequently did fulfill this function that very name came to be used alongside *Bet ha-K'nesset.* For Professor Zeitlin the word "synagogue" has other far-reaching implications. He rejects the widely held notion that the synagogue emerged in Babylonia, and he denies that it was an institution supported by the Aaronide theocracy. Rather does he insist that it is the creation of the Pharisees who, in their efforts to weaken the cultic monopoly of the Aaronides, instituted the *ma'amadot.* It was because the *ma'amadot* gathered in the secular meeting houses to read the Torah in conjunction with *korban tamid* that the synagogue came to be a permanent institution for reading the Torah.

Virtually everything that Zeitlin has written testifies to the crucial role he assigns to the significance of words. Thus he was struck by the fact that Bet Din and not Sanhedrin is the term used in tannaitic texts that have their origin in the pre-70 period. Indeed, throughout the tannaitic literature Bet Din is used much more frequently than Sanhedrin. He was so struck by this phenomenon that he advanced the brilliant hypothesis that at the time of Jesus the Bet Din was not the Sanhedrin. The latter was a council that served the interests of the state, whether Hasmonean, Herodian, or Roman, while the former was an autonomous court that had jurisdiction in the religious realm. The Gospel writers did not use either the Hebrew word Bet Din nor its Greek equivalent, *diakasterion,* because Jesus was brought before a political Sanhedrin and not before the religious Bet Din. Only after the Temple was destroyed in the year 70 did the name Sanhedrin begin to appear as synonymous with Bet Din, and then for a very good historical reason: the Roman emperors viewed the Bet Din at Yabneh as serving their political purposes and hence functioning as a Sanhedrin, a council. As telling evidence demonstrating that the Bet Din was not originally called a Sanhedrin, Zeitlin offers proof of the title Ab Bet Din. The second highest dignitary of the institution is the Ab of the Bet Din, not Ab of the Sanhedrin.

Perhaps nowhere has Zeitlin been more persistent and more unheeded than in his refusal to identify the Zealots with the Fourth Philosophy. Here we have a problem that seemingly is no problem at all, for Josephus uses the name Zealots for those who rose up against the provisional revolutionary government for its failure to prosecute the war against Rome with sufficient vigor. Josephus asserts that the name "Zealots" was a name by which the pro-war, anti-provisional-government faction called themselves, and he uses this designation in his *War* only *after* it was coined, not before. The so-called Fourth Philosophy or the Sicarii, on the other hand, had come into existence long before, when Judas of Galilee urged the Jews not to submit to the census ordered by Quirinius. The Zealots are no more identical with the Fourth Philosophy than the Jacobins are identical with the Sans-culottes, or the Mensheviks with the Bolsheviks. Zeitlin, sensitive to the manner in which political nomenclature emerges spontaneously out of a crisis situation, has seen in the term "Zealots" an indication of a new phase in a complex revolutionary syndrome and not a synonym for the Sicarii or Fourth Philosophy.

Zeitlin is always alert to the terminology used in the sources. He is stirred to speculation by the rise and fall of key words. Thus he was troubled by the shifts in usage of the term "Israel." Here we have a word that is biblical, and hence available for use by all post-biblical Jews. Yet he points out that "Judaean" tends to replace "Israel" during the period of the Second Temple. Thus in the Book of Esther we learn that many *mityahadim* pretended to be Judaeans. Similarly, Zeitlin points out, the *ketubah* of the Second Commonwealth read *ke-dat mosheh ve-Yehudaioi* and not, as at present, *ke-dat moshe ve-Yisrael.* So, too, in the Graeco-Roman documents of the epoch the Jews are referred to as the *ethnos judaion.*

Why, Zeitlin asks, did the customary usage of *Yehudim* in the period of the Second Temple give way to Israel? How is it that in the tannaitic literature *Yisrael,* and only *Yisrael*, is used to designate both the collectivity of Jews (*k'nesset Yisrael*), and the individual Jew himself? For Zeitlin such a shift cannot be gratuitous. His concept of history as a structured continuum demands that he seek out an answer in some major radical change in the historical process itself. He sees such a change in the destruction of the Second Temple and in the emergence of Christianity. The former shattered the reality of an ethnos and compelled Jews to orient themselves towards those Pharisaic concepts stressing the community of fellow-believers rather than of fellow-nationals. As for Christianity, Paul's claim that the followers of Jesus alone were the true Israel necessitated a denial in the most forceful manner possible: a determined effort to use the term "Israel," and Israel alone, as the designation for the Jews. *Yehudim* carried with it an ethnic, non-universalist connotation, and therefore must be studiously avoided. Israel, on the other hand, had always been linked with the one God's concern for His people.

Zeitlin's sensitivity to words continuously opens up new possibilities for an intelligible comprehension of the Second Commonwealth. He notes, for example, that prior to the destruction of the Temple, *Pesah* was applied only to the day of the slaughtering of the Paschal lamb, whereas the holiday itself was always referred to as *Hag ha-Matzot*. Only after the destruction of the Second Temple did *Pesah* come to be used for the entire holiday. He points out that in Josephus' *War* and in the Synoptic Gospels this distinction between the day of the Paschal-lamb sacrifice and the holiday of unleavened bread is clearly evident. When, however, Josephus wrote his *Antiquities*, towards the end of his life, the new usage is already taking over, and he uses the two terms interchangeably. The Gospel of John, in contrast to the Synoptics, uses *Pesah* only. For Zeitlin this is decisive proof that John must have been written very late.

Zeitlin's total commitment to the principle that words are historically conditioned is nowhere more tenaciously evident than in his insistence that the Dead Sea Scrolls could not have been written in the pre-Christian period. He was struck at the very outset with a cluster of words that were out of joint with the language preserved in the literature of the inter-Testamental period and the literature of the Palestinian and Babylonian Talmuds. He noted such alien expressions as *moreh zedek, gemar ketz,* and *pesher*. He immediately recognized them as belonging to a literary corpus of a much later vintage, that of the Karaitic age. For him the usage was decisive, and he has refused to budge from his methodological stronghold, however determinedly besieged by scholars great in number and towering in reputation. Though these latter show little or no respect for Zeitlin's methodological principle, and though they make light of his erudition, they have quietly taken over the linguistic discovery that Zeitlin was the first to make—a discovery that has subsequently been confirmed by students of Karaitica—namely, that the Scrolls do indeed use expressions that abound in Karaitic literature. The scholars now readily agree that the affinity is evident, though they attribute this to a long literary tradition which had its origins in the inter-Testamental period.

Professor Zeitlin has that rare gift for sensing a fruitful historical analogy. He generally offers historical examples that have more than superficial similarities in common with the phenomena that he is seeking to clarify. They thus serve a most valuable function. In his efforts, for example, to explain how the term Pharisees came to be applied to those who, according to Zeitlin, never referred to themselves as such, he appeals to analogous situations. History, he affirms, is replete with instances where a term of opprobrium is used in the heat of controversy and then becomes common usage, free of negative judgment. Thus the Protestants were called such by their Catholic enemies; it was not a name they chose for themselves. The Methodists owe their present name likewise to a reproach on the part of those hostile to them. And as for Jewish history, the *mitnagdim* most assuredly did not attach this label to themselves, yet *mitnagdim* in our own age are only too proud to bear it. So too with the Pharisees. They were called *perushim* (separatists, heretics) by their Sadducean opponents because they rejected the authority of the Zadokite high priesthood and because they affirmed the binding power of the Oral Law. The name first coined to degrade and humiliate gradually lost its negative meaning.

The reliance on analogy makes Zeitlin impatient of much of the scholarship dealing with the inter-Testamental period. He rejects so much of it because it is so patently unreal to a student of historical processes. He recognizes, for example, that the *semikhah* controversy between the Zugot must involve some major principle and not a dispute over a relatively insignificant point of law. He is struck by the fact that the *semikhah* issue was the only one which divided the Sages prior to the time of Hillel and Shammai. He notes that this disagreement was mandatory, for when Menahem did not differ on this issue with Shammai he could not hold the office of *Ab Bet Din*. Zeitlin is dissatisfied with the existing interpretations, not because a case cannot be made for them, but because they fly in the face of historical experience.

The clarifying brilliance of Zeitlin's insistence that basic principles underlie complex historical phenomena is nowhere more evident than in his analysis of the controversies between the Pharisees and the Sadducees. He demonstrates that these controversies reveal the Pharisees as the democratizers of Judaean society, as champion of a living Oral Law, and as the firm opponents of Aaronide supremacy. The Pharisees were no sect of ritual purists, separated from the masses, but the beloved leaders of the people, whose concept of the twofold Law enabled Judaism to cope with the bewildering problems of the Graeco-Roman world. Far from seeking to make the laws of ritual purity more severe, they took decisive steps to ameliorate them. The Sadducees were the defenders of the strict Pentateuchal laws of ritual purity against the Pharisees. Zeitlin's insight into the nature of the Sadducee-Pharisee conflict represents one of the major breakthroughs in making the history of the Second Commonwealth intelligible.

Zeitlin's lifelong search for an intelligible reconstruction of the history of the inter-Testamental period is reflected in numberless articles and in critical reviews. The clarifying role of his methods is most in evidence when he clearly focuses his attention on a single problem. There is scarcely an article or review that does not provoke the reader to serious thought and that does not open for him new angles of vision. This prying loose of the rigid mind-set is of even greater significance than the rightness or wrongness of Zeitlin's own solution. By focusing on the problem in a novel way, he compels a reorientation of thinking which may very well end up with solutions that were not only not anticipated by him, but which he may even reject. For this he can only hold himself responsible; for by unleashing methodological principles, he invites other scholars to take them up and push them to their logical conclusions. He thus sets in motion the process of reconceptualization and the dialectic of reordering and reshaping the contours of the past. Zeitlin's contribution to Jewish historiography lies in his courageous effort to develop new concepts, and new tools for the assault on a chaotic, disordered, jumbled, and meaningless past.

PRINCIPLES OF ACADEMIC RESEARCH

By JUDAH M. ROSENTHAL

Israel

Professor Solomon Zeitlin made his first appearance on the stage of Jewish scholarship in 1915. He then wrote his well-known study on the Eighteen Decrees that were enacted in 65 C.E. in the upper chamber of Hananiah ben Hezekiah ben Gorion. This study marks the beginning of his career as the leading student of the history of the Second Jewish Commonwealth.

The main contributions of Zeitlin in the field of the history of the Second Commonwealth lie in the following areas: The historical development of the Halakhah; Jewish Sects of the Second Temple era; Jesus and Early Christianity as seen within the context of their own times as well as against the background of contemporary Jewish life.

He had already at the outset of his academic career established the scholarly principles to which he has remained loyal and by which he has been guided to this very day. They include the desire to find the earliest versions of the primary sources. Zeitlin rightly has assumed that Jewish sources (the apocryphal, the Hellenistic and the Talmudic) as well as Christian sources (the New Testament and the Patristic Literature) have become corrupt through their transmission during the early generations. It therefore becomes the task of the modern researcher to find the original text or version of the historical source. Many false theories have increasingly found their way into scholarship because they were based on corrupt texts. Thus the modern scholar is obligated to reconstruct the text and with it the historiographic structure of the period of the Second Commonwealth, based on a foundation of authentic and reliable sources, all the while destroying what requires wrecking as a prior step in rebuilding. Another of Zeitlin's early principles is his emphasis on the evolutionary development of Halakhah. He sees the Halakhah as a dynamic expression of the spiritual life of the Jewish people, which was never static. Rather it resulted from contemporary spiritual forces meeting the demands of history. Zeitlin proclaims again and again that it is manifestly impossible to understand the Halakhah without an understanding of contemporary economic conditions as well as a recognition of contemporary religious concepts that undergird the Halakhah.

These principles of scholarship are reflected in Zeitlin's numerous articles and monographs. They serve to buttress his great reconstruction of Judaism in the period of the Second Commonwealth. They are likewise the principal weapon in his ongoing valiant struggle against those scholars who refuse to accept his principles.

The scholarly world owes a debt of gratitude to Professor Zeitlin for his struggle to demand and gain for rabbinic literature the same recognition as a reliable and important source as other scholarly sources. Yet many scholars, Jewish as well as non-Jewish, refuse to accept Jewish sources as equally important as other sources. There is no doubt, however, that Zeitlin is right in his contention that it should be forbidden any scholar to express an opinion regarding the history of Jewish religous life during the Second Commonwealth, or any other period for that matter, unless he is able to deal with the original rabbinic sources. All too often scholars have promoted various hypotheses on the basis of opinions formed from facts gleaned from secondary sources that have proven to be erroneous.

Even his opponents—and their number is hardly small—acknowledge his special ability to reveal the inherent weaknesses in the scholarly research of others. Therefore, his critical articles are profound and sometimes devastating. We mention as an example his critique of the identification of Paul as a disciple of Rabban Gamaliel, the elder, who scoffed at several of the stories of his master (Shabbat 30b). Zeitlin proved that this identification was based on a misunderstanding of the true meaning of the talmudic passage. He further proved that, according to manuscripts, the name of the author of this Aggada should be Rabban Simeon ben Gamaliel and not Rabban Gamaliel. He stressed in this review, as in some of his other reviews, that it was the obligation of the scholar to seek the first or original version of the source, and not simply to depend on versions that are in print, which sometimes become erroneous in the process of transmission.

From another vantage point, he has struggled against the old-fashioned scholars and savants. This, in spite of the fact that he himself appreciates and honors the knowledge of the old-fashioned תלמיד חכם and his mastery of talmudic textual materials. But, as he clearly demonstrates, many of the old-fashioned scholars lack any understanding of the historical development of the Halakhah. Even in his very first scholarly article, mentioned above, he dwelt on the relationship between the Halakhah and the actual life of the period. He has continued to emphasize in all his writing that the Halakhah is not some ethereal creation that hovers in empty space. The Halakhah is a product of the spirit of the times and the direction of contemporary life. In this article on the Eighteen Decrees, Zeitlin demonstrated that some of the decrees were the natural result of the emigration from the land of Israel that took place in the period before the Great Rebellion. Several centuries later, however, at the time of the closing of the Talmud, the reason for these ordinances became obscure. Zeitlin thus sought to reveal the reason for the decrees in order to help the student better understand them in their historical context. The great difficulty which he faced in reconstructing the spiritual life of the past in order to illumine the reason and direction of the Halakhah is primarily due to the fact that every generation added its own contribution to its interpretation; in most cases we see the ancient period only through the eyes of medieval interpreters. The great German scholar, Theodore Nöldek, interestingly, already understood this fact—that students often uncritically accept later interpretations as original opinion. He therefore demanded from his Jewish students at the beginning of the century that they dedicate their time and effort to a scientific edition of the Talmud. Modern talmudic scholarship has made tremendous progress in the field of textual criticism. A great number of old talmudic sources appeared in academic editions based on manuscripts. However, a scientific edition of the Talmud based on manuscripts and various versions found in rabbinic literature still awaits another generation of scholars. This labor can only be undertaken by a large group of scholars with modern training in talmudic literature. The work, so necessary, cannot be done by those who must depend solely on their textual knowledge without any modern critical training. This discipline, especially, Zeitlin urges upon the scholarly world.

Similar exceptional awareness is likewise demonstrated in Zeitlin's energetic espousal of changes in contemporary Jewish life. In several of his articles he argues for a revival of the Sanhedrin in order to modify the Halakhah. He speaks out for abolition of the second day of the festivals. He challenges the religious leadership of the State of Israel who have stultified Jewish religious observance. The lack of vision on the part of the Israeli Rabbinate has reduced Judaism to a low estate and has alienated the youth of Israel from the spiritual inspiration which lies in Torah study. Yet Professor Zeitlin holds no brief for any specific Jewish religious movement or for any institution with vested interests. He is concerned with but one goal, providing a verdant and secure future for the Jewish people rooted in Jewish tradition. He has maintained a strict freedom to express his opinions regardless of which side of any question he has criticized. His great knowledge and understanding of the life of the polity, supported by his understanding of the ancient Halakhah and the knowledge of modern, contemporary religious problems have enabled him to strike deep and to penetrate incisively to the heart of any question.

Dr. Zeitlin has contributed actively toward furtherance of the goal of knowledge. He is one of the founders of the American Academy of Jewish Studies which began in 1919. And during his forty-five years of teaching at the Dropsie College, he has raised up a large number of students who have assumed important positions in numerous institutions of higher learning and research. Perhaps the appreciation and esteem which his students show him is his most permanent tribute; it is one of his most significant contributions to the strengthening of modern Jewish life and thought.

JEWISH LITURGY

By PHILIP BIRNBAUM

New York City

The Synagogue has always served as the historic communal institution for the Jewish people. The prayers recited therein express the people's past, their belief in monotheism, and their hopes and ideals. Accordingly, probing into the origins of the Synagogue and the background of prayer have been subjects of keen interest to scholars, and particular to Professor Solomon Zeitlin throughout his many years of research in Jewish law and lore.

Tefillah has been generally defined as thought, intercession, exhortation, prayer, hymn, judgment. But this does not explain its origin and basic meaning. According to Professor Solomon Zeitlin, the original signification is plea or argument, as in Jeremiah (32:16–25). Clearly, this prayer is in the form of an argument on the part of Jeremiah, who could not reconcile the obvious sense of making a purchase transaction with the imminent overthrow of the city.

Similarly, Abraham's fervent plea on behalf of Sodom (Genesis 18:23–25) was in the form of an eloquent argument. Moses, too (Deuteronomy 9:26–28), argued with God not to destroy His people. Another instance of *Tefillah* argument is that of King Hezekiah (II Kings 20:2–3), who set forth the reasons that he did not deserve to die. The passage in I Samuel 2:25 likewise reveals the interpretation of *Tefillah* as "argument" in the original Hebrew. So, also, the expression in Psalm 106:30 is explained in the Talmud to the effect that Phineas argued with his Maker (Sanhedrin 44a). From all this, prayer emerged.

Dr. Zeitlin maintains that the term "tefillah" passed through a process of evolution, until it finally acquired the connotation of supplication, petition, beseeching, as well as that of an act of offering adoration, thanksgiving, or praise.

Dr. Zeitlin has also shown that the group of psalms (113–118) known as the *Hallel,* which is liturgically chanted at feasts and festivals, was entirely omitted in Judaea on the last six days of Passover and on Rosh Ḥodesh. Tosefta Pesaḥim 10:8 clearly asserts that the *Hallel* must not be recited liturgically in abridgment. The Jews in Babylonia, however, instituted the recital of the *Hallel* on the last six days of Passover and on Rosh Ḥodesh, and "to distinguish the reciting of the *Hallel* on these days . . . they abridged it." When Rav, the founder of the academy of Sura, arrived in Babylonia, he sought to prevent such liturgical use, but finally allowed the practice since they recited the *Hallel* only in an abridged form (Taanit 28b).

Since the abridged *Hallel* was never part of the Judaean liturgy, but merely a Babylonian custom, some medieval authorities maintained that the recital required no introductory benediction on Rosh Ḥodesh and the last six days of Passover. Dr. Zeitlin concludes therefrom that "there is no reason why" the abridged *Hallel* can not be recited in commemoration of joyous occasions, such as on the Independence Day of Israel.

Writing on the Haggadah and its origin, Dr. Zeitlin points out that the passage עבדים היינו, which follows the Four Questions, contains the phrase, הקדוש ברוך הוא. Since this phrase was used at a later period than the Second Commonwealth, it must have been inserted after the destruction of the Second Temple.

As to the Ten Commandments, we are told that they were recited in the Temple daily before the *Shema.* This practice was abolished in Palestine on account of the heretics (Berakhot 12a). Dr. Zeitlin explains this by pointing out that the Decalogue is preserved in two versions, in Exodus 20:1–21 and in Deuteronomy 5:6–21; the main divergences occur in the fourth and fifth comandments. "As long as the Decalogue was read in the Temple by the priests, the sages saw no danger from the heretics. With the introduction of the reading of the Decalogue in the synagogues, the sages feared that some heretics would proclaim that the Decalogue was not given by God, because of the contradiction."

In view of the fact that the phrase "ten martyrs" occurs nowhere in the Talmud, Dr. Zeitlin insists that neither the *Eleh Ezkerah* midrash nor the liturgic poem of Yom Kippur, concerning the ten martyrs, has anything of the spirit of Rabbinic Judaism.

To the question: Did the Jews in ancient times pray with heads covered or uncovered, Dr. Zeitlin replies that "the Jews did not cover their heads while praying. Even the *Shema* could be recited by men with uncovered heads," though some were opposed to this practice (Soferim 14:15). In Biblical times, prayers were rendered while standing, kneeling, or prostrate. The hands were raised heavenward, so much so that "spreading the hands" became synonymous with prayer. Generally, prayers were intoned loudly, but following the canonization of prayers the Rabbis were opposed to their loud recital (Berakhot 24b; 31a). Dr. Zeitlin sums this up: "Since the rabbis canonized the prayers and made them communal rather than individual, they naturally expected to have order in the synagogue."

Reflecting on Professor Zeitlin and his many original theories, it may well be said that we learn most from those whose opinions are not identical with our own. He has been justly described among contemporary scholars as the *Meorer* (Rouser) *par excellence.* Hundreds of articles and books would never have been written in various languages if not for Professor Zeitlin's continuous contention and strife in the name of truth and authenticity. May God grant him strength to keep stimulating a new generation of scholars in the field of his endeavors.

RABBINIC RESEARCH AND SCROLL STUDIES

By SIDNEY B. HOENIG

Yeshiva University

A. *Talmudic Lore*

To this day Talmudic study is carried on in the traditional manner, as it was once followed in the Yeshivot of Poland and Russia. The text is analyzed and the student seeks to reconcile discrepancies, to find the *Peshat* and to build up a keen structure of casuistry and dialectics. Rarely is the text studied to ascertain its historical base or to determine its original meaning. Rather, the conformity of the text to Maimonidean concepts or to the opinions of other sages (*Rishonim* and *Aḥaronim*—earlier and later Rabbinic Commentators) is the academic Yeshiva approach.

Though the Haskalah pioneers and students of the historical method often sought to find a scientific basis of the text, their stress was mostly on readings, on manuscripts and on comparison of notations. They did not aim to discover whether the original and correct sense was found in a Mishnah or in a Tosefta. The amoraic interpretation was accepted and contradictions were generally solved by variant textual reading or by a pilpulistic search for fundamentals (*shitot*).

Professor Zeitlin, however, in his study of the Talmud, has always favored internal evidence as the criterion of research, even above textual readings. From the very first essay in 1914 to the present day, he has demonstrated that a dogmatic approach is not the historico-critical method. Contradictions in readings between the two Talmuds, he points out, were not particularly due to scribal errors, but were a result of differences in locality. One example is the variation pertaining to the law of possession of land in years of *orlah,* when one cannot utilize the produce of the land. Were these years included in the reckoning for the purpose of establishing the right of possession in three years? A Babylonian source denies it, whereas a Palestinian source upholds this right. The simple conclusion that agrarian laws were not applicable to the Diaspora solves this problem of the contradictions found in the reading of the Talmudic texts.

So too, Zeitlin reiterates, one must differentiate clearly between tannaitic, amoraic or late geonic sources. One cannot and should not interpret the tannaitic texts only as given by the Amoraim; the latter often gave the opinions of their own times; they did not reflect the actual situation, the practice or the law that had been current in the Second Commonwealth or Mishnaic periods. It is this recognition of the time element in the text that gives, above all, the fundamental approach to clarity and that aids in understanding as to whether certain halakhot, such as *Tevillat Gerim* and *Erub,* were of the early period or whether they belonged to later generations of teachers. Similarly, a mere term like "Israelite" or "Yom tov" in a text, when traced to its basic usage and meaning, will explain even difficult Talmudic readings. Such, for example may be found in Mishnah Taanit IV (pertaining to the festivities on "Yom Kippur").

Explaining the Zugot controversies or the *takkanot* of Ezra, Zeitlin stressed that one should not be misled by amoraic interpretation. The *Semikhah* problem of the Zugot is not the same as that of the *Semikhah* of Temple sacrifice, nor does the amoraic explanation of *shum* (garlic) appertain to any practice of cohabitation on the Sabbath. It refers only to a question of susceptibility of foods to impurity. In all of these instances Zeitlin demonstrated that, in a critical investigation of a text, one is not bound to the traditional explanation.

One of the greatest of Dr. Zeitlin's contributions in Talmudic analysis was to point out the significance of the element of intention in rabbinic law. This tannaitic principle was set by *Hillel* and his school as against the Shammaites. Zeitlin showed that this basic principle—that only one's act should be the criterion of decision—can explain many Talmudic discussions. *Bererah, asmakhta,* etc., are only amoraic corollaries, derived from this tannaitic principle. They are not fundamental or original factors in themselves. Moreover, the principle of intention in Talmudic jurisprudence helps interpret numerous laws in civil matters: sales, marriage, torts, *hefker* (*res nullius*) capital cases, etc. Recognition that R. Jose followed the Hillelite School and that R. Judah the Shammaite School will further clarify the basic issues. So, too, the differences of opinion between R. Joshua and R. Eliezer are best understood from this perspective.

Demonstrating further that Shammai never set any determination of halakhah on hermeneutics, Dr. Zeitlin proved how a particular text (e.g., Shabbat 19a), originally attributed to Shammai, really is that of

Hillel. Thus Zeitlin always emphasizes that correctness in names, generation, geography, and also the knowledge of changes introduced by later commentators or such as are to be found in glosses will likewise help establish an exact text. He has shown that often a slight emendation based on internal evidence as well as on historical background will clarify a difficult context. Thus שירי in Abot changed to רישי explains the leadership of the Great Assembly; ערב (evening) instead of ערבי (Arab) elucidates a Mishnah pertaining to the High Priest's purity on the Eve of Yom Kippur; השם instead of משה in Yadaim IV. 8, interprets the use of the divine name in documents. Talmudic texts with words like *meshumad* and *mumar* have often been distorted. Original texts had first the correct reading, *meshumad,* as in the Palestinian Talmud. *Meshumad* applied to one forced, under threat of death, to accept another religion. *Mumar,* however, meant one who changed to a different faith of his own free will. Hence, a clear understanding of basic usage and meaning is most urgent in the scholarly discipline of talmudic study.

Professor Zeitlin has also explained such subjects as the "18 gezerot, the defilement of hands by Scriptures or by *basar ta'avah,* the steps in the intercalation of the calendar, and also the Passover ritual in which there were three and not four questions. Knowledge of history and calendation, for example, will reveal why and how the Passover incident of Bnai Batyra and Hillel occurred on a Sabbath. Similarly, the interpretation of the difference between *shtar Kiddushin* and *ketubah* results in a better recognition of what constitutes the basic talmudic law. Analysis of Hillel's *Prosbol,* or his three explanations of different laws when he came from Babylon, or the meaning of *demai,* or the laws of *peah* (*res nullius* or *res communis*) similarly give a clearer understanding of the historic development of talmudic jurisprudence.

One of the greatest of Zeitlin's contributions deals with the halakhic differences between the Pharisees and Sadducees and the reasons thereof. One finds here the explanation of the *maamadot* and *mishmarot,* alibi witness, the manumission of slaves, *shi'abud haguf, lex talionis, korban,* and the contrasts between the Palestinian and Babylonian customs. A misunderstanding of these concepts may befuddle the rabbinic student seeking clarity in his texts.

Another important feature is the differentiation between "midrash" and "mishnah," showing that the Mishnah form is the earliest and that "midrash torah" refers definitely to biblical exegesis. "Midrash halakhah," however, a later term, refers only to exposition of the halakhah, the common or oral law. Most interesting is it that Dr. Zeitlin insists that the correct reading of the word is Mishné (second law), and that this Mishne was already written down very early, even as Maimonides held. He shows that the earliest manuscript of Abodah Zarah, dated 1290, substantiates this view.

In textual readings Zeitlin proves from internal evidence that the Bet Din ha-Gadol of Jerusalem existed till the end of Temple days. The phrase "forty years before" is a later change. Originally it was "four years." Moreover, certain phrases in the Talmud are only explanatory or redundant interpolations, such as גוי עובד עבודה זרה. Similarly, for a better understanding of Talmudic texts, Dr. Zeitlin has enunciated the difference between משכון and ערבון in the laws of possession, as well as the differences between private and public wrongs in the determination of punishment. He has likewise made definite distinctions between such terms as *gezerah, takkanot, ha'arama,* etc. in his critical study, thereby giving fuller comprehension to many abstruse talmudic problems.

The knowledge of Rabbi Akiba's principle of יש אם למקרא, he indicates, adds much to the clarification of many texts. A comprehension of the historical nature of the Sukkot *Bet hasho'ebah* ceremony or the Hanukkah festival explains the early origins of my observances. Terms like "Judah" and "Israel" are best understood in their true background, giving added meaning to the metamorphosis of the phrase כדת משה וישראל and the reason for it. The benediction over luminaries, the observance of one day of Rosh Hashanah in Palestine, the morning benedictions in the Temple, and the development of many prayers and rituals also attain full clarity in halakhic perspective only when studied in a historico-critical fashion. Similarly, the principle of דינא דמלכותא, that "the law of the government is law" is explained from its source in Babylonia, since it was not maintained in Palestine. The analysis of the statement pertaining to different texts of Torot in the Azarah reveals the extent of Masorah tradition. A historic investigation of readings, moreover, explains the notion of immortality or bodily resurrection as propounded in the Talmud in different periods.

Zeitlin's study of rabbinics also reveals that until the age of twenty a person was not qualified as a witness in real-estate transactions, and that bar mitzvah is truly not a Talmudic requisite. In a like manner, studying the *takkanot* of Rabban Johanan ben Zakkai, he showed how the Sage decreed that the new harvest may be eaten immediately on the 16th of Nisan. An erroneous change in present Talmudic texts, namely, that it is forbidden, is only due to a saboraic revision. Similarly he demonstrated that, since the sacrificial aspects of bringing *Bikkurim* on Shabuot had been discontinued with the Temple destruction, later Talmudic sources, consequently, in time associated the Revelation with Shabuot, giving the festival added meaning.

Zeitlin has often stressed that, unlike the Pentateuch which was considered divine and unlike the Roman code which was derived from secular authority, the Rabbis considered the authority of the Mishnah as derived fundamentally from their own interpretation and knowledge. Therefore, to establish a systematic legal system of interpretation, Hillel applied hermeneutic devices. These were later expanded by rabbinic teachers who succeeded him, and aided in furthering rabbinic investigation and legislation.

In all, Zeitlin seeks in his study of Talmud, not a dogmatic approach, but a critical one. He sees in rabbinic lore the basis for a new code for modern Judaism, harmonizing law and life.

B. *The Battle of the Scrolls*

In the past two decades Professor Solomon Zeitlin's name has been closely associated with the Dead Sea Scrolls. Thus, A. Dupont-Sommer in his book, *The Essene Writings from Qumran,* writes (p. 394):

> Ever since 1949 Zeitlin has defended this thesis unceasingly in the *JQR,* whose editor he is, with an obstinacy and aggressiveness which cannot unfortunately take the place of proof. . . . Zeitlin's theory is no longer credited in the scientific world and for good reasons; but the author continues to complain bitterly that his arguments have not been refuted.

But even such deplorable remarks about him have not stopped Zeitlin, who comes up again and again with questions about the authenticity of the Scrolls—their mode of discovery, the scientific value of its paleography, the internal evidence and, especially, the Karaitic allusions, all matters which the biblical or Christian scholar cannot appreciate. Zeitlin has opposed the hasty pronouncements of scholars and the sensationalism connected with the scholarly finds, which smack of the advertising methods of Madison Avenue. He sticks to his guns—that the photostatic evidences should first be published. Where, for instance, are the Haftarah Scrolls which were first seen in 1947? Zeitlin made the bold suggestion, first to Professor Eliezer Lipa Sukenik, that many of the early discovered Bible scrolls may have been part of the Hebrew MSS obtained during the 1929 riots in Hebron. He still insists that the purchase of the Scrolls by Hebrew University, and the creating of a Shrine, a היכל הספר, was indiscreet; this is most distressing to Zeitlin, who loves the truth and wishes to see it prevail in Judaism and in Israel.

One of his opponents, Professor Millar Burrows, writes of him:

> Professor Zeitlin's independence of judgment and good sportsmanship in debate add zest to the search for truth. He renders at least the Socratic service of the gadfly and, of course, there is always the possibility that he may be right.

It is well known that the paleography of the Scrolls has been dependent upon the identification of the date of the Nash Papyrus, as recognized by Professor W. F. Albright. Zeitlin maintains, however, that the Nash Papyrus is of the third century C.E., when there was a movement to restore the Decalogue into the Jewish liturgy. Appropriately, this also explains the "discovery of Tefillin (phylacteries)"—texts of Shema and the Decalogue together in a scroll. Moreover, Zeitlin has demonstrated that these "Tefillin" are only sectarian amulets belonging to an early Karaite.

There are persons who complain that Zeitlin's stubbornness results from the fact that he has a medium of communication of his own; he is the editor of *JQR* and has utilized the journal for his own purposes. In this connection, it is interesting to recall that Dr. Cyrus Adler had served as editor until 1940. In February 1940, Dr. Adler was ill and wanted to discontinue the *JQR*; but Zeitlin, visiting him, pleaded for its continuance, on the ground that its absence could diminish the prestige of American Jewish scholarship. At Adler's request, therefore, since July 1940 Zeitlin expanded the *Jewish Quarterly Review;* it became the only English scholarly quarterly of note under Jewish auspices. Professor Zeitlin has completed thirty years of uninterrupted editorial supervision of the *JQR,* through turbulent times in world and Jewish history.

In addition to writing, Zeitlin has not feared to come into the "lion's den," and has delivered lectures on the Scrolls in the Hebrew University of Jerusalem, in the New York Public Library, in Münich, as well as in Moscow, in the face of many antagonists. He has questioned Professor Cecil Roth's contention that the Scrolls are of Zealot origin, reiterated by that scholar in the Masada finds; and he has questioned Professor Yigael Yadin's identification of the Bar Kokhba letters. Zeitlin puts these letters in the realm of fiction, asserting, for example, that the text contains the word רבינו, "Rabbenu," which did not became a title until the early part of the Middle Ages.

Zeitlin's obstinacy in the dating of the Scrolls and his determination in academic battle are not new aspects of his personality. He writes, "Harkavy had the courage to brand the Firkovitch discovery as forgeries; Clermont-Ganneau recognized the forgeries of Shapira. To some extent both of these scholars [Harkavy and Clermont-Ganneau] were my teachers." In his search for truth Zeitlin even opposed his own teacher, Salomon Reinach, who, upholding Professor Robert Eisler, believed that the Slavonic Josephus was a translation of the Aramaic or Greek Josephus, and that it revealed an authentic Christ passage from the historian's own hand. Zeitlin successfully disproved this fallacy. Dr. Cyrus Adler was then asked to curb Zeitlin. But academic freedom was fully allowed at the Dropsie College. Adler did not yield to the pressure even of James Loeb, the Maecenas of the Loeb Classics. Zeitlin won his point, now accepted by all, that the famous Christ passage was interpolated by a Church Father, probably Eusebius.

Zeitlin is convinced of the lateness of the Scrolls; there may be many who agree with him but hesitate to undermine their own popularity by siding with him. He and only one or two of his disciples have the fortitude to face the disdain which scholars silently show by their refusal to answer Zeitlin's queries. Zeitlin maintains that the Dead Sea Scrolls were written long after the destruction of the Temple, and are not of the early Christian era. He has unceasingly requested that Professors Dupont-Sommer, Albright, Burrows, Cross, Yadin, and deVaux answer his questions and refute his opinion, but they have failed to do so. He has shown that the translations of these scholars are faulty and deceptive; some of the Hebrew in the Scrolls is unintelligible. To him, the Scrolls fit into the Karaitic period when the Persians captured Palestine from the Byzantine Empire and promised the Jews an independent state in the early part of the seventh century. He questions the genuineness of the Zadokite Fragment (Damascus Document), believing it to be very late, as did also Professors Adolph Büchler and Arthur Marmorstein. The discovery of the phrase *b'talmud* in *Pesher Nahum* substantiates his contention that these Scrolls are not of the inter-Testamental era.

Some scholars think that Zeitlin, in persistently upholding his opinion, is "fighting windmills," and they ignore his arguments that "history is being falsified by the propaganda of the Scrolls." Zeitlin insists that the paleography of the Scrolls cannot be a criterion since we have no manuscripts of the pre-Christian period to make comparisons. The archaic writing therein is like that of the medieval age. Moreover, the Scrolls generally were not found by archaeologists, but bought from Bedouins who gave contradictory reports about the discoveries. The carbon-14 test was not applied to the scrolls, but to the linen. No scholar saw the scrolls wrapped in linen, and many scientists also maintain that the carbon-14 test is unreliable, since other tests which were made produced variant dates.

Zeitlin also points out that the ideas in the Scrolls are not in accord with those maintained by the Essenes. Immortality of the soul and reward and punishment after death are not mentioned. The Scrolls cannot be Essene, for this sect did not believe in Messianism nor in the idea of redemption, namely, that the Messiah died for the sins of the people. Being individualists, the Essenes did not support the idea of *proselytism.* Thus, to equate the Teacher of Righteousness with the Messiah is far-fetched. Similarly, Zeitlin stresses that one cannot associate the Sicarii with the Zealots, as do Professors G. R. Driver and Cecil Roth. The origins and philosophic perspectives of these two sects were definitely in conflict.

Zeitlin has also demonstrated that the *matres lectionis* in biblical texts were adopted in the time of Rabbi Akiba, not earlier. Erasures, parentheses, connecting lines between words or ellipses for phrases omitted, and the salutation "from," giving the name of a sender in a letter, also indicate medievalism; all these signs only came into usage later. The use of *El* or dots for the name of God also indicates a later period, for the Tetragrammaton was no longer used by traditionalists after the Second Temple era. The different readings of the Isaiah Scroll likewise do not prove the provenance of an early text. Many of the biblical readings in rabbinic literature are even preferable to the Masorah which was adopted in the medieval age.

No commentaries on biblical books were written during the Second Temple era. Many of the Scroll phrases can be traced back to Targum Jonathan, or to the Midrash, or to early Karaitic writings. The portrayals of the wars and the battle standards are only patterned after the medieval *Sefer ha-yashar.* Terms like *Moreh Zedek,* "brit (covenant) of Abraham," "time of final redemption" likewise indicate late writing. Certain references to laws pertaining to the Sabbath (*Erub*) and to purification were not at all in vogue during the pre-Christian era, but were enacted later. Terms like ערב שמיטה instead of ערב שביעית also indicate a later time.

The *Genesis Apocryphon,* with its mixture of Aramaic and Hebrew, and following late rabbinic interpretations of Genesis 12, reveals that it is a medieval composition. The halakhot of the Manual of Discipline are like those of the Zadokite Fragment of the medieval Genizah. The term *kittim* in the Middle Ages referred to those living in Italy and in the Byzantine Roman empire. Baptism is not mentioned in the Scrolls to associate it with Christianity. The calendar in the Zadokite Fragment is not a basic solar one and cannot be compared to the Book of Jubilees; it follows a Karaitic reckoning.

Interestingly, Professor Zeitlin was the first scholar to publish photostats of the Damascus Scroll (Zadokite Fragment). In so doing he showed that many scholars who relied on copyists erred in details of interpretation.

The recent excavations at Masada have led many to assume that this was the last stand of the Sicarii. Zeitlin insists that the story of Masada is not one of glory; rather, here in this fortress the Sicarii, with their philosophy of self-annihilation and individualism, contributed to the destruction of the national state. The Ben Sira text found there belongs to the medieval period, as is also evidenced by the use of such Talmudic words as שותף *shutaf* (partner), etc. During the early Middle Ages in the time of Heraclius, the time of the Parthian-Byzantine wars, many Jews found refuge in Masada. In general, the caves were a genizah of the sectarians and of the "mourners of Zion" during these wars.

It should also be stressed that New Testament fragments of the medieval period, Arabic papyri of the ninth century, as well as coins of the Arab period were found in the caves. All this negates a pre- or early Christian dating.

Moreover, the medieval Rabbis had copies of the Apocrypha and Jubilees. The Ben Sira text in Hebrew is one that was translated from the Greek and the Syriac, and the present discoveries are only copies of those renderings.

The sincere search for truth is the greatest asset one can possess. Professor Solomon Zeitlin has never relinquished this goal. His demand that scholars examine every facet and that they answer his relevant questions still holds. He has never declared that the Scrolls were a hoax; only that the initial discovery is a hoax. The Scrolls may indeed give a picture of the medieval period and throw light on sectarian phases of that time; but definitely, Zeitlin continues to assert, they do not have any historical value for the origins of Judaism and early Christianity, for they do not belong to the inter-Testamental period.

ANNOTATED BIBLIOGRAPHY

ABBREVIATIONS USED IN THIS BIBLIOGRAPHY

HUCA	*Hebrew Union College Annual*
JBL	*Journal of Biblical Literature*
JQR	*Jewish Quarterly Review,* New Series
MGWJ	*Monatsschrift für Geschichte und Wissenschaft des Judentums*
PAAJR	*Proceedings of the American Academy for Jewish Research*
PAJHS	*Publication of American Jewish Historical Society*
REJ	*Revue des Études Juives*

ANNOTATED BIBLIOGRAPHY

1914 - 1915

1. "Les Dix-huit mesures," *REJ,* Vol. 68 (1914), pp. 22–36. (See also no. 343.)

The record of the Eighteen Decrees in Shabbat 14a reveals that each decree had historical implications. The arrangement of the Decrees is still questionable; even the Amoraim could not make it specific and clear. It is apparent that sixteen of these Decrees were directed against the Romans to prevent relations with pagans, and not to offer sacrifices on their behalf. The decree relating to pagan lands was renewed because of emigration due to the war of 65 C.E. In many instances the severity of the Eighteen Decrees was a result of the insistence of Bet Shammai who aimed to maintain the conservative view of impurity based on the act and not on the intent.

There are other Eighteen Decrees with which both the Schools of Hillel and Shammai concurred. These applied to rules of purity directed not against the Romans, but against the priestly Sadducees, and were enacted in 65 CE. before Ananias (Hananiah) was killed and after Gessius Florus had massacred many in Jerusalem. The Assembly was in Hananiah's home. It was his son, Eleazar, who first succeeded in abolishing the peace-offering usually offered for Rome. With these enactments the war against Rome began.

1917

2. "The Semikhah Controversy between the Zugoth," *JQR,* Vol. VIII, No. 4 (April 1917), pp. 499–517. (See no. 358.)

It is the opinion of the commentators that the controversy of the Zugot (Hag. 2:2) is identical with the controversy of Shammai and Hillel as stated in the succeeding Mishnah, i.e., whether or not one is permitted to "lay the hands" upon the sacrificial animal in the Temple court on holidays. The Tosefta, the Palestinian Talmud, and the statements of the Zugot themselves, however, show that the controversy centered on whether or not reliance could be placed upon the authority of the Hakhamim in their innovations upon the Torah.

3. "Takkanot Ezra," *JQR,* Vol. VIII, No. 1 (July 1917), pp. 61–74.
The sources underlying the causes and reasons for the ten *takkanot* ascribed by the Talmud (B.K. 82a) to Ezra are reexamined in light of the difficulties posed by the Talmud itself. They were not instituted by any one man nor in any one period, though, for various reasons, they were ascribed to Ezra. The *takkanot* of purity and impurity are most ancient, but the *takkanot* amending the laws of the Sabbath stem from the Schools of Shammai and Hillel. The purpose of *takkanot* was to bring religion into consonance with life. (See no. 15.)

1918

4. "The Great Political Struggle. An Account of the Last Days of Jerusalem," *Jewish Forum,* Vol. I, No. 3 (April 1918), pp. 138–147.

It is a misconception to regard the Sicarii as "robbers." These revolutionaries were motivated by an inviolable attachment to liberty, and fought any tyrannic rule. In addition there was the Apocalyptic group which opposed all violence. Christianity owes its origin to the Apocalyptists. The request for Bar-Abbas, rather than for Jesus, reflects sympathy of some of the people with the Sicarii.

In the beginning of the War a coalition government was formed (presumably to obtain peace with Rome). The Zealots, who were democratically orientated, overthrew the aristocracy. They sought to limit the High Priests' term to one year at a time; they also established seventy of the *demos* as a court (*B.J.* 4.5.4 [336]). Rabban Johanan ben Zakkai was in sympathy with the peace party. It was John of Gischala, on the other hand, who sought to establish a dictatorship in opposition to the Zealots' (demos) party. All the sects were in constant internal conflict; they forgot partisan strife only when the Romans besieged the city (cf., no. 393).

5. "The Last Days of Jerusalem," *Jewish Forum,* Vol. I, No. 3 (April 1918), 12 pp. Reprint of no. 4.

6. "Megillat Taanit as a Source for Jewish Chronology and History in the Hellenistic and Roman Periods. Chapters I–III." *JQR,* Vol. IX, No. 1 (July 1918), pp. 71–102. (Cf., no. 16.)

7. "Judas of Galilee and Jesus of Nazareth," *Jewish Forum,* Vol. I, No. 9 (October 1918) pp. 514–521.

Initially the Jews (particularly the Sadducees) preferred a theocracy. In time, other political philosophies emerged. The Sicarii, founded by Judas the Galilean, maintained "no lordship of man over man," and that "terror must oppose terror"; the Pharisees, in response, stressed loyalty; the Apocalyptists, who believed in the equality of mankind, sought to estabish the Kingdom of Heaven by preaching the practice of nonresistance.

There are many similarities between the ideals of the Sicarii and the Apocalyptists, who were the followers of Jesus. They differed in method, but both opposed the rich, the Apocalyptists invoking upon them divine punishment, and the Sicarii, using actual violence. Both held a contempt of death. At Masada the Sicarii committed suicide, for to them, "life [without liberty] was considered a calamity." Jesus, though opposed to payment of taxes to authority, yielded to the pressure of circumstances. (Cf., no. 51.)

8. "When Did Jerusalem Surrender to Antiochus Sidetes?" *PAJHS,* No. 26 (1918), pp. 165–171.

Josephus notes that Antiochus invaded Judaea in the fourth year of his reign and in the first of Hyrcanus' rule, in the 162nd Olympiad. These dates do not agree: The former, 136–135 B.C.E., does not fall within the same period as the latter, 132–128 B.C.E. It is suggested that the invasion came in the fourth year of the rule of Hyrcanus I (distinguishing him from his grandson). This occurred in 133–132 B.C.E. With this amended textual reading, the dates are no longer contradictory.

1919

9. "Megillat Taanit as a Source for Jewish Chronology and History in the Hellenistic and Roman Periods. Chapters IV–VI," *JQR,* Vol. X, No. 1 (July 1919), pp. 49–80. (Cf., no. 16.)

10. "Sameias and Pollion," *Journal of Jewish Lore and Philosophy,* Vol. I, No. 1 (1919), pp. 61–67.

There are three references to Sameias in *Antiquities.* The first two refer to Shemaiah and the third to Shammai. According to Shemaiah,

Herod was guilty (cf., Kid. 43a). In all cases Pollion is Hillel, but a scribal error crept into the second passage describing Sameias as the pupil of Pollion, whereas it should read Sameias (Shemaiah), the teacher of Pollion-Hillel.

11. "Studies in Tannaitic Jurisprudence. Intention as a Legal Principle," *Journal of Jewish Lore and Philosophy,* Vol. I, Nos. 3–4 (1919), pp. 297–311.

An act is a result of volition. Intention relates to the consequences. A person may will an act, but at times he may not intend to produce the consequences of that act, i.e., plan for a particular result. Hillel was the first to recognize intention as a factor in Jewish law.

Understanding the principle of intention sheds light on many aspects of tannaitic jurisprudence, such as ritual purity, Sabbath, civil law, sales, marriage and divorce, torts, and even capital cases, where the main consideration is not the act but the intention. Among the Tannaim, R. Judah followed the Shammaitic view stressing the act itself; R. Joshua, a Hillelite, insisted on the prior intention of the act. (See also no. 26.)

1920

12. "Megillat Taanit as a Source for Jewish Chronology and History in the Hellenistic and Roman Periods. Chapters VIII–XII," *JQR,* Vol. X, No. 2 (October 1919) and No. 3 (January 1920), pp. 237–290. (Cf., no. 16.)

13. "The Secret of Badu: A Specimen of Jewish Camouflage," *American Journal of Theology*, Vol. 24, No. 4 (October 1920), pp. 502–512.

The contradiction of the dates of the crucifixion of Jesus in the Synoptic and non-Synoptic Gospels is not due to any "occult rule of *Badu.*" The system of *Badu,* בדו (Mon., Wed., Fri.), was arranged after the calendar was fixed, as a mnemonic device to indicate on which days Passover cannot fall. It was revised to *Adu,* אדו so that the Day of Atonement will not fall on Sunday or Friday, nor the "Day of the Willow" on the Sabbath. *Badu* could not have been a camouflage, for at the time of Jesus the fixed calendar was not yet in existence. (See no. 360.)

14. *Studies in Tannaitic Jurisprudence,* Ark Publishing Co. (Cincinnati: 1920), pp. 15f. Reprint of no. 11.

15. "The Takkanot of Ezra," *JQR,* Vol. X, Nos. 2 and 3 (October and January 1919–1920), pp. 367–371. (See no. 3.) A reply to Professor A. Marmorstein.

The fifth *takkanah* of Ezra, dealing with *shum,* eating garlic on the eve of the Sabbath, was not directed against the Samaritans who were opposed to cohabitation on the Sabbath. The edict deals with the rules of food becoming susceptible to impurity when water falls upon it (*nizzuk*) and is part of the basic halakhic differences between the Pharisees and Sadducees.

1922

16. *Megillat Taanit as a Source for Jewish Chronology and History in the Hellenistic and Roman Periods,* a Thesis submitted, February 1917, in partial fulfillment of the requirements for the degree of Doctor of Philosophy in the Dropsie College for Hebrew and Cognate Learning. Printed in England at the Oxford University Press, by Frederick Hall (Philadelphia: 1922), pp. xi, 118 + [2]. (See nos. 6, 9, 12.)

Originally the name was simply *Megillah; Megillat Taanit* is a later term. The scholion thereto is not authentic, for it belongs to the Talmudic period. Its contents include dates of events of the periods of the Hasmoneans, the Romans, and the Great War against the Romans. The last recorded event is that of 17 Adar 66 C.E.; thereafter Vespasian overcame the resistance in Galilee. Eleazar ben Ḥananiah circulated the Scroll to show that even as the Hasmoneans had overthrown the Syrian Greeks, the Jews should battle the Romans and preserve the national festive days. After 70 C.E., the Jews did not observe the list of national holidays except for Purim and Ḥanukkah. Because the Seleucidan battle of 312 B.C.E. was in the summer, the Palestinian Jews reckoned the year, beginning in the autumn, as year II of the Seleucidan era. I Maccabees follows this method, while II Maccabees counts 312 B.C.E. as the year I. However, all the cities around Palestine, following the Seleucidan era, fixed the beginning of the year according to the traditional New Year prevailing in their respective countries. In Damascus, for example, the era was counted from the spring of 312 B.C.E. I Maccabees (written in Hebrew) used the chronology of the Jews; II Maccabees, written in the Diaspora, follows the calculation current there.

The Sabbatical cycles all conform to the reckoning of the Seleucidan era as found in the incidents recorded in Josephus. This correct order was preserved by the Geonim. (Cf., no. 122.)

In *Bellum Judaicum* (B.J.) Josephus used the Tyrian (Syrian) calendar.

Many historical meanings of events are interpreted here; for example, the Second Temple was really finished on 23 Adar, the Revolt broke out in 65 C.E., not in 66. None of the holidays in the Megillah are to be traced to controversies between the Pharisees and Sadducees. (See no. 70.)

1923

17. "Studies in the Beginnings of Christianity," *JQR,* Vol. XIV, No. 1 (July 1923), pp. 111–139. Reviews of: Foakes-Jackson and Lake, *The Beginnings of Christianity*; Eduard Meyer, *Ursprung und Anfänge des Christentums*; Joseph Klausner, ישו הנוצרי.

Disastrous are the results when one writes the history of a people without being familiar with its literature and spirit, or if one is prejudiced against Jews and Judaism and follows the stereotype of condemning the Pharisees, e.g., picturing the Hasmoneans as "echt-jüdische Fanatiker," or praising Jason and Menelaus as "Reform Jews."

Jesus' basic teachings about God did not differ essentially from those of his contemporaries. The differences of opinion centered about three subjects: a) the method of resistance to the oppressors of Israel; b) the ultimate fate of the People of the Land; and c) the correct observance of the Law. On the first, Jesus opposed the tendency to rebel; on the second and third he conflicted with the Scribes.

1924

18. "The Halakhah in the Gospels and its Relation to the Jewish Law at the Time of Jesus," *HUCA,* Vol. I (1924), pp. 357–373.

Many halakhot, as the washing of hands before meals, and the institution of baptism for proselytes, did not exist during Jesus' time;

their inclusion only reflects the time of the compilation of the Gospels. Were baptism necessary in the Second Commonwealth, Josephus would have mentioned it with reference to the conversion of Izates. Early immersion was for purity, but not for proselytism. A halakhic controversy pertaining to such immersion, and a reference in the Sibylline oracles, belong only to the second century C.E.

During the Second Temple era the laws of purity did not apply to non-Jews; such a rule was promulgated in 65 C.E., when it was decreed that pagans were in the category of uncleanness like a *zab*. They then had to be immersed and also bring a sacrifice (cf., no 1). The Christians adopted the practice of baptism from the Jews after 65 C.E. (Cf. also no. 351.) Before 65, as Rabbi Akiba pointed out, there was no defilement of hands in the sanctuary. The Eighteen Decrees put every Jew into a status of ritual uncleanness. To mitigate this severity, the Rabbis declared that washing of the hands was sufficient, and *tevilah* (immersion) unnecessary. Some Rabbis, like R. Eliezer b. Ḥanokh, opposed this decree. The later Rabbis speak of *tebul yom* and *netilat yadaim* as new institutions.

19. שמעון הצדיק וכנסת הגדולה, *Ner Maaravi* (Kislev 5684-1924), pp. 137–142.

"Simon, son of Johanan," mentioned in Ben Sira ch. 50, is a portrayal of a contemporary (*ca.* 180 B.C.E.), and cannot be Simon I. According to Talmud Menahot 109a, Oniah III succeeded Simon. Hence, the reference is only to Simon II, in the time of Antiochus III.

The story in Yoma 69b, pertaining to Alexander the Great, refers to Antiochus III and to Simon II who repaired the walls of Jerusalem. The Abot reference to Simon the Just is to Simon II. The term שירי "remnant," should be read רישי, "head." The Great Assembly was a temporary body convened for special purposes, like the gathering by Ezra and Nehemiah and the conclave of 65 C.E., whose purpose was to act on extraordinary religious or political changes.

20. "The Napoleonic Sanhedrin and the Russian Government. A Critical Study in Modern Jewish History," *Ner Maaravi,* English Section, (Kislev 5684-1924), pp. 11–14. This is a paper read before the 28th annual meeting of the American Jewish Historical Society at New York, February 23, 1920.

It is generally held that Napoleon's action in 1804 troubled the Russian government, and that Russia therefore postponed the decree of expulsion of the Jews. The delay was, however, due rather to internal economic reasons. Russia recognized that the expulsion would cause an economic crisis; Napoleon's Sanhedrin and an apparent contact with Russian Jewry was used as an excuse to justify the postponement.

1926

21. "Origine de la divergence entre les Évangiles synoptiques et l'Évangile non-synoptique quant à la date de la crucifixion de Jésus," *REJ,* (Mélanges offerts à Israel Lévi . . .), Vol. 82, Nos. 163–164 (1926), pp. 199–208.

According to the Synoptic Gospels, the crucifixion took place on Passover; according to John, on the eve of Passover. The divergence does not involve the question of the historicity of the crucifixion of Jesus, but rather a difference of theological emphasis. All sources agree that the crucifixion was on Friday, the day of Adam's creation, and that Jesus came to atone for the original sin. The question pertains only to the date of the month. John maintained that Jesus was a paschal lamb, the sacrifice ordained for the fourteenth. The Synoptic writers held that Jesus personified the Passover—the redemption from bondage—which occurred on the fifteenth of Nisan.

The offering of the paschal lamb continued even after 70 C.E. as is evident in the words of R. Joshua (Eduyot 3:6) and in the action of Rabban Gamaliel (Pes. 7:2). Likewise, the pagan who was put to death for requesting the sacrificial portion of the Passover lamb (Pes. 3b) was one suspected of espionage by R. Judah b. Batyra (c. 120 C.E.).

22. "Regarding Eisler's discovery of the Slavonic Josephus," *REJ,* Vol. 82, Nos. 163–164, pp. 208–209. Postscript, unsigned. (Cf., no. 37.)

23. Review of: *The Pharisees* by R. Travers Herford, *JQR,* Vol. XVI, No. 4 (April 1926), pp. 383–394.

The division between the Pharisees and the Sadducees lay not only in their respective attitudes to the oral law, but also in their different concepts of social and political life. That Pharisaism was no "organized hypocrisy" and no "dead corpse of a once living religion," is correct.

1928

24. "The Christ Passage in Josephus," *JQR,* Vol. XVIII, No. 3 (January 1928), pp. 231–255. (Cf., no. 37.)

25. "Note on the Relation of the Slavonic Josephus to Jossipon," *JQR,* Vol. XIX, No. 1 (July 1928), pp. 77–78. (Cf., no. 37.)

1929

26. "Asmakta or Intention. A Study in Tannaitic Jurisprudence," *JQR,* Vol. XIX, No. 3 (January 1929), pp. 263–273.

Two controversies of R. Jose and R. Judah (cited in B.M. 48b, 77b and B.B. 10:5) led the Amoraim to conclude that the focal point of contention was the concept of *Asmakhta.* Many contradictory passages led to great confusion regarding this concept in the Amoraic and rabbinic literature. A critical analysis shows that the controversy of the Tannaim revolves about the principle of intention. The concept of *Asmakhta* was unknown to the Tannaim and never mentioned in the Mishnah. (Cf., no. 11.)

27. "The Slavonic Josephus and its Relation to Josippon and Hegessippus," *JQR,* Vol. XX, No. 1 (July 1929), pp. 1–50. (Cf., no. 37.)

28. "Some Stages of the Jewish Calendar," *Society for the Advancement of Judaism Review,* Vol. 8, No. 38 (May 31, 1929).

The calendar of the very early Hebrews was lunar, as indicated by the word *yerah* (moon). The biblical calendar, however, was a solar one (364 days). There is no mention of any intercalated month in the Bible. The month had thirty days, the day beginning with sunrise. The Day of Atonement consisted of two half-days—from evening to evening (the second part of the ninth, and the first part of the tenth). The solar year of the Egyptians was intercalated by a "little year" of five days. The Israelites added a day to every quarter, thus keeping the days of the week intact. The quarter-season consisted of 7x13=91; 30+30+31. (See no. 35.) The fifteenth day of the first and seventh months (Passover and Sukkot) occurred on Sundays. The Jubilee year—inserted between Yom Kippur and Sukkot—was only a "little year" of forty-nine days, added after forty-nine years, because of the one missing day (the 365th). Sabbatical years—not Jubilee years—were observed in the Second Commonwealth.

After the Restoration, the Jews adopted a lunar-solar calendar with Babylonian names for the months. These are mentioned only in post-Exilic literature. Intercalation was introduced to keep the festivals in the proper season rather than on established days of the week. Thus Shabuot, which had no fixed date, biblically, was arranged to be fifty days after Passover, regardless of the day of the week.

The change to a lunar-solar system eliminated the necessity for the Jubilee. The Jews also adopted the Greek system of three intercalated months in eight years, to prevent Sabbatical and post-Sabbatical years from being intercalated. (Cf., no. 122.) The New Year was changed to the fall. Thus, the Sabbatical year coincided with the beginning of the regular new year. The order of the week was always kept intact by Jews and Christians. In the fourth century the calendar was fixed by setting the years as full, normal, or defective, based on the number of days in Heshvan, Kislev, Tebet, so that the Festival of Shabuot occurred only on the sixth of Sivan. Also the system of *Adu* and *Badu* was then introduced, supported by the Metonic system of intercalating seven years in a nineteen-year cycle (3, 6, 8, 11, 14, 17, 19). (See nos. 13, 360.)

29. "Some Stages of the Jewish Calendar," *Society for the Advancement of Judaism Review,* Vol. 8, No. 38 (May 31, 1929), p. 12. Reprint. (See no. 28.)

30. "'Un témoignage pour eux,' Exemple de l'importance de la Halacha pour l'intelligence des Évangiles," *REJ,* Vol. 87, No. 173 (January–March, 1929), pp. 79–82.

One must recognize the significance of the Halakhah for the understanding of the Gospels. The phrase "a testimony for you," in Matthew 7.4, refers only to a harmonizing with the biblical law as interpreted by Hillel—that is, although a leper had become pure, he still needed priestly sanction. Thus, Jesus noted that though he cured the leper, it was still necessary, according to the Bible, to obtain the approval of the priest. The text should read "show yourself to the priest for his testimony" and "offer the sacrifice." "Testimony" here refers neither to leprosy nor to the sacrifice, but to the priestly declaration.

1930

31. "A Critical Edition of the Talmud. An Appreciation of Malter's *Text of Tractate Taanit*," *JQR*, Vol. XXI, Nos. 1 & 2 (July–October 1930), pp. 61–73.

One must always be careful about textual changes introduced by later commentators, and have a correct knowledge of names, generations, geography, etc., pertaining to the context. Striking examples may be found in the readings of Mishnah Eduyot 2.3 (and Pes. 19a) pertaining to the nondefilement of hands in the Temple, and in Mishnah Erubin 6.1, where "Sadducee" means a Jewish-Christian because, before the Temple's destruction, a non-Jew could not invalidate any *Erub* arrangement.

Another example of critical internal evaluation pertains to Sabbath fighting. Shammai never based Halakhah on biblical hermeneutics. Thus the Shabbat 19a dictum referring to battle on the Sabbath must be attributed only to Hillel's opinion. Likewise, Josephus renders 14 Lous (10 Elul) as the "wood-festival," evidencing that sometimes, even without any MSS or internal evidence, an extraneous source might be helpful for Talmudic interpretation.

32. Corrections to the article, "The Slavonic Josephus and its Relation to Josippon and Hegesippus," (*JQR*, Vol. XX, No. 1, July 1929), *JQR*, Vol. XX, No. 3 (January 1930), p. 281. (Cf., no. 37.)

33. "Chassidism: A Revolt of the Masses. The Origin of a Popular Religious Movement Among the Jews," *The Jewish Tribune* (August 1, 1930), p. 2.

Hasidism was a revolution of the masses against the intellectual aristocracy. Polish Jewry was then a state within a state, and Talmudic study was the very essence of life in the cities. On the other hand, the Ukraine was steeped in superstition and its aristocratic intellectuals disdained the ignorant Ukrainian Jews. As long as the Council of Four Lands was dominant, the Ukrainians could not revolt against rabbinic authority, but with its decline, the masses pressed their claim that all Jews were alike; no distinction should exist between those who were scholars and those who served God with their hearts. Although they introduced the revolt, the Hasidim called their opponents, "Mitnagdim." Similarly, in the Second Temple, those who opposed the aristocratic Sadducees were called "Perushim"—separatists. The Rabbis combated the Hasidic revolt because they feared that it would destroy the tradition of learning, and with it the essence of Judaism. Hasidism sought to replace the Rabbi with the Tzaddik, and the Talmud with Kabbalah—mysticism. Instead of asceticism, joy became the key, stressing the superiority of prayer over Talmudic study, and the sufficiency of simple repentance (without punishment for sin). Hasidism could not, however, displace the Talmud, and did not seek to do so. It strengthened the notion of equality in Judaism and the concern of one person for the other. At first it repudiated intellectualism, but later strengthened religious enthusiasm and devotion to God and man. (See no. 68.)

34. "La Révolution juive de 65–70, La Révolution française, et la Révolution russe. (Étude comparative.) Communication faite à la Convention de l'American Historical Association, à Indianapolis (U.S.A.)," *L'Univers Israélite* (Paris: 1930), p. 23.

The War of 65–70 C.E. went through phases similar to the French and Russian Revolutions. Josephus blames the destruction of Jerusalem upon the Apocalyptists and the Sicarii, calling the first "fools" and the second "bandits." Naturally, Josephus, as an "émigré," detested the "patriots," those who, as he himself noted, "loved liberty."

When the provisional coalition government was organized, those who had been the props of the Revolution were not recognized for their successes in the battle against Cestius. A Zealot party was organized under the direction of Eleazar ben Simon. He demanded that the provisional government be dismissed because of the people's lack of confidence in it, on the basis that the government did not prosecute the war vigorously. (Cf., no. 4.) There is here a resemblance to the actions of the Montagnards and the Bolsheviks.

The Zealot faction carried on a reign of terror, as did the Jacobins during the French Revolution, and destroyed the nobility, bringing on the civil war, and leading to the destruction of the state. The Pharisees retired to Jamnia; the Sicarii committed suicide in

Masada; the Apocalyptists, who did not fight, broke up into groups—one of which became the Christians. They retired to Pella, following their concept of non-resistance, and later propagated their views among the pagans of the Roman Empire.

35. "Notes relatives au calendrier juif," *REJ,* Vol. LXXXIX, Nos. 177–178 (1930), pp. 349–359.

Tannaitic literature makes no mention of laws of the Jubilee year. Certainly the Tannaim did not abolish these, for they only interpreted the law, and they considered these laws divine. Had a Jubilee existed during the Second Temple, and had difficulties arisen, the Tannaim would only have modified the laws without abrogating the institution itself.

Though there was no Jubilee year during the Second Commonwealth, there was observance of the Shemittah year. A calculation of the chronology, divisible by seven, demonstrates this, and it is borne out by Josephus, tannaitic literature, and even the Book of Jubilees, revealing that there was no separate Jubilee year. (Cf., no. 28.) Because of agricultural pursuits, and in accord with neighboring Hellenistic countries, the year was set according to the Shemittah period which began in the autumn. The Tannaim interpreted the Bible so that Nisan, the month of Abib, was the one used for counting months, but the civil year really began with Tishri. This is but another example of not abrogating the law or its institution, but only of interpreting and harmonizing it with actual life. To strengthen their position, the Sages stressed in calendation the element of testimony given by witnesses, who could even violate the Sabbath to do so.

Reference to chronological counting in the Bible dated from Exodus; Persian and Greek eras were used in post-biblical times. Counting in I and II Maccabees was not from Nisan, but followed the Seleucidan system. The reference to Rosh Hashanah, in Ezek. 40:1, is only to the 10th of Ab, the anniversary of the Temple's destruction. Symmachus and Karaitic writers support this explanation.

1931

36. "Josephus on Jesus," *JQR,* Vol. XXI, No. 4 (April 1931), pp. 377–417. A reply to the criticism by R. Eisler (in *JQR,* Vol. XXI, Nos. 1–2), of the author's article, "The Slavonic Josephus," in *JQR* (1928). (Cf., no. 37.)

37. *Josephus on Jesus. With Particular Reference to the Slavonic Josephus and the Hebrew Josippon.* Dropsie College for Hebrew and Cognate Learning (Philadelphia: 1931), pp. v–118, and 6 fascicles. Bibliography, pp. 117–118. (See nos. 22, 24, 25, 27, 32, 36.)

The *Jewish War* was Josephus' official report of his Galilee activity, and *Antiquities* was written to demonstrate the ancient glory of the Jews. In *Vita,* written later, Josephus divulged his true position in Galilee. In *Contra Apionem,* he aimed to refute the then current anti-Semitism. (Cf. no. 393.)

It is wrong to say that the Slavonic Josephus is a Khazar translation, or that it was based on a book called "Capture of Jerusalem," presumably written by Josephus for the Parthian Jews. Syrian-Macedonian names for the months found therein would not have been used in reference to the Parthians. No such book existed. Neither the Church Fathers nor the Talmud mention it. The Russian (Slavonic) version merely translated the text from the Byzantine Greek of Josephus, which in turn paraphrased *Bellum;* as witness the use of the term "Latins" instead of "Romans." There are no traces of Hebraisms in the Slavonic MSS. The Slavonic text made use of the Latin *Hegesippus* and the Hebrew *Yosippon.* The writer was acquainted with the Apocryphal Gospels, the Church Fathers, and the "Acts of Pilate."

The author of *Yosippon,* penned in the fifth century, was aware of tannaitic sources, but not of the Talmud. A Byzantine Jew, he also made use of the Greek Church Fathers. He does not mention the Temple dedication for Ḥanukkah, but obtained the story of the fire on the altar from II Maccabees. Many additions to *Yosippon* were made later. There is no Christ passage in *Ur-Yosippon.* The early Byzantine Greek text did not have the Christ passage. It was translated into old Russian in the twelfth century. The "Christ passage" in Josephus' *Antiquities* was interpolated by Eusebius. He was the first to use the phrase "tribe of Christians," found in the James context.

Josephus always repeated a characteristic phrase in any of his narratives: "this is the same man," as when writing of Sameias, Judah of Galilee, and Menaḥem. Such a phrase is not to be found in the Christ passage. The Church Fathers always refer to Josephus. Were the Christ passage authentic, they surely would have mentioned its source.

Until the destruction of the Temple, Jews did not believe in a supernatural Messiah; they held that deliverance would be by God Himself; Josephus also believed this. Messianic expectation was only popular with the Apocalyptists (cf., no. 7). There is no reference to the Messiah in the Apocrypha and in tannaitic literature before the destruction of the Temple.

38. "The Origin of the Synagogue. A Study in the Development of Jewish Institutions," *PAAJR*, Vol. II (1931), pp. 69–81. Traces the origin of the synagogue as an institution, not the origin of public worship (from author's note).

The origin of the Synagogue is to be found in the Pharisaic introduction of the daily sacrifice as a communal offering, and in their attempt to democratize the Temple procedures, for which they organized the Maamadot. Representatives of the people went to Jerusalem to take part in the daily sacrifice; others, at home, gathered in their own towns to read portions of the Torah relating to the sacrifice. Later a permanent place of assembly was established which became the forerunner of the Synagogue. (Cf., nos. 62, 157.)

1932

39. "The Am ha-aretz. A Study in the Social and Economic Life of the Jews Before and After the Destruction of the Second Temple," *JQR,* Vol. XXIII, No. 1 (July 1932), pp. 45–61.

The term *am ha-aretz* was applied to farmers, whereas the term *ḥaber* referred to one who participated in city government. With the creation of the Commonwealth, animosity developed between the inhabitants of the cities and the farmers, for the latter bore the full responsibility of supporting the priests and the levites. The *takkanah* of John Hyrcanus regarding *demai* reveals the reluctance on the part of the am ha-aretz to continue this support. (See nos. 50, 323.) The ḥaberim looked down on the farmers, and their cultural differences grew. In later tannaitic literature the term "am ha-aretz" became a by-word of contempt, while "ḥaber" referred to the scholar who observed the law and adhered to the laws of purity.

40. "Les Principes des controverses halachiques entre les écoles de Schammai et de Hillel. Étude sur la jurisprudence tannaïtique," *REJ*, Vol. XCIII, No. 185 (July–September 1932), pp. 73–83.

The controversies between R. Eliezer and R. Joshua, as well as those of R. Judah with R. Jose, may be traced to the disputes between the schools of Shammai and Hillel. R. Judah, though a disciple of R. Akiba, followed Shammaitic principles. The basis of the argument was the principle of intention. Intention does not mean desire; it pertains to the consequence of an act. (Cf., nos. 11, 26.)

The halakhot pertaining to ritual impurity (in Tractate Makhshirim), or preparation of food for the holiday (in Bezah), or acquisition of property (in Peah) are among the disputes involving the principle of intention. *Res nullius* (Hebrew, *hefker*) was also a matter of contention in the Roman schools of law. Tannaitic jurisprudence was enacted in a period of Jewish sovereignty in Palestine, whereas amoraic law developed in the Diaspora under different conditions. Hence, tannaitic law is not always academic; it is a vital and pertinent example even for contemporary situations in Israel.

41. "The Date of the Crucifixion According to the Fourth Gospel," *JBL,* Vol. LI, Part III (September 1932), pp. 263–271. (See also no. 344.)

Nisan was never intercalated, even when the determination was by eyewitnesses; hence, there could be no shifting of days affecting Passover. Even the Sadducees followed the Pharisaic calendrical practices for the Passover observance. The day of the Omer was fixed for 16 Nisan, regardless of the day of the week. The Pharisees would never shift the first day of Passover to prevent the day of the Omer from falling on Sunday.

The word *paraskeue* is not a technical term for "eve of Sabbath." It simply means "preparation." It became a pagan technical term for the eve of all holidays, as evident in the edict of Augustus (*Ant.* 16,6,2). A peace offering (*shelamin*) brought during the week of Passover could not be offered as a paschal lamb. The latter was limited only to the 14th of Nisan.

42. "A Historical Study of the Canonization of the Hebrew Scriptures," *PAAJR,* Vol. III (1931–1932), pp. 121–156.

The Pentateuch was canonized in the time of Ezra, and the Prophetic books in the Hellenistic period, as is evident in Ben Sira and II Maccabees. The Hagiographa was canonized in 65 C.E.

The word *ganaz* in talmudic literature does not mean "excluding, removing a book or hiding it," but "storing it away, preserving it." Though not fit for public reading, it should not be destroyed.

The Rabbis sought to oppose the study of the Book of Ezekiel in the schools because of the first chapter, the esoteric *Maaseh Merkabah;* Joshua b. Gamla prevented such action. Others wished to "store it away" because of apparent interpretive contradictions with the Pentateuch.

Josephus mentions twenty-two books in his canon. There was never a controversy concerning Song of Songs, but a difference of opinion existed about Ecclesiastes. It was added to the canon by the Academy of Jabneh; Esther was added by the Academy of Usha only because of the pressure of popular opinion, thus totalling twenty-four books.

Canonization was associated with the Great Assembly. This was an actual constitutional gathering even in 65 C.E. (cf., no. 19). A canonical book was declared as "defiling the hands." Ben Sira was excluded from the canon because it was written after prophecy had ceased, that is in the Hellenistic period. Tobit was written in the time of revolt against the Syrians. Its exclusion was due to its discrepancy with the later rabbinic *takkanah* of *ketubah,* set by Simon ben Shetaḥ. (See no. 47.) Susanna was written before there was a Great Sanhedrin (Bet Din ha-Gadol); it stresses an element of false witness which was contrary to the notion of the halakhah of alibi witnesses (*hazamah*). (Cf., no. 62.) Judith was written before the destruction of the Temple (not in the Trajan period), i.e., when baptism was not yet a requisite for conversion. There were early doubts about its value as there were, also, about the Book of Esther. The Book of Jubilees, though one of the earliest, dating from the time of Ezra, was excluded from the canon because it opposed the rabbinic calendar. (Cf. also nos. 77, 173.)

43. Additional note to article no. 42, *PAAJR,* Vol. III (1931–1932), pp. 157–158.

Anything which was sacred, but could not be used, defiles the hands. In this category is *ba'sar ta'avah,* "meat of desire," bought with second-tithe money.

44. "Le Hassidisme ou les origines d'un mouvement religieux populaire chez les Juifs" (author's name spelled Salomon Zeitlin), *L'Univers Israélite* (Paris: 1932), pp. 16. (Cf., no. 33.)

1933

45. "Intention as One of the Controversial Points between Jose and Judah (A Reply to Professor L. Blau)," *JQR,* Vol. XXIII, No. 4 (April 1933), pp. 369–371.

The controversy between R. Jose and R. Judah in B.M. 48b, 77b, is not centered on a difference of interpretation of "a fine by agreement." The focal point is intention or act. (Cf., nos. 26, 40, 180.)

46. "A Note on Baptism for Proselytes," *JBL,* Vol. LII, Part I (April 1933, pp. 78–79.

Baptism was not required for converts to Judaism until a few years before the destruction of the Second Temple. The early Talmudic instances refer only to the purification of the levitically unclean.

The reference in Testament of the Twelve Patriarchs (T.L. 14.6) does not contain the word "baptism." There is no proof of baptism from the fact that all who entered the Azarah were required to undergo ritual immersion. (Cf., no. 18.)

47. "The Origin of Ketubah. A Study in the Institution of Marriage," *JQR,* Vol. XXIV, No. 1 (July 1933), pp. 1–7.

Ketubah is not to be identified with *Shetar Kiddushin* (M.Kidd., I.I.), mentioned as one of the methods of acquiring a wife. It was never meant to be a document validating a marriage, it was a *takkanah* by Simon b. Shetaḥ improving the status of women, and making divorce by the husband more difficult to obtain.

48. *A Historical Study of the Canonization of the Hebrew Scriptures* (1933), pp. viii–38. Reprint of nos. 42, 43.

49. "The Tobias Family and the Hasmoneans. A Historical Study in the Political and Economic Life of the Jews of the Hellenistic Period," *PAAJR,* Vol. IV (1932–1933), pp. 169–223. (Cf., no. 50.)

This essay contains an analysis of the early Hellenistic period, the activity of the sons of Joseph ben Tobias, the Letters of Lysias and of Antiochus to the Jews, and the etymology of the term *demai.* (See no. 39.)

50. *The History of the Second Jewish Commonwealth,* Dropsie College for Hebrew and Cognate Learning (Philadelphia: 1933), pp. xii–78.

The volume describes the political and economic forces that divided the Jewish factions favoring either Syria or Egypt—the Seleucids or Ptolemies.

Alexander the Great favored the Jews above the Samaritans because of his desire to win over the Jews of Babylonia and Persia. The Ptolemies followed Alexander's policy of tolerance towards other religions; they sought only to spread Hellenistic culture as a unifying measure. The Septuagint served a need of the Jews in Alexandria: it was an answer to anti-Jewish charges, and fit in with the Ptolemaic policy of cultural Hellenization.

Jews in Alexandria from early times possessed equal rights with the Greeks, and had special privileges, being called Alexandrians, and being able to worship their own God. The Hellenes did not yet know of separation of religion and state, and they, also, had their own religious and cultural institutions. According to Claudius' letter, the native Jews enjoyed full citizenship and were part of the *polis* and gymnasium.

The bulk of the Jews in Judaea favored Syrian-Seleucid rule because of the similarity in language and thought, whereas Alexandrian Jewry was Greek. Joseph, son of Tobias, supported commercial ties with Egypt, although the High Priest opposed it. As the collector for the Ptolemaic court Joseph introduced Hellenism into Palestine and also curtailed the power of the High Priest. The sons of Joseph favored Seleucidan rule, yet strengthened the Hellenistic party, and aimed to make Jerusalem a Hellenistic metropolis.

This is the background for the priestly decline and the beginnings of the Hasmonean revolt. Aimed against Hellenistic assimilation, the revolt arrested national suicide by the Hasidim. The Hasmoneans ultimately saved the land. After their success they set up the new democratic government. As a result a Bet Din ha-Gadol, a Great Sanhedrin, came into being. (Cf., no. 131.)

Many economic, social, and religious changes resulted from the new assertiveness of the *am ha-aretz.* A clash between the "ḥaberim" (the urban population) and the "demoi" (people of the land) began to develop (cf., no. 39). *Demai* is equivalent to "am ha-aretz" (demoi, "people"). *Demai* does not appear in all tannaitic literature in the sense of "doubt," it only refers to the produce of a farmer; here it pertains to the question of whether or not the *am ha-aretz* gave his tithe.

This period saw the existence of several factions at variance with each other. The Sadducees held only the Torah to be binding, and believed in the priestly aristocratic leadership of the High Priest, the House of Zadok. They called those who opposed them separatists, "Perushim," as an epithet, and the term was retained. There was no Pharisaic "sect." (Cf., no. 73.) In Talmudic literature the leaders are called *Ḥakhamim.* The Pharisees upheld many liberal notions in the laws of Sabbath, levitical uncleanness, calendrical reckoning, etc., and they sought the democratization of the institutions of Jewish life. They also held to the belief in the doctrine of reward and punishment. (Cf., no. 62.) The Pharisees originated during the Ezra period. (See also no. 388.) The Essenes were the successors of the Hasidim of the Hasmonean period; they were individualists; they opposed all priests not of the Zadokite family. The Sadducees followed the Tobias family. Later, they supported the Hasmoneans and Herodians when they became the ruling class.

The Pharisees were interested in the middle class, and consisted of the people at large. The Hasmoneans made it possible for the Jews to gain independence, but the Pharisees made Jewish survival possible and, eventually, determined the turn taken in the development of Western civilization as a result of the influence of Judaism.

51. "Jesus in the Early Tannaitic Literature," *Abhandlungen zur Erinnerung an Hirsch Perez Chajes* (Wien: 1933), pp. 295–308.

All rabbinic passages pertaining to Jesus are of a later period, brought in under the influence of the Gospels. Jews learned from the Gospels the allusion to an execution on the eve of Passover. The reference that Jesus was close to civil authority also comes from the Gospel notion that Jesus was of the family of David. The stories of Joshua ben Perahiah (c. 100 B.C.E.) and Jesus (c. 33 C.E.) do not fit chronologically.

Before 70 C.E. the Sages knew nothing of Jesus. In the early Halakhah there is no trace of any of his controversies with the Pharisees. On the other hand, we find references to a contemporary, Judah the Galilean, the founder of the Fourth Philosophy, (cf., no. 7), and to Eleazer ben Dama, whom Josephus mentions as rebels against authority.

1934

52. "Judaism and Christianity," *JQR,* Vol. XXV, No. 1 (July 1934), pp. 19–26. Reviews of: *Neutestamentliche Zeitgeschichte . . .* von Joseph Felten; *Le Judaïsme avant Jésus-Christ,* le M.-J. Lagrange; *Beiträge zur syrichen und jüdischen Geschichte . . .* von Walther Kolbe; *Oeuvres Complètes de Flavius Josèphe,* traduites en français sous la direction de Théodore Reinach. Tomes I–VI.

Messianic expectation was not a common notion among the Jews. It was accepted only by the Apocalyptists, the forerunners of Christianity. (Cf., end of no. 37.)

53. "Josephus—Patriot or Traitor?" *The Jewish Chronicle,* September 7, 1934.

The provisional government officially sent Josephus to Galilee to fight the Romans. This is recorded in *War.* In *Vita,* written towards the end of his life, Josephus revealed the truth, that he had been sent to disarm the revolutionaries and to endeavor to maintain peace. Thus, officially, he was commissioned to defend Galilee; unofficially, to suppress the revolution, playing a dual role. Later he defected to the Romans. (Cf., also no. 393.)

54. "Josephus—Patriot or Traitor?" Reprint of no. 53.

55. "L'Origine de l'institution de baptême pour les prosélytes," *REJ,* Vol. 98, Nos. 193–194 (July–December 1934), pp. 61–68.

Baptism for proselytes is not mentioned in the Bible, Josephus, Philo, or the Apocryphal literature. Only in 65 C.E., with the growing animosity towards Rome, was it enacted that pagans be regarded as in the state of a *zab.* When baptism became a requisite for conversion, R. Eliezer, a Shammaite, held that circumcision, too, was required, baptism alone being insufficient. R. Joshua, a Hillelite, maintained that with baptism the person became a convert; hence, if he were uncircumcized, he would be reckoned only as an 'uncircumcized Jew.' All Talmudic notations pertaining to baptism of proselytes, therefore, belong to the period after 65 C.E. (Cf., nos. 18, 46.)

1935

56. "Maimonides," *American Jewish Year Book* (5696-1935), Vol. 37, pp. 61–97.

No Hebrew scholar exerted a more profound influence on Jewish life or aroused as much controversy as Maimonides. His *Mishneh Torah* was in line with his belief that the Messianic age was near, with the return of the Jew to Palestine expected shortly. Therefore, he prepared a Jewish constitution, without referring to the names of Tannaim, Amoraim, etc.

Strangely, the *Shulhan Arukh* was accepted as "the decisive word in Jewish law" more than the *Mishneh Torah*. Nevertheless, it is to be remembered that Jewish law is elastic and is always subject to interpretation. Believing in the divine origin of the Torah, Maimonides, unlike Spinoza, saw the need in any contradiction between Torah and reason, to explain the words of the Torah allegorically. He held that Jewish law was immutable.

The vision that Maimonides cherished of the return to Palestine has been realized. Yet, if the *Mishneh Torah* must be replaced as a constitution, it must be by a document that reflects the spirit of Maimonides—one faithful to the concepts of historical Judaism and of authority. (See also no. 57.)

57. *Maimonides. A Biography,* Bloch Publishing Co. (New York: 1935), pp. xi–234 + 1 ill.

A full biography and analysis of the works of the great sage reveal that Maimonides was a nationalist. In his opinion, Jewish law must be universally applied, since the precepts were given for the perfection of the people. The controversy between Maimonides and Samuel ben Ali resulted from his view that supreme leadership among the Jews should be vested in the Exilarch and not in the religious head of the Academy. Opposition to Maimonides was not specifically because of his philosophic views, but primarily because he gave reasons for the precepts.

The volume contains an elaborate discussion of Maimonides as a thinker and statesman in all fields of knowledge—revealing his intellectual daring, when he omitted laws contrary to science and reason. His *Mishneh Torah* may be a guide to bring into consonance

Jewish life and religion in the Diaspora and in the Land of Israel. (See also nos. 71, 361.)

58. "Remarks on the Sabbatai Zevi Movement," *Gibeath Saul, Essays Contributed in Honor of Rabbi Saul Silber* (Chicago: 1935), pp. 34–36.

Three causes for the false Messianism are generally given: the Kabbalistic movement, the expectation of the millenium, and the catastrophe of 1648. In the West Kabbalism, and even the millennial notions of the English people, did not find an echo.

The calamity of the Jews in 1648 was due not only to political and economic causes, but also to religious motives. The Ukrainians fought against the Uniat Church, and Chmielnitzki was their religious hero. They opposed heretics and non-Christians; to them, the Jews represented both. Jews could save their lives only by baptism into the Greek Orthodox Church.

The Tartars sold many Jews to the Turks. When ransomed, these returnees brought back messianic messages to the Polish Jews. Also, the victory of the Ukrainians against the Poles made an impression on the Jews, who likewise awaited salvation.

59. ברור הלכות: א) מחלוקת ב"ש וב"ה בדין פאה. ב) שלש הלכות שנתקשה בהן הלל. *Horeb,* Vol. II (1935), pp. 280–283.

The laws of the "corner tithe" are concerned with the problem of *res nullius.* Bet Shammai held that *peah* was similar to lost articles found. Bet Hillel said that *peah* is not *res nullius* but *res communis.*

In the three instances that Hillel expounded—leprosy, Passover offering, and matzah observance—he reconciled contradictory verses and then found his views confirmed by "common practice"—the Halakhah. Previously, in Babylon, he had not been aware of the practice. This is evidence that the Halakhah (common law) preceded the Midrash (expository) form. (Cf., nos. 160, 208.)

1936

60. "The Jews: Race, Nation or Religion—Which? A Study Based on the Literature of the Second Jewish Commonwealth," *JQR,* Vol. XXVI, No. 4 (April 1936), pp. 313–347.

During the Second Commonwealth the term *Judaean* had a national connotation and referred to the citizens of Judaea. The Babylonian Jews, though united with their Judaean brethren in a common religion, designated themselves as Hebrews or Israelites. The Idumaeans and Adiabenes, who accepted Judaism, are referred to by Josephus as "co-religionists," for they still maintained their distinct ethnos. They are not called Judaeans. After the Destruction, when the nation, as such, was eliminated, all Jews were united by a common culture. "Israel" had a universal religious connotation. The Christians referred to the Jews as Judaeans, insisting that they were an ethnic group. The Jews called themselves *Knesset Yisrael,* indicating that they represented a universal culture and religious philosophy. (Cf., also no. 123.)

61. *The Jews: Race, Nation, or Religion? A Study Based on the Literature of the Second Jewish Commonwealth,* Dropsie College for Hebrew and Cognate Learning, (Philadelphia: 1936), pp. v–41. Reprint of no. 60.

62. הצדוקים והפרושים, פרק בהתפתחות ההלכה. *Horeb,* Vol. III, Nos. 5–6 (Nisan 5696–Tishri 5697-1936), pp. 56–89.

The sects first mentioned by Josephus in his narrative about Jonathan emerged long before that era. The Sadducees were the aristocratic priests of the Zadok family. When Ezra sought to guide Judaism on the basis of the tradition of the elders, and not merely by Pentateuchal laws, they opposed him, calling his group, "Perushim," separatists from the norm. Though the term is found often in the Talmud, it does not always refer to the Pharisees, excepting where we specifically find a dialogue with the Sadducees.

Herod sought to curb the Sadducean priests who were the leaders in the government. He did not oppress persons who did not participate in politics: thus, Hillel and Shammai were free to direct the Sanhedrin.

The basic differences between the Pharisees and Sadducees as indicated in the Halakhah may be divided into three categories: a) religious; b) social; and c) dogmatic.

A. Religious:

1) The controversy pertaining to the daily offering (Tamid) reveals that the democratic Pharisees wished the costs for the offerings

to come from the public coffers. This approach was the basis for the emergence of the Synagogue, first evident in the practices of the Maamadot, as complementary lay services parallel to the Temple service of the priests. (Cf., no. 38.)

2) The controversy pertaining to Shabuot was connected with the calendar. The Sadducees sought to retain the old calendrical practices of the Omer on Sunday, though the calendar had already been changed. (Cf., nos. 28, 41.)

3) The Pharisees also insisted that the Omer be prepared even on the Sabbath, and regarded the act as not being limited to the Temple. They aimed at full participation of the people, even on the Sabbath.

4) The Pharisaic rule that "the willow overrides the Sabbath" was opposed by the Sadducees since it is not mentioned in the Pentateuch, and because they maintained that the service was permitted only within the Temple. But the farmers (the common people) felt that such a service was vital to their existence as evidence that God would give them the necessary rain in good time (cf. no. 39). There are many instances recorded in the Talmud wherein the Pharisees sought to curb Sadducean Temple service, as in the question of the purity of vessels. (Cf., no. 1.)

5) The Pharisaic rule of rendering defiled the priest who was to prepare the red heifer was designed to emphasize the ordinances of immersion and purity as taught by them, namely, that it was unnecessary to wait until dusk for purification.

6) The *nizzuk* controversy refers not to any pouring from vessels, but to the law that food becomes susceptible to uncleanness only if unattached. The early Sadducees held that even standing wheat, if water fell on it, became susceptible to uncleanness. (Cf., nos. 1, 15.)

7) The decree that "the Scriptures defile the hands" was intended to curb the priests from eating *terumah* after they touched the Torah Scroll, unless they immersed themselves fully. This was also a demonstration of canonization (cf., no. 42). Because the Hagiographa was not included in the canon until 65 C.E., we have no Haftarot from this section.

8) The controversy pertaining to the libation of water referred to the Sadducean belief that, for the divine gift of water, the pouring should be on the ground. The Pharisees, opposed to superstition, insisted that the hands be raised and the libation be on the altar, as in all sacrifices. (See no. 75.)

9) The controversy pertaining to entrance into the Holy of Holies by the High Priest on the Day of Atonement was based on the Sadducean view that this could be effected only by a smokescreen, to prevent seeing the Divine Presence. The Pharisees believed in His omnipresence, and opposed superstitions.

B. Social:

1) The controversy pertaining to alibi witnesses indicates that the Sadducees still retained the old biblical law of false witnesses, whereas the Pharisees limited it only to those who claimed an alibi. This delineation aimed at avoiding indiscriminate killing of false witnesses.

2) The Sadducees regarded slaves as mere chattel. The Pharisees insisted on their personal rights and responsibilities.

3) The Sadducees upheld the rule of female inheritance. The Pharisees maintained that inheritance passes on to the daughter of a deceased son, but not to her aunt, the sister of a deceased son.

Controversies concerning meal offering, *talio,* virginity proof, etc., are not found in the Talmud. They are only additions in the scholia of Megillat Taanit. (Cf., no. 16.)

C. Dogma and Beliefs:

The Pharisees believed in resurrection, free will, and reward and punishment. The Sadducees denied the latter for the individual person, since there is no reference to this specifically recorded in the Torah. They believed it applied only to the State. The Pharisees sought to reassure the average person by means of the promise of future rewards for his observance of the precepts. (See also no. 268.)

In general the Sadducees denied "deduction" from oral tradition for any normative practices. Judaism has survived only because of the Pharisaic interpretation of the law. (Cf. also nos. 74, 75, 305.)

1937

63. הצדוקים והפרושים : פרק בהתפתחות ההלכה, *Horeb,* at Salomon's Press in Jerusalem (New York: 1936). Reprint of no. 62.

64. "Minkin's Hassidism," *JQR,* Vol. XXVII, No. 3 (January 1937), pp. 249–252. Review of: *The Romance of Hassidism,* by J. S. Minkin.

Hasidism is not an outgrowth of the Kabbalah. Whereas Kabbalah stressed asceticism, Hasidism emphasized the importance of *simḥa* (rejoicing). Hasidism was a revolt of the masses against an overemphasis on intellectualism and scholarship. (Cf., nos. 33, 68.)

65. "Beginnings of Christianity and Judaism," *JQR,* Vol. XXXVII, No. 4 (April 1937), pp. 385–398. Reviews of: M. Goguel, *The Life of Jesus;* F. J. Foakes-Jackson and K. Lake: *The Beginnings of Christianity*; J. Bonsirven, *Le Judaïsme Palestinien au temps de Jésus-Christ*; H. Danby, *The Mishnah*; R. Travers-Herford, *Talmud and Apocrypha.*

A proper comprehension of early Christianity demands a thorough study of Judaism and an understanding of its sources. (Cf. nos. 17, 76, 81, 82.)

66. טומאת נכרים בזמן הבית השני, *Horeb,* Vol. IV, Nos. 7–8 (Nisan 5697, Tishri 5698-1937), pp. 29–40.

Gentiles did not impart uncleanness (cf., nos. 18, 46, 55). The text dealing with uncleanness contracted by the High Priest should not read an "Arab" [king], but "Erev" [Yom Kippur]. The king was Agrippa II.

67. Review of: *A Social and Religious History of the Jews,* by Salo W. Baron. *REJ,* Nouvelle Série, II (CII), Nos. 1–2 (July–December 1937), pp. 141–143.

Social items and the institutions that affected Jewish history such as the status of women, the influence of the law on economics, and the history of the Synagogue, should receive greater stress in the study of the Second Temple era. (Cf., no. 80.)

68. "Hassidism," *The Jewish Forum,* Vol. XX, No. 11 (November 1937), pp. 201–202.

Hasidism developed differently in the period of Rabbi Schneur Zalman in White Russia, where Lithuanian scholarship was all-important. It cannot be compared to the ignorance prevalent in the Ukraine during the time of R. Jacob Joseph. (See also nos. 33, 64.)

69. Foreword to *Jacob Emden,* by Mortimer J. Cohen. The Dropsie College for Hebrew and Cognate Learning (Philadelphia: 1937) pp. 11–15.

The controversy between Jacob Emden and Jonathan Eibeschütz was not the direct result of personal hostility; it also involved social, economic, and psychological forces. The lower classes supported Eibeschütz, and the upper classes stood behind Emden. In evaluating a leader, even the inner and personal aspects of his life should be studied. The amulet phase of the controversy was only a smokescreen. After the Shabbatai Zevi movement, the poorer classes sought to snatch the leadership from the wealthy and from the Rabbis. This factional controversy may have been a prelude to the rise of Hasidism. (See no. 33.)

70. "Nennt Megillat Taanit antisadduzäische Gedenktage?" *MGWJ*, new series, Vol. 45 (1937), pp. 351–355.

Megillat Taanit does not record any dates pertaining to Sadducean-Pharisaic controversies (cf., no. 16.). The victory over Cestius was on 8 Dies-7 Kislev-November 25, 65 C.E.

1938

71. "Maimonides," *JQR*, Vol. XXVIIII, No. 3 (January 1938), pp. 273–278. Reviews of: *Maimonides*, by Abraham Heschel; *Moses Maimonides*, 1135–1204, *Anglo-Jewish Papers in Connection with the Eighth Centenary of His Birth*, edited by I. Epstein; *Faith and Reason: The Conflict Over the Rationalism of Maimonides*, by Joseph Sarachek.

As a result of the wide acceptance of Maimonides' magnum opus, the *Mishneh Torah*, his *Guide for the Perplexed* was also read. The purpose of the *Mishneh Torah* was not so much to counteract the Karaitic approach, but to serve as a constitution for the Jews upon their return to Palestine. Maimonides anticipated the return because of the persecution the Jews suffered in the Diaspora. (Cf., nos. 56, 57, 361.)

72. "Ḥanukkah. Its Origin and its Significance," *JQR*, Vol. XXIX, No. 1 (July 1938), pp. 1–36.

The celebration of Ḥanukkah was both religious and nationalistic. In the Temple the holiday was commemorated with prayers and sacrifices, while parades of torches were the symbols of its national character. Josephus refers to it as the "festival of lights," giving its name a nationalistic and historical explanation. The menorah-lighting was instituted at a later time when public national parades were no longer possible. The "miracle of the oil," recorded in the Babylonian Talmud (Shabbat 21b), was a later explanation, whereas the Palestinian sources, Pesikta Rabbati, preserving the tradition of the spears and torches, is closer to the original. (Cf., also nos. 181, 254.)

73. על השם "פרושים", *Hadoar,* Vol. XVIII, No. 41 (October 21, 1938), pp. 691–692.

The term "Perushim" does not refer to a sect, but to those who "separate," as from defilement. The division into patrician and plebeian has no Talmudic basis in interpretation. (Cf., no. 50.)

74. "The Pharisees and the Gospels," *Essays and Studies in Memory of Linda R. Miller,* (New York: 1938), pp. 235–286.

The Halakhot recorded in the scholia of Megillat Taanit, and those which emanated from the school of Hillel, and from Rabbis Akiba and Eliezer cannot be ascribed to the Pharisees.

The Pharisees abolished *lex talionis* by means of a legal fiction. Jesus, as a moralist, only appealed to the plaintiff not to make demands and to abstain from evil so that there should be no need of litigation.

Jesus held that permission to divorce was to be granted as the consequence of a sinful act, and hence to be limited to the instance of adultery. Moralists and conservatists often arrive at the same conclusions, though from different points of view. Jesus, as a moralist, would punish a man for his intention, e.g., coveting, whereas the Pharisees punished only the act of adultery. Similarly with oaths, Jesus held that one had no right to swear at all, whereas the Pharisees sought only to curb swearing. The ethical teachings of the Rabbis were more practicable; Jesus showed that he did not comprehend the nature of human beings by saying "love thine enemy." The dicta in the Sermon on the Mount illustrated that the Pharisees were concerned with the equity of the law whereas Jesus, not being interested in the State, only appealed to the individual to refrain from evil, thus seeking to change man's nature.

The Rabbis did not consider Jesus' followers as Temple priests, to be permitted to do work on the Sabbath, nor did they regard him as

"Lord of the Sabbath" or consider that he possessed the art of healing. Jews continued to observe the national fasts during the Second Commonwealth in memory of the First Temple's destruction. Regarding himself as a Messiah (i.e., "the bridegroom"), Jesus held there was no need of fasting while he was alive. In his preachment of a new ethical and social order, Jesus denied the "tradition of the elders" and the rabbinic laws of impurity. Hence the elders opposed his association with sinners and publicans. The Gospels record that Jesus overstepped the "tradition of the elders by eating with unwashed hands," but this decree was instituted some years before the Destruction. (Cf., no. 18.) The word *Korban* in the Gospels, as in tannaitic literature, means vow. (Cf., no. 380.) If a man took a vow not to honor parents, the Pharisees declared by legal fiction, that the vow could be absolved. This was in accord with the Pharisaic regard for the power of "tradition of the elders" to annul a vow. Jesus, however, maintained that no vow could be taken contrary to a biblical precept.

The entire Chapter 23 of Matthew is a later interpolation. The words "Pharisees, hypocrites," never came from the mouth of Jesus. Similarly, the word "Rabbi" in the first two Gospels is a later usage. (Cf. nos. 381 and 404.)

There are no halakhic differences recorded in the Gospel of John. We do not find therein the animosity between the Pharisees and Jesus as seen in the Synoptic Gospels. John was written for Gentile Christians, and the halakhic aspects had no meaning for them. The Synoptic Gospels, however, were directed to the Jewish Christians. Matthew and Luke were written for Jews; Mark was written in Rome for Jewish Christians. It contains the geography of Palestine and the designation of God as *Geburah* (Power), an expression that only Jews would comprehend. These points reveal not only the differences between the Pharisees and Jesus, but also disclose the basic elements in the Gospels. (See also no. 397.)

1939

75. הפרושים, Horeb, Vol. V, Nos. 9–10 (Nisan 5699-1939), pp. 27–42. Review of L. Finkelstein's *Pharisees, JPS* (Philadelphia: 1938).

It is erroneous to divide the biblical and apocryphal books into categories of patrician and plebeian, and the Tannaim into caste systems. (Cf., no. 73.)

A Greek name is not in any way evidence of aristocracy. Abtalion is Aramaic, from *talya*—child.

For a historic recognition one must carefully distinguish between the various Rabban Gamaliels mentioned in the texts.

The term *b'nai Knesset* has no affinity to Pharisees and Sadducees, nor is "Pharisee" in opposition to "am ha-aretz." Neither is "ḥaber" a synonym of Pharisee. "Ḥaber" is a person scrupulous in matters of purity, in contrast to the "am ha-aretz," who was not. (Cf., no. 39.)

To declare that the Sadducean landowners did not pray for rain because it would spoil the festival in Jerusalem and that they therefore objected to the water libation is farfetched. That the Pharisees, especially in Jerusalem, needed water is controverted by the fact that Jerusalem never suffered drought; one cannot associate the water libation incident with the Alexander Jannai episode. (Cf., no. 62.)

It is incorrect to maintain that the Shammai-Hillel controversies were based fundamentally on economic motives when, in fact, religious principles dominated.

To assume that Simon ben Shetaḥ (not Judah ben Tabbai) killed *one* false witness is contrary to internal evidence.

To declare that there was a Pharisaic-Sadducean controversy about lighting candles on Friday night is baseless; it merely follows Geiger's theory.

Intercalation of the calendar was set by those invited by the Nasi.

In the time of the Hasmoneans the Sanhedrin displaced the earlier Gerousia (cf., no. 50).

Phule in the case of Simon, the Temple captain, means "family" (not tribe).

The abolition of "Trajan day" was not due to the emperor's unfulfilled promise to rebuild the Temple. Permission to rebuild the Temple was not given by Trajan, but by Hadrian (117–118 C.E.), and he retracted it in 121–122 C.E. Hence, preparations for the rebellion were begun, breaking into the open under Bar Kokhba in 132 C.E.

To say that a fast day was decreed on Ḥanukkah in Lud because of the war is unacceptable, for the fast may have actually been ordained because of a lack of rain.

76. "Historical Books on Judea, the Second Commonwealth, the Pharisees and Josephus," *JQR,* Vol. XXIX, No. 4 (April 1939), pp. 409–14. Reviews of: א. שליט: המשטר הרומי בארץ ישראל *Studien der jüdischen Selbstverwaltung im Altertum,* von Hans Zucker; *Judaism and Christianity, Essays,* Vol. I, edited by William Oscar E. Oesterley; Vol. II, edited by H. Loewe; *Flavius Josephus,* by Leon Bernstein.

Rabbinic and tannaitic sources are as vitally important for the study of the Second Commonwealth as are the secular Hellenistic and Roman literatures. (Cf. no. 65.)

77. "The Book of Jubilees, its Character and its Significance," *JQR,* Vol. XXX, No. 1 (July 1939), pp. 1–31.

The strong arguments preserved in Jubilees against calendar reform and in support of the observance of the Jubilee years give indications of the early origin of the book. It is a composition dating back to the pre-Hellenistic period, when the changes had not yet been introduced. (Cf., no. 209.)

The Book of Jubilees was not composed by a Pharisee, a Sadducee, or any other sectarian, but by those who opposed the Pentateuch, and hoped to gain acceptance for their own views with the introduction of a new text. (See also nos. 128, 146.)

78. *The Book of Jubilees, its Character and its Significance,* The Dropsie College for Hebrew and Cognate Learning (Philadelphia: 1939), pp. vii–31. Reprint of no. 77.

79. "Rashi (Rabbi Solomon of France). On the Occasion of the 900th Anniversary of His Birth," *American Jewish Year Book* (5700-1939), Vol. 41, pp. 111–140.

A comparison of Maimonides and Rashi reveals the differences between the philosopher-codifier and the commentator *par excellence.* Without Rashi's *magnum opus,* the commentary on the Talmud, the Babylonian Talmud would have remained a closed book.

Before the eighth century, France was influenced by Palestinian traditions. This included communal life and the study of Aggadah and Midrash. Later the Babylonian Gaonate began to dominate, and the Babylonian Talmud became the authoritative word.

Whereas Spanish Jewry followed religious leadership, French Jews chose lay leaders. In the eleventh century the Rabbinate became more powerful because of the influence of Rashi and his descendants. He believed that decisions of a local court based on Gemara were valid and no other authority could reverse them. (See also no. 94.)

Troyes was an important city in Champagne and among its industries was the manufacturing of parchment, which aided the growth of literary pursuits. The great fairs held there encouraged intellectual communication.

Rashi wrote his Bible commentary for the masses (not for scholars) and he followed the Masoretic text. He felt the need for a synthesis of *Peshat* and *Derash.* He also wanted Talmudic learning to be the possession of the masses. Before undertaking the task, he had to have a definite text; he, therefore, traveled to various academies to obtain manuscripts as well as the commentary notes current in those schools. The first draft of the commentary was written after visiting the academies of Troyes.

Some of the interpretations of Rashi are an answer to christological renditions of biblical texts. An example is found in a Rashi manuscript on Chapter 53 of Isaiah, in the library of Moscow. He did not consider Christianity to be an idolatrous religion, and held that Christians could be employed by Jews in making wine. He also permitted a creditor to charge interest if money were loaned through a third party, and he was very solicitous in his legal decisions on the rights of Jewish women. Many of these aspects of his thought are emphasized in his Responsa.

Rashi also wrote liturgical pieces. His commentaries are an important source for the cultural and linguistic history of France, which have not, as yet, been fully utilized.

His sway over Judaism was greater than that of any other Jew since Talmudic days. He democratized the Talmud and Jewish learning. Even Christian theology was affected by Rashi's Commentary. Through Nicholas de Lyra, it was the channel for Reuchlin and Luther; it also influenced the King James Version of the Bible; and recognition of its importance caused the Commentary to be burned together with the Talmud. As a halakhist, Rashi made Jewish law a living force applicable to the needs of his time.

1940

80. Review of: *A Social and Religious History of the Jews,* by Salo Baron, *Journal of Jewish Bibliography,* Vol. II (January 1940), pp. 12–17. (See also no. 198.)

Tannaitic literature shows that the Jews of the Diaspora were exempt from the religious duty of making pilgrimages to Jerusalem, though they may have come voluntarily. References to prevention from making pilgrimages refer to curbs on the Palestinians by civil authorities.

Only the Jews of Babylonia used the Seleucidan era for reckoning.

Mar Samuel was not against the institution of the Prosbol, but against the method of its writing (Yer. Shebiit 39c). He held that even a symbolic pledge of a needle which was received by the creditor for a loan of thousands of dollars, allowed him to reclaim his loan, regardless of the Sabbatical year. (Cf., no. 149.)

According to R. Jose, a priest may marry a daughter of a proselyte. The priests themselves, however, followed stricter practice. The basic manuscripts read, "a person who does not have a wife is not a man." Because of Christian celibacy it was changed to read, "a Jew who does not have a wife . . ." (See no. 67.)

The term *soferim* refers to Pharisees and to the Oral Law. It cannot refer to Sadducean Scribes.

81. "Jesus in Modern Jewish Literature," *JQR,* Vol. XXX, No. 4 (April 1940), pp. 407–409. Review of: *Die Jesusfrage im neuzeitlichen Judentum,* von Gosta Lindeskog.

Jewish scholarship did not base its research on Jesus and Christianity solely upon apologetics; it resulted, rather, from a quest for scientific historical information. (Cf., no. 65.)

82. "Jewish History at the Time of Jesus," *JQR,* Vol. XXX, No. 4 (April, 1940), pp. 409–414. Review of: *The Jewish World in Time of Jesus,* by Ch. Guignebert.

One should not minimize the importance of rabbinic sources in writing an inter-Testamental history, for only this literature reflects the spirit of the people of the Second Commonweatlh. Herod, for example, is not to be referred to as an Arab. Although he was not of the Jewish race, he did accept the Jewish religion. During the Second Commonwealth Jews were not racially minded. Proselytes were accepted as equals, as "co-religionists," and were not frowned upon.

83. *The Jewish Quarterly Review,* New Series, established by Cyrus Adler, edited by Abraham A. Neuman and Solomon Zeitlin. Vol. XXXI (1940–1941). Philadelphia: The Dropsie College for Hebrew and Cognate Learning, London: Macmillan & Co., Ltd. With this volume, Dr. Zeitlin assumed editorship of the *JQR.*

84. "Rashi and the Rabbinate. The Struggle between Secular and Religious Forces for Leadership," *JQR,* Vol. XXXI, No. 1 (July 1940), pp. 1–58. (Cf., no. 114.)

85. "The Maccabean Struggle," *JQR,* Vol. XXXI, No. 2 (October 1940), pp. 199–204. Review of: *Der Gott der Makkabäer,* von Elias Bickermann.

It is wrong to assume that the Maccabean struggle was based primarily on a religious strife between the two elements within the Judaean population, for even the liberal group was not prepared to accept polytheism in place of monotheism. The struggle was in reality political and economic.

86. "The Jews in the Byzantine Empire," *JQR,* Vol. XXXI, No. 2 (October 1940), pp. 204–206. Review of: *The Jews in the Byzantine Empire*—641–1204, by Joshua Starr.

The Jewish communal leaders in the Byzantine period were not Rabbis, but Elders and Parnasim. The term "Rav," found on tombstone inscriptions, does not refer to a rabbi in a leadership role, but to his scholarship.

87. "The Differences between Babylonian and Palestinian Customs," *JQR,* Vol. XXXI, No. 2 (October 1940), pp. 206–208. Review of: *The Differences between Babylonian and Palestinian Jews,* by Mordecai Margulies.

The purpose of the Geonic Document, which sets forth the differences in approach between Palestine and Babylonia, totalling some fifty-six customs, was not to oppose Babylonian tradition. It sought rather to convince Babylonian Jews who migrated to Palestine to accept the Palestinian tradition.

1941

88. "The Opposition of the Spiritual Leaders Appointed by the Government," *JQR,* Vol. XXXI, No. 3 (January 1941), pp. 287–300. (Cf., no. 114.)

89. "From Jesus to Paul," *JQR,* Vol. XXXI, No. 3 (January 1941), pp. 309–314. Review of: מישו עד פאולוס, מאת יוסף קלויזנר.

It is the result of a misinterpretation to claim that Paul was a disciple of Rabban Gamaliel I, and that the Talmud records that he who maintains that there is no mention of the Resurrection in the Torah will not have a portion in the World to Come. (See also no. 111.)

90. "Philo Judaeus," *JQR,* Vol. XXXI, No. 4 (April 1941), pp. 314–321. Review of: *An Introduction to Philo Judaeus,* by Erwin Ramsdell Goodenough.

It is difficult to find a basis for the suggestion that Philo was politically motivated in writing his *Against Flaccus* and *The Embassy to Gaius.* His purpose was theological—to impress upon the Jews that, though God may punish them, He would not permit them to be destroyed. He illustrated this by the examples of Flaccus, Sejanus, and the Emperor Caligula. In like manner, the Jewish objection to the introduction of Caligula's image into the Temple was theological, and was not politically motivated.

91. "The Crucifixion of Jesus Reexamined," *JQR,* Vol. XXXI, No. 4 (April 1941), pp. 327–369; Vol. XXXII, No. 2 (October 1941), pp. 175–189. (Cf., no. 98.) [For comments on Sholem Asch's *The Nazarene,* see *ibid.,* p. 327.]

92. Review of: *The Main Institutions of Jewish Law,* Vol. II, by Isaac Herzog. *JQR,* Vol. XXXII, No. 1 (July 1941), pp. 103–107.

The laws of obligation include such legal concepts as *shibud* and *asmakhta.* Even with a dogmatic approach to legal decisions, one must be cognizant that development in Jewish law is a vital process.

93. Review of: *Essays on Maimonides. An Octocentennial Volume,* edited by Salo Wittmayer Baron. *JQR,* Vol. XXXII, No. 1 (July 1941), pp. 107–114.

Maimonides, in his *Mishneh Torah,* did not reflect his own views, but codified the approaches to be found in Talmudic law. To identify Talmudic principles as the personal views of the Rambam is a fallacy. (Cf., nos. 56, 57.)

94. פירוש רש״י על התורה והירושלמי. *Horeb,* Vol. VI, Nos. 11–12 (November 1941-5702), pp. 188–191.

Rashi used the term "Bet Din" instead of "Parnas," for he was opposed to the laity as rulers. Rabbenu Gershom, however, had issued his decrees in the name of the community. Though the Babli has "Parnas," Rashi used the wording of the Yerushalmi—"Bet Din." (Cf., no. 79.)

95. תשובה לבקרת, *Hadoar,* Vol. XXI, No. 43 (1013), (October 31, 1941), p. 792. Rejoinder: re *synedrion.*

Herod did not kill all the members of the Sanhedrin. Jesus was only examined, not tried, by the synedrion.

96. הסנהדרין בימי בית שני, *Hadoar,* Vol. XXII, No. 7 (1020) (December 19, 1941), p. 109.

The religious Sanhedrin functioned until 70 C.E.; Herod did not abolish the Sanhedrin.

The Mekhilta of R. Simon, mentioning an abolition "forty years before the Destruction," is late and is contradictory to the phrase אלא בפני הבית. The phrase בית שני in a text indicates its lateness as used by the Amoraim. The Tannaim used simply הבית. This article also aims to weigh the views of Dr. Chaim Tchernowitz (Rav Tzair).

1942

97. "Correspondence, Rejoinder." *JQR,* Vol. XXXII, No. 3 (January 1942), pp. 326–336. (To Dr. Salo W. Baron, regarding his criticism of a review of *Essays on Maimonides.*)

Maimonides was a codifier. As such, he incorporated the laws of the Mishnah into his legal code. To study his personal approach one must first collect his decisions by the side of the Talmudic controversies on the subject, and thereby determine what Maimonides' personal views were, and any laws he introduced. (See no. 93.)

98. "The Crucifixion of Jesus Reexamined" (continued from *JQR*, XXXII, 1941–42, 175–89), *JQR*, Vol. XXXII, No. 3 (January 1942), pp. 279–301.

There were two types of courts during the Second Commonwealth. A religious Sanhedrin tried offenders against biblical law, and was governed by the regulations recorded in the Mishnah. It was presided over by scholars in Jewish law. The political synedrion did not have a regular meeting date, but was summoned by the High Priest when an offender against the state had to be tried. The members of this synedrion were not necessarily scholars of Jewish law, for this court was not governed by Jewish legal principle.

Jesus could not have been tried by a religious Sanhedrin. The claim of Messiahship and to being the Son of God was not punishable by death, according to religious law. He was arrested and examined by the political synedrion as a political offender against Rome, and was condemned and crucified by Pilate. Peter was tried by the political synedrion that was summoned to adjudicate his political offense, i.e., for teaching that Jesus was the King of the Jews. The nature of the offense is alluded to by Gamaliel in his speech, as he compared Peter's action to that of Theudas and Judas the Galilean, both of whom were guilty of state offenses. Stephen, however, was tried for a religious offense, for blasphemy against God and Moses. He was brought before the permanent religious Sanhedrin. Paul was tried for a political offense, for degrading the Temple by bringing pagans into its court, an offense that was associated with a death penalty even for a Roman citizen. The Jewish leaders may have been guilty of bringing Paul to the Roman authorities, but even this act was associated with the political circumstances of the day, for the Jews were held responsible for the tranquillity of the community. (See also no. 105.)

99. Review of: *Rashi Anniversary Volume. Essays on Rabbi Solomon ben Isaac of Troyes, France;* ed. by H. L. Ginsberg, *Journal of*

Jewish Bibliography, Vol. III, Nos. 1–2 (January–April 1942), pp. 48–51.

Though Rashi relied on MSS, when internal evidence proved that the text was wrong, he did not hesitate to amend it, e.g., Kiddushin 22a. (Cf., no. 79.) Joseph Bonfils and Rabbenu Gershom were the only two authorities to issue ordinances, but these were always with the consent of the community (see no. 94).

The *Ḥerem ha-Yishub* was practiced only by Franco-German Jewry, and not among the Jews in Spain (cf., no. 150).

100. "Aramaic Gospels in the Synagogue," *JQR,* Vol. XXXII, No. 4 (April 1942), pp. 427–431. Review of: *Documents of the Primitive Church,* by Charles Cutler Torrey.

The Synoptic Gospels were most probably written in Aramaic, some decades after Jesus. The frequent reference in John to "Passover, the name used after the Destruction, rather than to the "Feast of Unleavened Bread," indicates a late date of composition. During the Second Commonwealth, "Passover" referred to the sacrifice of the paschal lamb on the 14th day of Nisan, while the rest of the festival was known as Ḥag ha-Matzot.

101. Review of: *Essays on Anti-Semitism,* edited by Koppel S. Pinson, *JQR,* Vol. XXXII, No. 4 (April 1942), pp. 431–435.

A primary reason for the animosity of the ancient pagan world towards the Jews was the Jews' uncompromising insistence that their God was the true God of the universe, and their refusal to recognize the gods of the cities in which they lived.

It is difficult to believe that the basic reason for the Church's blaming of the Jews for the execution of Jesus was to facilitate conversion among the Gentiles. The Apostolic Fathers never raised this argument.

102. Correction to the article "The Crucifixion of Jesus Reexamined," in *JQR,* Vol. XXXII, p. 301: *JQR,* Vol. XXXII, No. 4 (April 1942), p. 435. (See no. 98.)

103. "Ginzberg's Studies on the Palestinian Talmud," *JQR,* Vol. XXXIII, No. 1 (July 1942), pp. 83–88. (See no. 109.)

104. Correction to review of *Essays on Anti-Semitism* (in *JQR,* XXXII), *JQR,* Vol. XXXIII, No. 1 (July 1942), p. 107. (See no. 101.)

105. *Who Crucified Jesus?* New York: Harper & Brothers, Publishers (1942), pp. xv–240.

Neither the modern Jew nor his ancestors are responsible for the death of Jesus. In order to understand the events of the Crucifixion, the historical background of the Jewish people up to the time of Jesus must be reconstructed. This includes the development of Judaea from theocracy to commonwealth, the Restoration and the Davidic dynasty, the theocracy and the canonization of the Pentateuch, the Oral Law, the Pharisees and Sadducees, the influence of, and the revolt against Hellenistic assimilation, the establishment of the Commonwealth, the dominance of the Pharisees, and the democratization of Judaism. The events that led from the commonwealth to the end of the Hasmonean dynasty, the reign of Herod, and Judaea as a Roman province under the procurators reveal the social classes and the strife of the period. This includes the two Sanhedrins—religious and political, and the different parties and beliefs—Pharisees, Sadducees, Essenes, Fourth Philosophy (Sicarii), and the Apocalyptic Pharisees.

Other chapters analyze the Gospels as sources for history, showing their stress on theology, and for whom and when they were written. In discussing the Sermon on the Mount (see no. 397), distinctions are made between public and private wrongs, and between ethics and law. Jesus' controversies pertaining to Sabbath, fasting, *korban,* washing the hands, and his association with publicans and sinners, are reviewed along with the phases of animosity expressed against the Pharisees.

Special emphasis is laid in this volume on the explanation of the story of the Passion, and the discrepancies involved. The Trial and the Crucifixion of Jesus are reconstructed. The conclusion is reached that the Jews did not crucify Jesus and should not bear the blame for his death. (Cf., nos. 74, 98.)

1943

106. "Saadia Gaon—Champion for Jewish Unity under Religious Leadership," *JQR,* Vol. XXXIII, Nos. 2–3 (October 1942–January 1943), pp. 265–401. (Cf., no. 114.)

107. *Saadia Studies. Published by the Jewish Quarterly Review in Commemoration of the Thousandth Anniversary of the Death of Saadia Gaon,* edited by Abraham Aaron Neuman and Solomon Zeitlin. Dropsie College for Hebrew and Cognate Learning (Philadelphia: 1943) pp. [3] 1–293.

108. "Saadia Gaon—Champion for Jewish Unity under Religious Leadership," in *Saadia Studies* (Philadelphia: 1943), pp. 257–293. (See nos. 106 and 107; cf., no. 114.)

109. "Ginzberg's Studies on the Palestinian Talmud," (continued from *JQR,* XXXIII, 1942, 83–88), *JQR,* Vol. XXXIII, No. 4 (April 1943), pp. 419–434.

Gemara has the connotation of finality: the Geonim meant the Babylonian Talmud to be the final word in Halakhah. Although the Babylonian Talmud was accepted by the Geonim and the Rabbis of the Middle Ages as the authority for legal decisions, the Palestinian Talmud is important as a prime source for the development of the early Halakhah and for Jewish history. Because it records conditions of an earlier period, the time before the Temple's destruction, the Mishnah in the Palestinian Talmud is valuable as an early redaction.

110. "Judaism as a Religion. A Historical Study," *JQR,* Vol. XXXIV, No. 1 (July 1943), pp. 1–40, and No. 2 (October 1943), pp. 207–241. (See no. 123.)

111. "Erroneous Statements on Paul in Doctor Klausner's Book," *JQR,* Vol. XXXIV, No. 1 (July 1943), pp. 117–121. Remarks about the English version of *From Jesus to Paul,* by Joseph Klausner. The Hebrew edition was reviewed in 1941. (Cf., no. 89.)

The suggestion that the phrase "that pupil," in B. Shabbat 30b, refers to Paul and identifies him as a disciple of Rabban Gamaliel, is erroneous. This notion is a result of misreading a Talmudic text. A reference to Jesus in terms of "that man" is found only in later rabbinic literature.

112. Correction to article, "Judaism as a Religion," (see no. 110). *JQR,* Vol. XXXIV, No. 2 (October 1943), p. 241; unsigned. (Cf., no. 123.)

113. Short Notices. Reviews of: *Social Thought Among the Early Greeks,* by Joseph B. Gittler; *Overcoming Anti-Semitism,* by Solomon Fineberg; *Jewish Migration, Past Experiences and Post-War Prospects,* by Eugene M. Kulischer, pp. 1–51. *JQR,* Vol. XXXIV, No. 2 (October 1943), pp. 264–265.

Social thought is already revealed in early Greek literature. To understand anti-Semitism, one must also comprehend the historical impacts of Jewish migration.

114. *Religious and Secular Leadership,* Part I, The Dropsie College for Hebrew and Cognate Learning (Philadelphia: 1943), pp. xvi–117 + [1]. (See nos. 84, 88, 106.)

This volume consists of three articles formerly published in the *JQR* and entitled: "Rashi and the Rabbinate," "The Opposition to the Spiritual Leaders Appointed by the Government," and "Saadia Gaon—Champion for Jewish Unity under Religious Leadership." To these was added a chapter, "The Struggle Between Babylonia and Palestine for Hegemony."

1. Rashi and the Rabbinate:

In Palestine after the Destruction, Jewish leadership—both secular and religious—was vested in the Nasi, who traced his genealogy to the Davidic dynasty. In Babylonia leadership was divided, with religious authority in the hands of the scholars, the heads of the academies, and secular duties under the control of the Exilarch. Eventually with the ascendency of Sherira and Ḥai Gaon, who traced their ancestry to David, the scholars gained supremacy.

Rashi attempted a change in the community leadership structure in France, where the lay leadership was vested in the Parnasim. His responsa evidence a conscious effort, at the expense of a secular leadership, to raise the prestige of the Rabbinate which claimed an unbroken chain of spiritual authority from Ḥai Gaon and the Babylonian academies. (Cf. also nos. 79, 94.)

2. The Conflict among Spiritual Leaders:

Rabbi Isaac ben Sheshet (Ribash, 1326–1408) reports a struggle for the rabbinical post in France between Johanan, the son of Mattitiahu, the previous Chief Rabbi of France, and Joshua, the disciple of the late Chief Rabbi. The former had been sanctioned by the government and approved by the community to succeed his father. Isaac ben Sheshet of Spain supported Johanan, while Meir ha-Levi of Vienna upheld Joshua's claim. This conflict reveals the different approaches of the communities. Germany and France strongly adhered to the *takkanah* that no Jew should accept a position, religious or secular, from the government. Meir ha-Levi therefore opposed Johanan, who was approved by the government. In Spain, however, a rabbi appointed by the government was recognized as the Jewish leader. Hence, Isaac ben Sheshet not only supported Johanan, but opposed the Franco-German approach.

3. Saadia Gaon:

Although Saadia's controversy with the Palestinian scholar, Ben Meir (c. 921), seemingly centered around the problem of calendar intercalation, the underlying issue was rabbinic authority in legal interpretation—namely, Ben Meir's assertion of Palestinian supremacy vs. Saadia's claim for Babylonian Jewish authority.

The conflict of religious and secular forces may be traced throughout Jewish history. Initially, there was the struggle for hegemony between the Jewish center of Babylon and the Holy Land. After the Destruction the Jews in Babylonia sought to establish their own hegemony—not to be dependent on Palestine. In later times, Saadia and Rashi believed that leadership should be vested in a spiritual authority, for they considered the Jews to be a religious community. Maimonides believed in an Exilarch, i.e., in a secular leadership.

Rashi was responsible for the institution of the Rabbinate and Jewish education in Ashkenazic countries. Saadia was responsible for Babylonian hegemony over Palestine. Maimonides, on the other hand, considering the Jews to be not merely a religious community, but a people, looked for the establishment of the Jewish people as a nation in Palestine, able to develop their culture based on Torah.

The title "Rabbi," derived from the Patriarchate, denoted scholarship and indicated Franco-German Jewry to be of Palestinian origin. "Rav" is a Babylonian title going back to the Geonim. It refers to authorization and status. Spain followed the Babylonian traditions.

The volume also contains a history of the development of *Semikhah,* practiced in Palestine and in Franco-German communities, but not in Babylonia and Spain. Isaac ben Sheshet held that with the disappearance of the Patriarchate and Exilarchate, *Semikhah* ceased to exist. Isaac Abarbanel, coming to Italy, was unaware of the Franco-German custom of *Semikhah.*

Herein is also included a history of the Jewish calendar (see also nos. 28, 35). From Saadia's time, the Jews of Babylonia accepted the Metonic system of intercalation, based on a nineteen-year reckoning. Many scholars opposed this view, insisting that the calendar should be based only on observation of the moon. In ancient days Jews had neither a fixed calendar nor fixed days. Observance of two days, even for Rosh Hashanah, is only rabbinical.

Saadia won authority for the Diaspora, but with the present establishment of Israel its leadership may perhaps reassert its influence. Saadia, by his battle against the Karaites, Ben Meir, and the Exilarch, sought to create unity in Judaism. He maintained that Jews were held together only by Torah.

1944

115. "Correspondence. Who Crucified Jesus?—A Reply to a Critic; *Catholic Biblical Quarterly,* Vol. VI, No. 1 (January 1944), pp. 104–110.

The Talmud speaks of a religious Sanhedrin, while Josephus and the New Testament deal with a political body. In John the contentions are not halakhic, but are based on miracles.

The Gospel of John lays the blame for the Crucifixion on the Jews. The historicity of this Fourth Gospel has been questioned; yet textbooks, today, still contain the accusation.

Jews in the Diaspora suffered even before the rise of Christianity; in a pagan world they were the only monotheists. The blood of the Jews was the seed of the Church because the Jews spread the idea of monotheism. A charge of guilt can be applied to the Christian world for using the Crucifixion as a pretext for persecuting the Jews throughout the ages. (See also nos. 98, 101, 105.)

116. "Judaism as a Religion. A Historical Survey" (continued from *JQR,* XXXIV [1943], 207–241), *JQR,* XXXIV, No. 3 (January 1944), pp. 321–364; Vol. XXXV, No. 1 (July 1944), pp. 85–116; No. 2 (October 1944), pp. 179–225. (Cf., no. 123.)

117. Review of: *The Jewish Community. Its History and Structure to the American Revolution,* by Salo Wittmayer Baron, *JQR,* Vol. XXXIV, No. 3 (January 1944), pp. 371–384.

Subjects such as *ḥeber ha-'ir,* the system of Jewish education begun in the days of Simon b. Shetaḥ, the historical development of the Synagogue, and the importance of the *Maamad* institution are vital to the study of Jewish communal life in the Second Temple era.

118. על המעשה ברבן גמליאל, *Talpioth,* Vol. I, No. 2 (Tebet-Adar 5704), pp. 450–452.

The story of Rabban Gamaliel II in Maaser Sheni 5.4 is intertwined with the story of the removal and distribution of tithes.

119. "Communication: The Editor," *Crozer Quarterly,* Vol. XXI, No. 2 (April 1944), pp. 148–149. In reply to Dr. Ralph Marcus' review of *Religious and Secular Leadership.* (See no. 114.)

Rabbinic knowledge is necessary in addition to historical insight for studies of early Judaism. The Great Sanhedrin had (religious) authority over the entire people. The High Priest's actual authority was in the Temple, but he also wielded a general influence. Onias allied himself with Seleucus against Ptolemy III. The Syrian-Babylonian authorities did not want any export of wealth from Babylonia to Palestine.

120. "Maimonides and the Mekilta of Rabbi Simon ben Yochai," *JQR,* Vol. XXXIV, No. 4 (April 1944), pp. 487–489. Review of: מקורי הרמב"ם והמכילתא דרשב"י עם מבוא, באורים והערות מאת מנחם כשר.

Maimonides often used the Mekhilta as a source for his decisions, but not all passages in this particular text are of tannaitic origin. There are interpolations from later rabbinic writings. This Mekhilta copied much from the *Mishneh Torah.*

The Tannaim always used the word הבית. Only in the amoraic period did the Jews begin to use the term "Second Temple" (cf. no. 96). A redundant expression like גוי עובד עבודה זרה was never used by the Tannaim. This phrase is proof that this Mekhilta is a copy from *Mishneh Torah.* (See also no. 127.)

121. "A Note on the Doctrine of Asmakhta," *JQR,* Vol. XXXIV, No. 4 (April 1944), pp. 491–495. An exchange between Jacob J. Rabinowitz and Solomon Zeitlin.

There is a difference between property designated as a mortgage (משכון) and a deposit given by a buyer (ערבון). In the first case the mortgagee retains the property, while in the latter the property is obtained by the seller. (See no. 396.)

Maimonides held that tannaitic statements were authoritative, even when quoted in a Baraita or Tosefta. But he favored the decision of the Babylonian Talmud above the Palestinian, when there was a difference of opinion among the Amoraim.

122. "A Note on the Sabbatical Cycles," *JQR,* Vol. XXXV, No. 2 (October 1944), pp. 238–239. (See also nos. 16, 28.)

The Geonim, not Maimonides, had the correct reckoning of the Sabbatical cycles; the year 4935 (1174–1175) was a Sabbatical year (divisible by seven). In Saadia's calendar, which we use, the Sabbatical years are sometimes intercalated, but this created a burden for the farmers.

1945

123. "Judaism as a Religion. A Historical Study," (continued from *JQR,* XXXV [1944], 179–225). *JQR,* Vol. XXXV, No. 3 (January 1945), pp. 303–349. (See nos. 60, 110, 112, 116.)

The Festivals (Passover, Shabuot, and Sukkot) that had been observed largely as agricultural and national commemorative holidays were imbued, after the Destruction, with a strong religious significance. Judaism became a universal religion, uniting all those who believe in the God of Israel.

The term *galut* (exile) reveals a metamorphosis: from its original reference, pertaining to the forced expulsion of the Jews from the Northern Kingdom by the Assyrians, to its later theological connotation, referring to all Jews who reside outside the boundaries of the Holy Land. A study of the references to the Jews in Graeco-Roman literature and in the writings of the early Church Fathers shows that the Jews were viewed as a religious community rather than as a nation. This concept saved the Palestinian Jewish community from extinction after the Temple's destruction.

An analysis of Jewish history from the time of the Exodus until the destruction of the Second Temple, with emphasis upon the developmental changes in the implications of Jewish nationalism, shows that during the First Temple era, the god-concept was closely identified with the land. When the two kingdoms existed each worshipped the god of its own area. In the Second Temple era, the Jews in Judaea, having their own land, considered themselves a nation, while the Jews in Babylonia were recognized as a religious community. Judaism was thus no longer limited to a land, but united all believers. After the Destruction the entire Jewish people was united as a religious people, and referred to itself as *Knesset Yisrael* (Community of Israel). The Jews were then termed "Israelites," in the religious sense. (Cf., no. 204.)

Although the early Christians defined the Jews by the term *laos* (people), in the third century the Church Fathers began to apply to them the term *ethnos* (nation), insisting that Christianity was the only universal religion, and that Judaism was the superstition of an ethnic group. Religious persecution followed. The Jews accepted this ethnic term "nation," but they did not surrender their belief in a universal Judaism. Whether the Jews were a nation or a religious people was discussed in France after the French Revolution, and in Holland, in 1796, at the Constitutional Assembly of Batavia. In the nineteenth century different views emerged regarding the nature of Judaism. Some leaders negated the Diaspora, stating that the future of the Jews lay only in Palestine. Others held that after the destruction of the Temple the Jews had lost their basic national character. (See no. 130.)

With the goals of emancipation frustrated, the nineteenth century witnessed a variety of approaches to Jewish nationalism. Although Peretz Smolenskin and Leo Pinsker were both nationalists, they differed; the former believed that the Jews were a spiritual nation on foreign soil, and the latter insisted that the Jews must be transformed into a nation. Theodor Herzl evolved the plan for political Zionism and the establishment of a Jewish state. Opponents of this concept were Aḥad Ha-Am and Simon Dubnow.

124. "Anti-Semitism," *Crozer Quarterly,* Vol. XXII, No. 2 (April 1945), pp. 134–149.

The Germans added the racial element to the already deep-rooted religious hatred. (See also no. 101.)

125. Three line note to: "The History of the Jews in Russia in Recent Publications." *JQR,* Vol. XXXV, No. 4 (April 1945), p. 393.

The Jewish population in Russia in 1914 reached seven million.

126. "Additional Remarks," *JQR,* Vol. XXXV, No. 4 (April 1945), pp. 414–419. Remarks on Wischnitzer's article, "History of the Jews in Russia in Recent Publications" (see no. 125), and re: Elbogen, *A Century of Jewish Life.*

Any history of Russian Jewry in the early twentieth century should stress the activities of the defense of the Jewish position in the Beilis case and also the role of the Russian Rabbinate.

127. Untitled Note. *JQR,* Vol. XXXV, No. 4 (April 1945), pp. 455–456. Reply to comments on review of *Maimonides and the Mekilta of Rabbi Simon ben Yochai,* by M. Kasher. (See no. 120.)

Additional evidence shows that some passages in Maimonides, seemingly taken from the Mekhilta, are not of tannaitic origin.

128. Short Notices. *JQR,* Vol. XXXV, No. 4 (April 1945), pp. 457–459. Reviews of: *The Babylonian Talmud in Selection,* edited and translated from the original Hebrew and Aramaic by Leo Auerbach; and *The Relevance of Apocalyptic, A Study of Jewish and Christian Apocalypses from Daniel to the Revelation,* by H. H. Rowley.

References in the Book of Jubilees to civil and ecclesiastical authority being in Levitical hands is not evidence of a post-Maccabean composition, (see no. 77). The High Priest, prior to the Hasmonean era, controlled both areas of authority. (Cf., no. 119.)

129. "The Legend of the Ten Martyrs and its Apocalyptic Origins, *JQR*, Vol. XXXVI, No. 1 (July 1945), pp. 1–16.

The source of the legend is the apocryphal *Midrash Eleh Ezkerah,* now part of the Yom Kippur liturgy. It correlates the event to the selling of Joseph by his ten brothers, a sin that required a martyrological form of atonement.

According to the Book of Jubilees, Joseph was sold on the tenth day of the seventh month.

The notion of martyrdom was accepted by the Apocalyptists, the forerunners of Christianity, but was rejected by the Pharisees and the talmudic Sages. The only martyrs referred to in the Talmud were R. Akiba, R. Hanina b. Teradyon, and R. Judah b. Baba. Mention is also made of the violent death of Huzpit and Judah b. ha-Nahtum, but there is no early reference to a group of ten martyrs. (See also no. 143.)

130. "Jewish National Minority Rights," *JQR,* Vol. XXXVI, No. 1 (July 1945), pp. 98–103. Reply to Bernard G. Richard's criticism of the essay entitled "Judaism as a Religion." (See no. 123.)

Historically, only the Jews in ancient Palestine were considered a nation. The Jews of the Diaspora were united by a common religion. The concept that the Jews are a separate nationality in the countries where they live represents a misconception of Jewish history, and is contrary to the spirit of Judaism.

131. "The Political Synedrion and the Religious Sanhedrin," *JQR,* Vol. XXXVI, No. 2 (October 1945), pp. 109–140.

In *Antiquities* Josephus uses the word *synedrion* for the first time when speaking of Herod's trial for the murder of Hezekias. In the Gospels and in the Talmud, which are post-70 C.E., it is used to connote a court. The judiciary system that was introduced when the Commonwealth was established in the days of the Hasmoneans included a lesser court (Bet Din) for trials, and a Great Court (Bet Din ha-Gadol) for legislation. (See also no. 50.) Religious courts did not assume the name Sanhedrin until after the Destruction; hence there is no reference to it in the early sources (cf., also no. 142). The *synedrion* that tried and convicted Jesus was not a religious court, but a state council that was assembled to try a political offender. (Cf., nos. 105, 136, 142.)

132. "Criteria for the Dating of Jubilees," *JQR,* Vol. XXXVI, No. 2 (October 1945), pp. 187–189. In reply to H. H. Rowley.

Evidence for an early pre-Hellenistic dating of the Book of Jubilees is the fact that the months are referred to not by name, as in the later Apocryphal works, but by number. (See also nos. 77, 128, 146.)

133. *Louis Ginzberg Jubilee Volume, on the Occasion of his Seventieth Birthday,* The American Academy for Jewish Research, English Section (New York: 1945), pp. ix–446 + 1 ill. Solomon Zeitlin, member of the Editorial Committee.

133a. "A Note on the Legend of the Ten Martyrs," *JQR,* Vol. XXXVI, No. 2 (October 1945), pp. 209–210.

In the *Midrash of Proverbs* and in *Yalkut Shimoni,* the supposed death of the ten martyrs is linked directly to the atonement for the sale of Joseph by his ten brothers. In the former volume it is in the name of R. Joshua b. Levi, and in the latter work, by Rav Yehuda. This evidences the great influence that apocalyptic literature had on the Midrash. (Cf., also no. 129.)

1946

134. Review of: *The Babylonian Talmud in Selection,* edited and translated by Leon Auerbach. *Crozer Quarterly,* Vol. XXIII, No. 1 (January 1946), pp. 100–102. (See also no. 128.)

Religious appeasement is an illusory policy. Many Jews write books (as on the Talmud) in apologetic tones to gain Christian good will. A devout Christian, however, does not seek apologetics.

135. "A Historical Study of the first Canonization of the Hebrew Liturgy," *JQR,* Vol. XXXVI, No. 3 (January 1946), pp. 211–229. To be continued. (Cf., no. 157.)

136. "Synedrion in the Judeo-Hellenistic Literature and Sanhedrin in the Tannaitic Literature," *JQR,* Vol. XXXVI, No. 3 (January 1946), pp. 307–315.

The term synedrion in LXX Proverbs does not have the connotation of "court of justice." The translator had texts with readings other than our masoretic version. Before the Destruction there was only one Jewish court, a *Bet din,* a *kriterion.* The term *synedrion* is used in Judeo-Hellenistic literature for the first time in the Book of Susanna. (Cf., no. 131.)

137. "The Beginning of the Jewish Day During the Second Commonwealth," *JQR,* Vol. XXXVI, No. 4 (April 1946), pp. 403–414.

The calendar during the Second Commonwealth was a fixed one, lunar-solar in nature, and was accepted in all parts of Judaea. The months were reckoned according to the moon, while the years were reckoned according to the sun. The day began with the evening. The holidays were arranged according to the solar seasons in their respec- lunar months. There were no arbitrary approaches to the Jewish calendar then. (See also nos. 28, 35, 154, 306.)

138. "The Jews in Egypt in the Hellenistic-Roman Period," *JQR,* Vol. XXVII, No. 1 (July 1946), pp. 89–93. Review of: היהודים במצרים בתקופה ההלניסטית-הרומית לאור הפאפירולוגיה, מאת אביגדור צ׳ריקובר.

The courtier Onias, mentioned in a papyrus dating back to the year 164 B.C.E., could well be a reference to Onias III, who built his temple in Egypt in 168–167 B.C.E. Onias IV was not the one who constructed the temple.

The *Fiscus Judaicus,* the Jewish tax imposed by Emperor Vespasian, aimed to symbolize the victory of Jupiter over the God of Israel, and not merely to obtain funds to rebuild the Temple of Jupiter. The tax was therefore removed when Christianity became the official religion of Rome.

139. *"Hatekufah,"* *JQR,* Vol. XXXVII, No. 1 (July 1946), pp. 95–98. Review of: התקופה, ספר ל-לא, העורכים — יצחק זילברשלג ואהרן ציטלין.

(Evaluation of Scholarly Articles by L. Finkelstein and S. Feigin.)

The contention that mention of Sameias and Pollion by Josephus refers to Shemaiah and Abtalion is questionable. (Cf., no. 10.) In the days of the Second Commonwealth the altar as a refuge for an unintentional murderer did not exist. Homicide was tried in court and the defendant was either sentenced or acquitted. (See also no. 160.)

140. Short notices. *JQR,* Vol. XXXVII, No. 1 (July 1946), pp. 99–102. Reviews of: *The Idea of Nationalism,* by Hans Kohn; *Nationalities and National Minorities,* by Oscar J. Janowsky; *Voix de l'Orient,* by Jacques D'Aumale.

The nationalism evident in the Pentateuch was not characteristic of the approach taken by the Jews in the Second Commonwealth. The Jews had then ceased to view themselves as an ethnic group. (Cf., no. 123.)

The Sephardic Jews are the descendants of Babylonian Jews who traveled to Spain with the Arabs, following the Arab conquest of Spain in 711. Ashkenazic Jewry has its source in the migration of Jews from Palestine to Europe in the days of the Roman Empire.

141. "A Note on the Chronology of the Destruction of the Second Temple," *JQR,* Vol. XXXVII, No. 2 (October 1946), pp. 165–167.

The Second Temple was destroyed in 69–70 C.E. Maimonides, Rashi, and Ibn Ezra, however, date it at 68–69. Their error is a result of the different calculations of the "Era of Contracts"—311, in Babylon, or 312 and 313 B.C.E., as calculated in Palestine. (See no. 16.)

142. "Synedrion in Greek Literature, the Gospels, and the Institution of the Sanhedrin," *JQR,* Vol. XXXVII, No. 2 (October 1946), pp. 189–198. (In reply to S. B. Hoenig, in the same issue.)

In his *Antiquities,* written in 93 C.E., Josephus used the term *synedrion* for the first time in reference to a trial court. In his earlier volume, *The Jewish War,* "synedrion" is still used to denote a council. (Cf., also no. 131, 136.)

143. "A Note on the Legend of the Ten Martyrs." Reprint of no. 133a, article in *JQR,* Vol. XXXVI, No. 2 (October 1945), pp. 209–210.

144. ספר היובל לכבוד לוי גינצברג למלאות לו שבעים שנה. חלק עברי ניו יורק, תש"ו [1946], האקדמיה האמריקנית למדעי היהדות. pp. ix–446. Solomon Zeitlin, member of the Editorial Committee. (See no. 145.)

145. הפקר ויאוש, מחקר עפ"י הספרות התנאית. ספר היובל לכבוד ל. גינזברג, ח"ב, pp. 365–380.

The basic difference between the schools of Shammai and Hillel in the laws of *res nullius* is that the former applied them even if there was a limitation set on the declaration of *hefker,* whereas the School of Hillel maintained that no limitation could be set. Many rules, such as those pertaining to divorce and slavery, also belong to the question of "limitation." (See also nos. 11, 59.)

1947

146. "The Apocrypha," *JQR,* Vol. XXXVII, No. 3 (January 1947), pp. 219–248. (Also a review of *The Apocryphal Literature,* by C. C. Torrey.)

The Book of Jubilees is an early composition (5th century B.C.E.). This is indicated by its reference to Shabuot as a festival not connected with the Omer, and by the solar calendar used therein. (Cf., also nos. 77, 128, 132.)

147. "A New Palestinian Edition of the Mishna," *JQR,* Vol. XXXVII, No. 3 (January 1947), pp. 301–305. Review of: משניות ברכות, פאה, דמאי... תרגום ומבואות ופירוש חדש באנגלית, מאת יעקב הלוי הרצוג.

There are no sources indicating that in pre-Second Temple days the Sanhedrin met in the Sanctuary. Whenever the term "Sanhedrin" is used in connection with Moses and the early biblical era, the reference is Aggadic in nature.

Shammai and Hillel are not to be classified as Tannaim. The period of the Soferim lasted until the Destruction, when the tannaitic era began.

148. "The Warning Inscription of the Temple," *JQR,* Vol. XXXVIII, No. 1 (July 1947), pp. 111–116. Remarks concerning Dr. E. J. Bickerman's article, "The Warning Inscription of Herod's Temple," *JQR,* (April 1947).

The reason for the prohibition was to maintain the sanctity of the Temple, not any notion of Gentile impurity. Even Israelites could not enter all areas.

149. "Prosbol: A Study in Tannaitic Jurisprudence," *JQR,* Vol. XXXVII, No. 4 (April 1947), pp. 341–362.

The *takkanah* of Prosbol, introduced by Hillel, served to encourage loans, while protecting the creditor against having the loan annulled by the Sabbatical year. The *Prosbol* could be prepared by the creditor even without the debtor's knowledge, and it had to be deposited within the court.

150. Review of: *The Herem Ha-yishub. A Contribution to the Medieval Economic History of the Jews,* by Rabbi L. Rabinowitz. *JQR,* Vol. XXXVII, No. 4 (April 1947), pp. 427–431.

The *Ḥerem ha-Yishub* was an innovation of the Middle Ages. It had no relation to any Talmudic dictum, hence a *ḥerem* was required. It was the result of a community organizational situation, and not an attempt to control economic competition. In France and Germany, which consisted of independent communities, the *ḥerem* was introduced to bar new settlers, for fear of antagonizing the local authorities. (See also nos. 99, 373.)

151. "The Assumption of Moses and the Revolt of Bar Kokhba. Studies in the Apocalyptic Literature," *JQR,* Vol. XXXVIII, No. 1 (July 1947), pp. 1–45.

The Assumption of Moses, believed to have been composed after the death of Herod, is actually the last composition in apocryphal literature. It was compiled in 140 C.E., after the Bar Kokhba revolt. The date is deduced from the author's passage regarding the year of the anticipated Messianic era. (Cf., nos. 224, 312.)

Taxo (a bow—sign of peace), the man referred to as one of the tribe of Levi who "will speak to them," can be identified as Rabbi Joshua ben Ḥananiah who opposed the revolt. This characterizes the book's approach, referring to the rebels as "pestilent and impious men."

152. "Jewish Rights in Palestine," *JQR,* Vol. XXXVIII, No. 2 (October 1947), pp. 119–134.

The Jewish claim to a homeland in Palestine is valid. Religiously, the Jews are the only people to whom the whole land is considered sacred. Historically, the Jews lived in Palestine from the days of Joshua. Even after the Temple destruction, Jewish communal life continued on Palestinian soil. Legally, they never surrendered title. Judaea was not annexed to the Roman Empire with the Destruction. (See nos. 304, 313.)

153. "Paganism to Christianity," *JQR*, Vol. XXXVIII, No. 2 (October 1947), pp. 205–208. Review of: *Paganism to Christianity in the Roman Empire*, by Walter Woodburn.

That there is an authentic Christ passage in *Antiquities* is erroneous. (See no. 37.) That Jesus was accused of a political crime is true. (Cf., no. 105 and no. 161.)

154. "Correspondence: The Beginning of the Jewish Day During the Second Commonwealth," *JQR*, Vol. XXXVIII, No. 2 (October 1947), pp. 215–219. "Correspondence between P. J. Heawood and S. Zeitlin."

Although circumstances at times necessitated the mention of day before night in the Mishnah (Ber. 4.1; Sukk. 2.6), in the Second Temple era, with a lunar-solar calendar in effect, the day began with the preceding evening. During biblical days, however, with a solar calendar in effect, the day began with sunrise. (See also no. 137.)

155. "What, Then, Are the Jews?—In the Light of History," *Menorah Journal*, Vol. XXXV, No. 3 (Autumn 1947), pp. 266–279.

A definition of the Jew cannot be made *de novo;* it must be based upon the experiences of the Jewish people throughout the centuries. A variety of theories consider the Jews as either a nation, a nationality, a civilization, a combination of all the above, or as individuals who do not constitute a people at all. All are historically inaccurate. The basis for political Zionism, namely, that the Jews are a nation, has no roots in history. Jews are united by religion alone. (Cf., also no. 123.)

156. *Who Crucified Jesus?* Harper and Bros., second edition (New York: 1947), pp. xv–250. (Cf., no. 105.)

Synedrion, in the Greek classical and Judaeo-Hellenistic literature, means only "council" or "conference." (Cf., no. 142.)

In early days, the kings were themselves the judges, or they appointed judges. With the Restoration, supreme authority was vested in the High Priests. The court was called Bet Din. The change from Theocracy to Commonwealth brought about also a change in the judiciary system. A court was established independent of the High

Priest and the Ethnarch. The supreme authority in religious law was now the Bet Din ha-Gadol.

After the destruction of the Temple and state, the religious court remained the only authority over all Jewry. The term, which before had been used in connection with summoned councils (*synedria*) was now used for the religious court. It also took up civil matters. The term "sanhedrin" does not occur in tannaitic literature prior to the Destruction. (Cf., no. 136.)

1948

157. "A Historical Study of the First Canonization of the Hebrew Liturgy," (continued from *JQR,* XXXVI [1946], 211–229; see no. 135), *JQR,* Vol. XXXVIII, No. 3 (January 1948), pp. 289–316. To be continued.

Originally prayer was a cry in time of distress. The principal vehicles of prayer were through *neder*, a vow or promise (as Jacob's *neder*), and by *tefillah,* argument (e.g., Moses' appeal to God not to destroy the Jews). The word *tefillah* in the sense of prayer arose only in a later period. Many examples are cited to show that *tefillah* originally meant plea (this is also the origin of *Muflah,* the pleader in a court). Prayer was effected by spreading the hands in a pleading attitude.

Besides prayer there were praises, doxologies, and penitential recitals. The destruction of the First Temple brought in the element of confession, as in Ezra. A study of the liturgy in tannaitic literature shows that there were no early organized prayers. Prayer could be offered anywhere; there was as yet no synagogue.

During the Second Temple era, prayers generally began with praise, followed by request, and then by phrases of thanks. It is so also in Apocryphal literature.

Prayers did not take the place of sacrifices. Only the time of prayer was derived from the time of sacrifices. Prayers were recited aloud while standing. After the canonization of prayers the rabbis opposed loud prayer. The Talmudic discussions about this belong to the period after 70 C.E., when prayers were being canonized.

The liturgy in the Temple was priestly, with daily recital of *Shema,* holiday recital of *Hallel,* and also a liturgy for fast days. In the Temple Court during the Second Commonwealth, there was no organized recital of prayer. (Cf., no. 219.) The Temple sacrificial worship, however, did have an organized mode, and included the participation of the assembled worshippers. The institution of the *maamadot* system necessitated that Jews in various communities assemble on designated days for Torah readings, thus representing the earliest form of formal gathering for liturgic worship.

It can be assumed that only the priests were required to wear head coverings in the course of their ministrations. After the liturgy was canonized and the mode of service organized, all were required to cover their heads during worship. Women, too, seem to have participated, even in the reading of the Torah.

(For the origin of the Synagogue, see no. 38; for the Passover liturgy, see no. 159; for Hallel see no. 315; for the Tefillah: Shemoneh Esreh, see no. 337.)

158. Short Notices: "The Schocken Library," *JQR,* Vol. XXXVIII, No. 3 (January 1948), pp. 349–351.

During the Second Commonwealth the Jews who lived in the Diaspora were not exiles. *Galut* received a theological meaning of awaiting the Messiah. Throughout history this concept contributed much to the survival of Judaism. (Cf., no. 123.)

The autobiography of Solomon Maimon is a classic, an important document on the history of the Jews in Poland in the eighteenth century.

159. "The Liturgy of the First Night of Passover" (continued from *JQR,* XXXVIII [1948], 289–316), *JQR,* Vol. XXXVIII, No. 4 (April 1948), pp. 431–460. (See no. 157.)

The dipping into *haroset* is symbolic of the biblical command to sprinkle some blood of the paschal sacrifice upon the doorposts. The rabbinic tradition to "dip twice" on Passover night has its source in the blood of the paschal lamb and in the blood of circumcision, both being elements in Jewish redemption.

During the Second Temple, three questions were asked, as recorded in the Palestinian Talmud. Rabban Gamaliel II added a fourth, relating to the eating of *maror* (bitter herbs). In the original liturgy only "three sons" were included, corresponding to the three questions, and only three cups of wine were used. When a fourth question was added, a fourth son (unable to formulate a question), and a fourth cup of wine were also added. (See also nos. 241, 283.)

160. "The Halakhah: Introduction to Tannaitic Jurisprudence," *JQR,* Vol. XXXIX, No. 1 (July 1948), pp. 1–40.

Herein is a discussion of tannaitic jurisprudence and its sources—the Mosaic laws, the *gezerah* (legislation promulgated for a specific reason), the *takkanah* (an amendment of an early law [cf., no. 185]), the *minhag* (the usage prevalent in a particular locality or group), and *siyug* ("a fence around the law").

Biblical laws greatly expanded as a result of tannaitic jurisprudence. Among the innovations were that crime (theft or homicide) was considered a state offense as well as a private wrong, and emphasis was also placed on the consideration of intention as a factor in a person's actions. (Cf., no. 40.)

161. "The Hoax of the 'Slavonic Josephus,' " *JQR*, Vol. XXXIX, No. 2 (October 1948), pp. 171–180. Refers to article by J. S. Kennard in *JQR,* XXXIX, 161–70.

There was no Christ passage written by Josephus. The paragraph in *Antiquities* was an interpolation by Eusebius who believed that such a reference must have existed, but had been deleted by the Jews. Christological references in the "Slavonic Josephus" are insertions by the Church Fathers. (See no. 37.)

162. "The Council of Four Lands," *JQR,* Vol. XXXIX, No. 2 (October 1948), pp. 211–214. Review of: פנקס ועד ארבע ארצות לקוטי תקנות, כתבים ורשימות, סדורים ומבוארים בידי ישראל היילפרין.

The collection of material pertaining to the Council's activities from 1580–1764, reflecting the religious, social, and economic life of Polish Jewry in the sixteenth, seventeenth, and eighteenth centuries, discloses the division that then existed between the religious and secular leadership. The Council attempted to forbid Rabbis to hold any post connected with taxation and to participate in any activity that was not of a religious nature. Although the Council was autocratic and curbed the freedom of the individual, it did keep the Jewish community intact.

163. Review of: "A Selected Bibliography (1920–1945) of the Jews in the Hellenistic-Roman Period," in *Proceedings of the American Academy for Jewish Research,* Vol. XVI (1946–47), *JQR,* Vol. XXXIX, No. 2 (October 1948), pp. 221–222.

A mere subject catalogue is insufficient to assist students of the Hellenistic-Roman periods. It is important to make the bibliography "more descriptive," that is, to give some "idea of its contents."

1949

164. "A Commentary on the Book of Habakkuk: Important Discovery or Hoax?" *JQR,* Vol. XXXIX, No. 3 (January 1949), pp. 235–247.

This scroll is a product of the Middle Ages. The title, *Moreh Tzedek* ("Teacher of Righteousness"), was not in use during the era of the Second Temple. The use of "El" (as in the Zadokite fragment) in reference to God indicates a late composition; "Yahweh" and "Adonai" were the terms used during the Second Commonwealth.

165. "The Cryptic Numbers in Daniel," *JQR,* Vol. XXXIX, No. 3 (January 1949), pp. 321–324. Refers to H. L. Ginsberg, *Studies in Daniel.*

The Sages in the Talmud did not occupy themselves with calculations on the coming of the Messiah based on cryptic numbers in this Apocalyptic book.

The restoration of the Temple service did not occur after 1072 days, but after 1092 days, consisting of two normal years of 354 days and an intercalated year of 384. Rededication of the Temple took place "on the same day"—to the exact day and month—as its desecration (25 Kislev). The defilement took place in 168 and the rededication in 165 B.C.E.

166. "Origin of Hebrew Scrolls. Authenticity of Manuscript Said Not to Be Established," To the Editor, *The New York Times,* April 2, 1949.

Internal evidence negates any early dating of the Scrolls. Scholarship would be best served if the discovery of these Scrolls were not surrounded by sensational publicity.

167. "Scholarship and the Hoax of the Recent Discoveries," *JQR,* Vol. XXXIX, No. 4 (April 1949), pp. 337–363 + 3 pl.

That the Scroll of the War of the Children of Light with the Children of Darkness dates back to the pre-Hasmonean era, and that the phrase, "Kittim of Egypt and Kittim of Assyria" refers to the division between the Ptolemies and the Seleucids, is a hasty and erroneous conclusion. (Cf., no. 253.) In the literature of the Second Commonwealth the Seleucids were never associated with the kings of Assyria, but rather with Syria or Aram. *Kohen ha-Rosh,* used in referring to the High Priest, was a term employed during the Middle Ages. During the Second Commonwealth *Kohen ha-Gadol* was the accepted usage.

168. "The Alleged Antiquity of the Scrolls," *JQR,* Vol. XL, No. 1 (July 1949), pp. 57–78.

The paleography and orthography of the Second Commonwealth era indicate that the discovered Scrolls do not date back to the pre-Christian era. The authors of the Scrolls used the five final letters in the Hebrew alphabet (מנצפ"ך), which were not introduced until the time of R. Akiba. (See no. 187.)

169. "Prayer in the Apocrypha and Pseudepigrapha," *JQR,* Vol. XL, No. 2 (October 1949), pp. 201–203. Review of: Norman B. Johnson's essay, "Prayer in the Apocrypha and Pseudepigrapha," Monograph Series of the Society of Biblical Literature and Exegesis.

The Books of the Apocrypha and Pseudepigrapha not only cover a span of half a millenium, but also represent different localities (Palestine and the Diaspora) and different approaches to Judaism. To consider this body of literature as belonging to one period and originating with one group, and to quote from the various volumes indiscriminately in order to determine forms of prayer is, historically, an invalid approach.

170. Review of: *Why Jesus Died* by Pierre van Paasen. *JQR,* Vol. XL, No. 2 (October 1949), pp. 217–218.

The Zealots were not Jesus' followers, nor did they believe in a Messiah; and the spurious Christ passage is not in *War,* but in *Antiquities.* (See no. 161.)

171. "Needed: A New Jewish History," *Menorah Journal,* Vol. XXXVII, No. 1 (Winter 1949), pp. 126–135. (See also no. 372.)

An analysis of Heinrich Graetz' volumes reveals that the work is now antiquated. New discoveries in the Genizah have added enormously to our knowledge. No one man could have mastered all the courses of Jewish history. Graetz was mistaken in writing that Judith was authored in the time of Trajan; the Apostolic Father Clement of Rome, (*ca.* 100 C.E.) mentioned the book much earlier. Simon Dubnow did not believe, as did Graetz, that literary productions should be the signposts of Jewish history. His own approach was a national-sociological one, not that of a classical halakhic scholar. Cecil Roth imitated Graetz and Dubnow and even adopted some non-Jewish notions, such as the theory that Menelaus was "an Israelite of the tribe of Benjamin," not recalling that "Binyamin" was the name of a priestly family. The Sicarii and the Zealots are incorrectly identified as being the same. Josephus never confused the two parties.

1950

172. "The Mystery of the Hebrew Scrolls," *Crozer Quarterly,* Vol. XXVII, No. 1 (January 1950), pp. 35–42.

The events surrounding the discovery of the Scrolls are still shrouded in mystery. A survey reveals discrepancies in the accounts of Dr. John C. Trever, the Metropolitan Yeshue Athanasius Samuel, Dr. E. L. Sukenik, O. R. Sellers, and G. L. Harding.

173. "Jewish Apocryphal Literature," *JQR,* Vol. XL, No. 3 (January 1950), pp. 223–250.

The term "Apocrypha," which means "hidden," was applied by the Church Fathers to spurious, heretical books, and to those not in the Hebrew canon; yet they esteemed and cited many books, considered them to be of divine inspiration, and applied the term "ecclesiastical" to them. There is a division between the Protestant and Catholic Churches as to what is regarded as Apocryphal. The Catholic Church incorporated the books into the Holy Scriptures. The leaders of the Reformation followed the Hebrew canon.

Only books that had religious pretensions were under the ban of being "outside books," not secular books like Homer. Ben Sira was first banned because it is similar to Proverbs. Later, there being no fear of its being introduced into the canon, Ben Sira was quoted in the Talmud.

Some books were banned because of a time element, or because they were written in a foreign language, or because they were produced by dissenters and opposed to normative halakhah. (Cf., no. 42.) These "outside books" influenced Apocalyptic and Midrashic literature and were popular in the Middle Ages.

Angelology is traceable to the Book of Enoch; two Messiahs, to Fourth Ezra; ten martyrs, to the Book of Jubilees and the Testament of the Twelve Patriarchs. Messianic revelations were drawn from the Assumption of Moses. Jewish mysticism, Kabbalah, and Hasidism can also be traced to Apocalyptic literature.

Charles' introduction to his edition of Pirke Abot was not correct. It is a rabbinic work, like other tractates of the Mishnah.

To include the medieval work, the Zadokite Fragments, was wrong, because it misled scholars into believing that this karaitic work of the ninth and tenth centuries belonged to the inter-Testamental period! (Cf., no. 201.)

174. "Where is the Scroll of the Haftarot?" *JQR,* Vol. XL, No. 3 (January 1950), pp. 291–296.

The "disappearance" of the Scroll of the Haftarot, which T. Wechsler examined together with the Scroll of Isaiah, casts further suspicion on the authenticity of the Scrolls. The suppression of this Scroll, which is obviously of late origin (for Haftarot were assigned to each Sabbath only in Babylonia, after the Temple destruction), may have been done to reflect the "antiquity" of the other Scrolls.

175. "When were the Hebrew Scrolls 'discovered'—in 1947 or 1907?" *JQR*, Vol. XL, No. 4 (April 1950), pp. 373–378.

Though it is generally accepted that the Scrolls were discovered in 1947, there is a notion that the Scrolls were found by the Bedouin forty years earlier, in 1907.

176. "The Hebrew Scrolls: Once More and Finally," *JQR,* Vol. XLI, No. 1 (July 1950), pp. 1–58.

The Isaiah Scroll does not include all the variations from the Masoretic text that are recorded in tannaitic literature. The numerous errors in the use of language point to the fact that this Scroll could not have been penned in the Hasmonean era, when Hebrew was a living language, but rather in the seventh or eighth century.

The Habakkuk Commentary (as well as The War of the Sons of Light with the Sons of Darkness, the Thanksgiving Psalms, and the Sectarian Manual) bears a close textual resemblance to the Zadokite Fragment found by Solomon Schechter.

177. "Goodwill and Scholarship.'" *JQR,* Vol. XLI, no. 2 (October 1950), pp. 225–241. Review of: L. Finkelstein, *The Jews: Their History, Culture, and Religion,* 1949.

To persist in the assertion that the Jews obtained their ideas from the Greeks, in the face of evidence, is obsessive. Scholars who maintain this are merely aping the notions of German scholars who were hostile to the Jews in their treatment of Jewish history. It is particularly incorrect to state that the Talmudic period ended in 1035 C.E.

Schools for advanced studies were already in existence before Simon ben Shetah (first century B.C.E.); Ben Sira (c. 170 B.C.E.) portrays an early system of Jewish education.

The concept of a Chosen People is biblical, and is based on the idea of a God of Israel who favored the patriarchs. The prophets, however, preached universality. The idea of chosenness was abandoned during the time of the Second Temple; normative Judaism did not stress it. Apocalyptic Judaism and Christianity, however, retained the concept that the Jews were, indeed, "chosen." The idea became popular with the Jews of the Middle Ages to counteract the hostility of the Christians, and was stressed by ethnic nationalists like Judah ha-Levi. (See also no. 205.)

The Jews of the Talmudic period believed that it was wrong to resort to the pagan courts, because they regarded Jewish law in all its branches as divinely inspired.

Jews were active in missionary work during the period of the Second Commonwealth. The Church later prohibited proselyting.

178. "A Chronological Error on a Stamp of Israel," *JQR,* Vol. XLI, No. 2 (October 1950), pp. 243–244.

The year 66 C.E. corresponded to 3826–27 A.M. The Revolt broke out in 65 C.E. on June 4, i.e., 13 or 14 Sivan, 3825 A.M., not in 66 C.E. The victory of Cestius was on 7 Kislev, 3826 A.M.

179. "Who Crucified Jesus?" Serialized in *The Jewish News,* Detroit (December 22 and 29, 1950). Reprint of no. 156. Articles appeared on the first page of *The Jewish News.*

180. "A Note on the Principle of Intention in Tannaitic Literature," *Alexander Marx Jubilee Volume,* 1950. pp. 631–646.

The views of R. Judah and R. Simon pertaining to "preparation" for the Sabbath are based on the principle of intention: R. Judah, a Shammaite, did not require it, whereas R. Simon, a Hillelite, did. Thus the school of Hillel was strict in this matter where the school of Shammai was lenient. Mishnah Eduyot does not record all the differences between the schools of Hillel and Shammai. (See nos. 11, 26, 40, 45.)

181. Jewish Apocryphal Literature, Solomon Zeitlin, editor-in-chief. *The First Book of Maccabees,* An English Translation by Sidney Tedesche, Introduction and Commentary by Solomon Zeitlin. Published for the Dropsie College for Hebrew and Cognate Learning by Harper & Brothers (New York: 1950), pp. xvi–291.

Preface: In many cases the translation and dating of the Apocryphal books are incorrect because of a lack in understanding Jewish background. In the main, Christian scholars interpreted these works in order to present early Christianity in the light of their beliefs, while Jewish scholars neglected them. A scientific edition is still to be issued. (See no. 173.)

Introduction: The series fittingly begins with I Maccabees because of its portrayal of the Hasmonean battle for freedom for conscience, a struggle which became the turning point for Jewish history and Western civilization.

The author of I Maccabees was a contemporary Palestinian, a supporter of strict Judaism, yet he did not attribute the Jewish victories to miracles but to Hasmonean valor. There is no hint of the doctrine of a "life after death" in the book. This concept was still new to Jewish thought.

Mattathias permitted Sabbath warfare because of the danger of annihilation. The principle that one Sabbath may be profaned in order to be able to keep others became a Pharisaic doctrine and was enunciated by Hillel. Such permission did not indicate any Sadducean tendencies. On the contrary, the Sadducees were stricter than the Pharisees in Sabbath observance.

The historical narrative of the author's own period is accurate, but there are some lapses in his handling of the earlier period of Alexander the Great—and his knowledge of the Romans is hazy. The fact that the Romans are described as being friendly presupposes the writing of the book before Pompey's capture of Jerusalem. Its time of composition was probably after John Hyrcanus' death.

The book deliberately avoids the use of the Divine Name, as well as "Hebrew" and "Jew"; "Israelites" is used to designate the people. "Jew" is only used in dealing with non-Jews. These elements indicate that I Maccabees was edited after the destruction of the Temple; yet, in Chapter 14, the term "Jews" is found. This may be an authentic copy of the document declaring Simon High Priest and Ethnarch. The use of the term "true prophet" in Chapter 14 also suggests a date in the first century C.E., designed to offset other prevailing notions.

There may be historical truth in the tradition that the Elders of the Schools of Hillel and Shammai edited I Maccabees. The Hebrew text was still extant in the third or fourth century. Polybius was the source for the early history of the Hellenistic world; I Maccabees is the only work contemporaneous with it, and is decisive and clear where the pagan authors (Livy, Appian, Justin) are often ambiguous.

The proem in II Maccabees, telling of the fire descending from Heaven, is designed to give universal (not local) significance to the festival of Hanukkah. (See also nos. 16, 72, 227.)

The Rabbis spoke highly of the Hasmoneans. The Talmud, and the Commentators, even interpreted biblical verses as allusions to them. The term "Maccabee" is not used because it alludes only to Judah, whereas the Rabbis attributed the success of the struggle to all the Hasmoneans. The Rabbinic stress is on the miracle—on the religious aspect, as in the proem, rather than on the secular.

Appendix: The original title of the book may have been *S'far bet sarché El,* "The Book of the House of the Princes of God." Simon was called "sar am El." The Hebrew term, *hasmonean,* means "prince." The Aramaic *S'far bet sarché El* is a translation of *Sefer bet Ḥashmonaim.* The title, Book of Maccabees, was originated by the Church.

Judah's name, Makkabi, indicates a physical characteristic: it means "the Hammer-headed." [See also F. Perles, "The Name Makkabios," *JQR,* XVII, No. 3 (January 1927), p. 404.]

1951

182. *Who Crucified Jesus?* Serialized in the *Jewish News,* Detroit (January 5, 12, and 19, 1951; Continued from December 29, 1950). All articles appeared on the first page of the *Jewish News.* (See no. 156.)

183. "The Hebrew Scrolls: A Challenge to Scholarship," *JQR,* Vol. XLI, No. 3 (January 1951), pp. 251–275.

Because of their lack of knowledge of rabbinic and karaitic literature, Scroll scholars often operate in a nebulous area. The inclusion, in the Zadokite Fragment, of a law concerning Sabbath journey enacted after the time of Rabban Gamaliel the Elder, proves that the work was compiled after the Destruction (see no. 184). It is a work of the tenth centry and is in accord with karaitic ideas in opposition to the rabbinic *Takkanah of Erub.* The reference in the Manual of Discipline to "spitting" also pertains to a Karaitic prohibition, that of spitting in the synagogue. The text is not an Essene document.

The view that *Pesher Habakkuk* deals with the capture of Jerusalem by Pompey on the Day of Atonement (a Sabbath day) cannot be correct, for that event took place on the ninth of Tammuz, 63 B.C.E., on a Wednesday. The *matres lectionis* in the Isaiah Scroll is evidence of the lateness of this copy. (Cf., no. 187.)

Professor Sukenik's report contains contradictions about the jars. The discrepancies cannot be assigned to the disturbances of 1947–1948.

184. "The Takkanot of Erubin. A Study in the Development of the Halakha," *JQR,* Vol. XLI, No. 4 (April 1951), pp. 351–361.

Originally, one could walk only four cubits from his house on the Sabbath. The Sages permitted walking through the entire city on the Sabbath, and new-moon witnesses were given the same privileges as residents in order to encourage them to come to testify. This *takkanah* of *Teḥum Shabbat* was introduced by Rabban Gamliel the Elder (20–50 C.E.), and was later extended by the Sages in the interpretation of *makom* ("place") to include 2,000 additional cubits beyond the city limits. The *takkanah* of Erub was based on the principle of intention. Naturally, one who denied its validity could not avail himself of it.

Another *takkanah* pertained to carrying anything from the courtyard of one house to another on the Sabbath; this could be arranged through the legal fiction of a partnership. Such association could not be established with a Jew who profaned the Sabbath publicly, or with a pagan; in their case, it was necessary that the property be actually rented for the purpose.

A third *takkanah* pertained to cooking. Since the law did not permit cooking on a holiday for the succeeding day, it was arranged that if a holiday fell on a Friday, the cooking on that day for the Sabbath was deemed a continuation of preparation from Thursday (the eve of the holiday).

All three types of *Erubin* were introduced before the Bar Kokhba period. A *takkanah* is a universal regulation, an amendment of early legal rules—pentateuchal or halakhic—in order to harmonize law and life. Generally it is lenient, and the Rabbis drew their support from the Bible. (Cf., no. 160.)

185. "A Note on 'The Manual of Discipline,'" *JQR,* Vol. XLI, No. 4 (April 1951), p. 449. Review of: *The Dead Sea Scrolls of St. Mark's Monastery,* Vol. II, Fascicle 2, Plates and Transcription of the Manual of Discipline, edited by Millar Burrows, etc.

The photostat of the Discipline Scroll substantiates the claim that it is a medieval concoction, written by a person of mediocre attainments, one not even well versed in medieval Hebrew. It is erroneous to deduce from it similarities to the Gospels.

186. "The Time of the Passover Meal," *JQR,* Vol. XLII, No. 1 (July 1951), pp. 45–50.

According to the Synoptic Gospels, the Last Supper was a paschal meal since Jesus was crucified on the first day of Passover. According to John, the Supper was an ordinary meal because the Crucifixion was on the eve of Passover. (Cf., also no. 189.)

In biblical days, Passover (14 Nisan) represented the spiritual redemption. The Festival of Matzot commemorated the physical exodus. After 70 C.E., the Pharisees laid greater stress on the religious significance of the holiday; hence the term "Passover" was applied to the entire festival. Since this was a new connotation, Josephus, in *Antiquities,* explained: "The festival which is called Passover."

It is wrong to state that in biblical days the normal day was reckoned "from evening to evening" or that there were then two "New Moon days." (See also no. 154.)

187. "The Hebrew Scrolls and the Status of Biblical Scholarship," *JQR*, Vol. XLII, No. 2 (October 1951), pp. 133–192.

The Isaiah Scroll demonstrates that the scribe copied the text mechanically and often misspelled the same words. It is disillusioning to see biblical scholarship give reliance to such texts. (Cf., no. 176.)

Daniel's prophecy is not dependent on Numbers 24:24. The word *Asshur* is not found in the Daniel verse, hence its author could not have anticipated the (medieval) Rabbis' interpretation that the Numbers text referred to Syria in the time of the Hasmoneans. (Cf., no. 165.)

Jesus, though called "teacher," was never called a "Teacher of Righteousness." To say that the Scrolls belong to the Ebionites is incorrect because neither Jesus nor the Davidic family are recorded therein. The Ebionites believed only Jesus to be the true Messiah. The Scrolls, however, look forward to the coming of a Messiah.

The quotation of Isaiah (61:1) in Luke 4:18 does not correspond to the Isaiah Scroll text, but to the Masoretic text.

The Manual of Discipline is a version of the medieval Zadokite Fragment. The Zadokites are glorified in the Scrolls because the Karaites prided themselves on being a continuation of that family. The Messiah, they believed, was to be of the family of Aaron.

The use of dots to indicate missing words, or the substitution of *Eli* (my God) for *Adonai* in a benediction, demonstrate lateness of composition. (See also nos. 164, 201.)

The phrase *Kohen ha-mashiaḥ* was not used to designate an office during the Second Commonwealth.

The Hasmoneans were of the family of Joarib and never claimed to be of the family of Melchizedek.

To assume that Second Commonwealth Jews wrote commentaries or midrashim like the *Pesher Habakkuk* is false.

The Masoretic text is an aggregate of readings found in many manuscripts. It is not based on internal evidence.

The system of drawing a line through a word to indicate a mistake, and writing above, is a late usage.

Final מנצפ"ך were introduced into the Bible after the Destruction.

The jars and the cloth must be disassociated from the Scrolls, as evidence of dating.

If the Qumran "brotherhood" in Palestine represented the forerunners of the Karaites, how do we explain that the Karaites originated in the East, in Babylon? Professor Kahle's associating the Scrolls with the Magharians, as forerunners of the Karaites, is guesswork; we know nothing about that sect.

If the exceptional terms in the Scrolls had been early, i.e., from the Second Commonwealth, they would have been mentioned in subsequent literature.

The phrase "House of Absalom" may pertain to the revolt of the followers of the new Exilarch against the legitimate heir of the House of David, namely, Anan, the Karaite.

Many (false) translations in LXX are due, undoubtedly, to the absence of the *matres lectionis* in the Bible. Before the time of Rabbis Akiba and Ishmael the Bible had no *matres lectionis*. Their controversy was as to whether to introduce vowels (Akiba's view, יש אם למקרא) or not (Ishmael's). Hence the final Masorah fixing came much later, long after the time of R. Akiba. (Cf., nos. 194, 247.)

188. Jewish Apocryphal Literature. Solomon Zeitlin, editor-in-chief. *Aristeas to Philocrates* (Letter of Aristeas), edited and translated by Moses Hadas. Published for the Dropsie College for Hebrew and Cognate Learning by Harper & Brothers, New York (1951), pp. vii–233. (Cf. no. 173.)

1952

189. "The Last Supper as an Ordinary Meal in the Fourth Gospel," *JQR*, Vol. XLII, No. 3 (January 1952), pp. 251–260.

The Gospel of John was written, not in Aramaic for Jewish Christians, but in Greek for Gentile Christians in the Diaspora. The expressions "their Law" or "Jewish Passover" indicate this. Hymn singing (*Hallel*) is mentioned in the Synoptic Gospels because the Last Supper was recognized as a Passover meal; in John, however, *Hallel* is not mentioned because in this Gospel the Last Supper was considered an ordinary meal. (Cf., no. 186.) The discrepancy is not based on history. It pertains to ideology: Does Jesus personify the Paschal lamb or Passover redemption?

190. "Reply to Dr. William Chomsky's 'Note on the Meaning of *Hediot* in Mishnaic Hebrew.'" *JQR,* Vol. XLII, No. 3 (January 1952), pp. 329–330.

During the Second Commonwealth the Greek word *idiotes* (Aramaic הדיוט) had the connotation, "commoner," in contrast to priesthood or royalty.

The Tannaim held the Aramaic language in great regard. Hence, *lashon hediot* cannot be interpreted in a derogatory sense.

191. היש הכרח בחדוש הסנהדרין בישראל להתאמת ההלכה לחיים, *Bitzaron,* Vol. XXV (Shevat-Adar, 1952), No. 4, pp. 225–227; Vol. XXVI (Nisan 1952), No. 5, pp. 22–31.

There is no concept of "permitted" or "kasher" in the Pentateuch. Everyone and everything was in a category of pure or impure. Such observances affected the rules of food and of personal purity and ultimately led to "washing of hands" as a modification of the need for full immersion in case of impurity. Thus, the Sages sought to ease the laws. Examples are the *Erub,* (see no. 184), and the *Prosbol.* (Cf. no. 149.) In the latter case, the Sages stressed the phase of *obligatio in rem,* allowing collection of a debt in a Sabbatical year. They also abolished the *talio,* and likewise instituted the *ketubah* as a financial guarantee for the wife. (Cf., no. 47.)

The Rabbis instituted inheritance by issuance of a will, thus permitting the granting of an inheritance even to persons not recognized by the Bible as heirs. (Cf., no. 367.) Similarly, partnership is not mentioned in the Bible, but the Rabbis sanctioned it.

After the Temple's destruction, the progressive mode declined. Rabbi Judah ha-Nasi had to adjust the Mishnah to the needs of the time. He omitted many halakhot practiced in Temple days. For example, there was no separation of the sexes in the Temple except for the Sukkot celebration. The Amoraim also instituted halakhot to separate the Jew from the non-Jew.

Spiritually, Judaism is a product of the teachings of the Prophets and the Pharisees; Jerusalem has always been its center. Israel Jewry, however, cannot force its opinion on the Diaspora, because Judaism is not a theocracy; that type of government was abolished in the Hasmonean period. Judaism is a nomocracy; the Law, as it is interpreted, serves as guide.

Many rabbis in Israel still retain the East European ghetto approach, as evidenced in their decision concerning *shemittah*—"selling" the land to an Arab in order to permit its cultivation during the seventh year. (The Passover "sale" is a legal fiction used by an individual, not by a community.) Were the rabbis in Israel of strong will, they would find talmudic precedent concerning the abolition of *shemittah,* as proposed by Rabbi Judah. With harmonization as a goal, the rabbis should follow the mode of interpretation practiced by the Sages of the Second Temple era. The creation of a new code, as Rabbi Judah ha-Nasi did with the Mishnah, is urgent. (See also no. 193.)

192. חדוש הסנהדרין והתאמת ההלכה לחיים, תדפים מבצרון. 20 pp. Offprint of no. 191. (Cf., also no. 193.)

193. "Is the Revival of a Sanhedrin in Israel Necessary for Modification of the Halakha?" *JQR,* Vol. XLII, No. 4 (April 1952), pp. 339–376.

With the election of Simon the Hasmonean, the theocracy was abolished and a commonwealth established. Religious power no longer rested in the hands of the High Priest: a Bet Din was established. The Pharisees, who believed in liberal interpretation of the Law, came into the ascendancy, since they had assisted the Hasmoneans. They strove to bring religion into consonance with life. Their legal principles represented the ideals of justice—Jewish law was elastic.

Naturally there was opposition from strict constructionists who disdained liberalism, and also from Apocalyptists who stressed ethics and conscience over the laws. The laws enacted after the Hadrianic period were not progressive in character because Jews had lost their political independence. It became necessary then to collect laws into one corpus, for their preservation.

Amoraic law is not as progressive as the tannaitic. The aim of the Amoraim was to save Judaism, and separate Jews from the pagan world. The Palestinian collection of Gemara (study, final) was not properly edited because the academies were closed after the Nicaean Council.

Jews all over the world are bound together by their religion. They owe allegiance to the countries in which they live, but Judaea has always been the holy land for all Jews. To the Christians, only the *loca sancta* connected with Jesus are important.

Israel dare not become a Levantine state. It must continue the teachings of the Second Commonwealth, but state and religion must be kept apart. Many laws have outlived their purpose. Present day Judaism is in chaotic state in Israel because of forced Sabbath observance and wrong application of the Sabbatical year. Religious leaders must have the courage to interpret the laws and make them applicable to life.

There is a crying need for a corpus of halakhot based on historical development, which hitherto has not been created. Dogmatic presentation of Jewish law is not the answer. (See no. 309.)

194. המגילות הגנוזות. השאלות השנויות במחלוקת. תמצית הרצאה באוניברסיטה העברית בי"ד סיון תשי"א, *Hadoar,* Vol. XXXII No. 22 (April 4, 1952), pp. 425–426; No. 23 (April 25, 1952), pp. 479–480; No. 24, pp. 501–502. See no. 195. (Includes a detailed summary of a Hebrew University lecture, 14 Sivan 5711—April 4, 1952.)

The Torah Scrolls may have been pillaged in the Hebron riots of 1929. This may be supported by Professor Hamilton who noted that some of the Scrolls were in the monastery for about twenty years. Professor Sellers declared that the cave was one which Origen had visited. Were this so, he would not have left Scrolls behind!

The archaeologists found only artifacts, and not Scrolls. The question is whether the Scrolls were in the jars or wrapped in the same cloth on which the carbon-14 test was made. There is no paleography of the Second Temple with which to make comparisons. The Nash papyrus is of the third century C.E.

The Masorah was not edited finally till after the fourth century—hence the different readings in the Isaiah Scroll. The author of *Pesher Habakkuk* was influenced by *Targum Jonathan.*

Only in the Middle Ages was "Asshur" used to describe nations persecuting Jews. This is based on Numbers 24:24. (See no. 187.)

195. המגילות הגנוזות. Reprinted from *Hadoar,* with an Introduction, Vol. XXXII, Nos. 22, 23, 24 (1952), pp. 27. (See no. 194.)

196. תשובה ל-א. מ. הברמן (Reply to A. M. Haberman's article entitled "Brith Damesek," in *Haaretz*), *Haaretz,* Tel Aviv: Friday, June 27, 1952.

The word מאד is never translated as "money" in LXX. The Scrolls do so. It is a late usage, based on the Talmud. The term משכיל, as used in the Scrolls, is karaitic.

197. "Bar Kokhba and Bar Kozeba," *JQR,* Vol. XLIII, No. 1 (July 1952), pp. 77–82.

Bar Kokhba is a surname. It was not based on the name of "a city," and does not mean the "son of Kokhba." Surely the person did not bear the name Bar Kozeba with a connotation of "liar." His name was Simon. Those Jews who proclaimed him a leader called him Bar Kokhba (star), but with his failure he was designated Bar Kozeba (deceiver).

Père de Vaux has conceded that the Scroll jars are only of the domestic type used in the vicinity in the latter part of the first century C.E.

198. Review of: *A Social History of the Jews,* by Salo Wittmayer Baron, Second Edition, Revised and Enlarged. *JQR,* Vol. XLIII, No. 1 (July 1952), pp. 97–110. (Cf., nos. 67, 80.)

A Jewish history can be written only with the cooperation of many experts in their respective fields; it is not a task for one man. (Cf., no. 171.) An author must set down events in chronological order and not in zigzag fashion. The sequence of historical development is important in studying the world of the Talmud. The *Mishneh Torah* of Maimonides is not a source for the laws of the Second Commonwealth. Certain historical features in this volume need a proper interpretation; for example: The letter in II Maccabees about the observance of the Festival of Dedication was not written by Jews in Jerusalem, but by the Antiochan epitomist. The principle of *hefker Bet Din* came into being after the Destruction, when the Bet Din exercised both civil and ecclesiastic authority.

199. "The Hebron Pogrom and the Hebrew Scrolls," *JQR,* Vol. XLIII, No. 2 (October 1952), pp. 140–152.

The question remains: How and when did the St. Mark's Monastery get possession of the Torah Scrolls? Originally they were brought to Hebron from Kurdistan. Wechsler suggests that they represent part of the loot from the Hebron pogroms of 1929. A great collection was in the library of Antiquites of Judah Bibos. The view that some Scrolls had been in the monastery for twenty years would coincide with the 1929 date. (See no. 194.)

How can it be that Bar Kokhba signed as a "Nasi of Israel," if the Jews began to call themselves "Israelites" only after the collapse of the revolt, in order to refute Christian claims?

The scholars' emendations to the Scrolls are arbitrary. Their use of *notarikon* and acrostics to explain the texts is preposterous, and displays a lack of knowledge of medieval Hebrew and sources. The methodology is one of obscurantism and new-occultism.

200. Review of: *Tannaitic Parallels to the Gospels,* by Morton Smith. *JQR,* Vol. XLIII, No. 2 (October 1952), pp. 196–199.

The Greek translator of Matthew 28:1 in his rendering of "end of Sabbath" (*opse de Sabbaton*) misunderstood the original Aramaic באפוקי דשבתא (מוצאי שבת), which means Saturday night and Sunday. In both tannaitic literature and in the Gospels the use of "Sabbath" also as "week" is common.

The passage in Mark 7:2 does not mean "defiled, unclean, unwashed hands." It only parallels ידים מסואבות, and follows the decree of 65 C.E. that washing of the hands was necessary before breaking bread.

201. *The Zadokite Fragments,* Facsimile of the Manuscripts in the Cairo Genizah Collection in the Possession of the University Library, Cambridge, England. With an Introduction by Solomon Zeitlin. *The Jewish Quarterly Review* . . . Monograph Series, No. 1 (1952), Philadelphia: The Dropsie College for Hebrew and Cognate Learning, pp. 2–32 + 20 pl.

Though translations by Schechter, Charles, and Levi appeared long ago, the facsimile of the text itself was not published until now. The fragment is a karaitic work, as is evidenced by expressions used in it, and by the inclusion of halakhot occurring only in the Mishnah and in rabbinic literature of the Middle Ages. Words like בית השתחות (house of worship) and ברית אברהם (circumcision) indicate lateness of composition (see nos. 187, 198). The prohibition against marrying a niece on the maternal side is from Anan.

The author followed a lunar-solar calendar contrary to the Book of Jubilees which uses a solar calendar. The "390 years" pertain to Hillel's ascendancy as head of the Sanhedrin. "Twenty years" refers to the joint rule of Menaḥem and Hillel. Thereafter, Shammai joined the Bet Din, and the Karaites commended the latter as their spiritual ancestor.

The Karaites sought their origin in the Jeraboam ben Nabot schism and regarded themselves as "Mourners of Zion." Some of them lived in Damascus.

The use of *El* was prevalent in the Middle Ages to avoid writing the Tetragrammaton. (See also nos. 164, 187.) Louis Ginzberg's emendations invalidate much of Schechter's work. Büchler and Marmorstein already demonstrated that the text is of the Middle Ages. (See also no. 183.)

1953

202. "The Bet ha-Shoebah and the Sacred Fire. A Historical Study of Religious Institutions During the Second Commonwealth." *JQR*, Vol. XLIII, No. 3 (January 1953), pp. 217–223.

The Bet ha-Shoebah ceremony, as can be seen in its use of torches in its celebration, is connected with fire and not with the libation of water (*nissukh ha-mayim*). It should read שובה (fire). [See *Arukh*.] Because of an amoraic misunderstanding, it became שואבה (drawing of water or "the Holy Spirit"), or חשובה (prominence).

The prologue in II Maccabees contains a letter asking the Jews to celebrate "the Festival of Purification like the Festival of Tabernacles and the Days of Fire." In the times of Moses and Solomon, and in the period of Ezra and Nehemiah, fire descended onto the altar. Similarly, in the time of Judah Maccabaeus, there was purification by the descent of the holy fire. Thus, with the Bet ha-Shoebah ceremony, the tradition about the celebration of the sacred fire observed during the Festival of Tabernacles was maintained. (Cf., no. 227.)

203. "The Mishna in Yadaim IV.8 and 'The Sectarians,'" *JQR*, Vol. XLIII, No. 3 (January 1953), pp. 297–300.

The textual reading is not "writing the name of Moses (משה) in a document," but "writing the divine name (השם) together with that of a mortal ruler." An objection to such a practice may have been raised by the Sicarii leader, Judas the Galilean, who was opposed to temporal rule. The Mishnah in Berakhot, indicating the decree that one should greet his fellows with the Divine Name, was enacted in opposition to the Judaeo-Christians. Ḥai Gaon had already noticed this. (See also no. 388.)

The Pharisees were not divided into seven categories. The term "Pharisees" is used only in dialogue with or in reference to the Sadducees. Otherwise it means, simply, "separatists." (Cf., no. 73.)

204. "The Names Hebrew, Jews, and Israel: A Historical Study," *JQR,* Vol. XLIII, No. 4 (April 1953), pp. 365–379.

The name of a nation has particular significance, especially when, due to historical reasons, there were changes. Originally "Israel" had a racial connotation. With the division of the kingdom, the North came to be called Israel, and the South, Judah; the language was "Yehudit." After the Restoration, the land was Judaea and the language was "Hebrew." The term "Knesset Yisrael" was coined later, in contrast to *ecclesia.*

The term "Israel" is never found in tannaitic literature to denote the people of Judaea. It was used only in contrast to priests and Levites. The name "Judaean" was also applied to Egyptian Jews, because of the Ptolemaic rule. Those in Antioch were called "Hebrews," for they were under the rule of the Seleucidan Empire. This is evident in II and IV Maccabees and in the letters of Paul.

The term "Judaism" (*Yahadut*), as found in Maccabees, became the designation for the religion followed by those who accepted the Jewish way of life. It was coined in Antioch, in contrast to Hellenism. In time, the word "Jew" became a term for the devotees of the same religion. (Cf., no. 123.)

After the catastrophe of Bar Kokhba, the Judaeans (Jews) changed their name to "Israelites" to counteract the contentions of the Christians. In Talmudic literature, the term "Israel" generally has a spiritual connotation, for all those united by the religion. The land was called *Eretz Yisrael* in contrast to the Roman designation—Palestine. The Roman emperors did not add "Judaicus" to their own titles because the word had a religious significance.

The modern State of Israel has chosen its name well, because the name now has not the religious connotation which Judaea or Judaism have. Nevertheless, *Shema Yisrael* and phrases in the Talmud referring to Israel include all Jews of the stock of Israel, not only the inhabitants of the land.

205. "Race Relations," *JQR*, Vol. XLIII, No. 4 (April 1953), pp. 388–391. Review of: *Race Relations in Ancient Egypt*, by S. Davis.

Isocrates, contrary to many Greeks, held that "Hellene" referred to cultural rather than racial superiority. Though ancient Jews maintained a concept of chosen peoplehood, and considered idol worshipers to be inferiors, the Pharisees laid stress on Judaism as a religion, and not as a blood relationship. Anyone who accepted Judaism was a spiritual descendant of Abraham and equal to all other Jews.

In Alexandria there were two classes of Jews; some enjoyed full citizenship, others did not. Hatred of the Jews developed, for political reasons, after Alexandria had been taken over by the Romans. The Aristocrats and Stoics disdained the Jews because they were fearful of rivalry with their religious philosophy. (Cf., no. 222.)

206. "The Theodosian Code," *JQR*, Vol. XLIII, No. 4 (April 1953), pp. 392–394. Review of: *The Theodosian Code and Novels and the Sirmondian Constitutions. A Translation with Commentary, Glossary, and Bibliography*, by Clyde Pharr.

Judaism was recognized as a lawful religion in the Roman Empire where Christianity had become the dominant religion. The government issued decrees for the protection of Jews against violence.

The Church Fathers stimulated accusations, and some called the Jews deicides. The Code, completed in 437, contains legislation dating from the time of Constantine (312 C.E.) when Jews were subject to all the laws of the State, but in religious matters were to be tried by judges appointed by the Jewish Patriarch. An edict of Theodosius (392 C.E.) reveals support of the Patriarch above the local Jewish authorities. The last Patriarch was Gamaliel VI, for the partriarchate was then abolished. Decrees are addressed to the Teacher (*Didascalus*), and each community leader was so called. The term "Rabbi" was adopted as a title only later. (See no. 329.)

207. "More Hebrew Scrolls," *JQR*, Vol. XLIII, No. 4 (April 1953), pp. 406–408.

The great financial value placed on the supposed discovered Scrolls has caused the Bedouins to seek further discoveries in caves. Are these the loot from *Genizot* in old libraries sacked in 1929 and in the later wars of the Arabs and Jews?

It is wrong to maintain that there have now been discovered, for the first time, a Hebrew translation of Ben Sira, an Aramaic translation of Tobit, the Testament of the Twelve Patriarchs, etc. These translations had already been known during the Middle Ages. Before any stamp of authenticity is given or implied, photostatic forms should be produced.

208. "Midrash: A Historical Study," *JQR,* Vol. XLIV, No. 1 (July 1953), pp. 21–36.

The term "midrash" means "to inquire of" or "interpret" biblical passages. There is *Midrash Torah,* which is the interpretation of the Torah, and is not to be confused with Midrash Halakhah. The sages who interpreted the Bible were *Darshanim.* The place of study was *Bet Midrash.*

Halakhot (common law) preceded the Midrash (hermeneutics) form of legislation. Some of the halakhot are as old as the Pentateuch; others preceded the interpretations by Hillel. For new halakhot (legislation), support has to be obtained from the Pentateuch. When the halakhot—the unwritten laws—were accepted, they became statutory laws. Rabbi Meir held that Mishnah—the corpus, second to the Torah—pertains to halakhot, subject form; Rabbi Judah said that Mishnah is Midrash Torah, i.e., an arrangement according to the interpretation of the verses. Thus the Mekhilta, Sifre, and Sifra are Midrash Torah. But Mishnah remained the collection of halakhot.

The Midrash of Genesis is basically eschatologic, and the Midrash of Lamentations deals with consolation—themes that concerned the Jews in the third century when these homilies were composed. During the Second Commonwealth there was no Midrash for any prophetic book.

209. Review of: גלות וגאולה בספרות ישראל מאת מאיר וכסמן, *JQR,* Vol. XLIV, No. 1 (July 1953), pp. 80–81.

There are no messianic allusions in the Book of Jubilees nor in I and II Maccabees.

The expression 'to this day" is biblical and hence, as used in Jubilees, it cannot fix the date of that book as of the time of John Hyrcanus. (See also no. 77.)

210. "The Fiction of the Recent Discoveries Near the Dead Sea," *JQR,* Vol. XLIV, No. 2 (October 1953), pp. 85–115.

In antiquity, letters began with the name of the sender, e.g., "King Demetrius to Simon the High Priest." The letter *mem* ("from") prefixed to the author's name came into use only in the Middle Ages, as did letters bearing signatures. (See nos. 255, 299.) Letters in Yosippon support the view that even in the third century Jews did not use the prefix *mem.* (See also no. 216.)

The Karaites used the title נשיא ישראל (see no. 199). Hence, the antiquity of the so-called Bar Kokhba letters cannot be authenticated through these forms.

The Hebrew text of Ben Sira found by S. Schechter is of the Middle Ages (see C. Torrey, in *Alexander Marx Jubilee Volume,* 1950). (Cf., also, no. 207.)

The Nash papyrus is of the third century C.E., when an attempt was made to reintroduce the recital of the Decalogue in Nehardea. (Cf., also no. 255.)

The old Hebrew script was still in use during the fourth century. The phrase "Covenant of Abraham" in the Zadokite Fragment came into use only after the Pauline period. (Cf., also no. 201.)

In an intercalated year it is the first Adar (of 30 days) that is always intercalated.

An analysis of the background of the halakhic differences between Rashi and R. Tam pertaining to the passages in the Tefillin reveals that Rashi followed the earlier Palestinian custom, whereas Rabbenu Tam accepted the later Babylonian custom of the Geonim who had altered the order. This custom was not fixed earlier than the fourth century C.E. The phylactery, discovered by the Bedouins, follows the Babylonian (and Egyptian) custom. How could this have come into a cave near the Dead Sea in ancient days? (See also nos. 387, 392.)

211. Foreword to: *Israel Salanter, Religious-Ethical Thinker; the Story of a Religious Ethical Current in Nineteenth-Century Judaism,* by Menahem Glenn (New York: 1953). Published for the Dropsie College for Hebrew and Cognate Learning by Bloch Publishing Co., pp. xi–xii.

Hasidism did not penetrate into the communities of Lithuania, which remained a citadel of the *Mitnagdim.* Jews in that area were more apt to be rationalists, and Haskalah made its imprint there. Dissension arose when the rabbis saw Haskalah as a danger to Judaism, and the Haskalah leaders accused the rabbis of siding with the wealthy and the well-established. (Cf., no. 33.) Rabbi Israel Salanter disapproved of the rabbis keeping aloof from the people and, therefore, initiated a new school stressing *Musar,* Jewish ethics, to unite rabbis and laymen. The *Epistle of Musar* is the credo of the great movement of the Lithuanian Jewish world, now extinct.

212. Foreword to: *Landmarks and Goals. Historical Studies and Addresses,* by Abraham A. Neuman, Dropsie College Press (Philadelphia: 1953), pp. xi–xv.

Dr. A. A. Neuman has demonstrated that the *Yosippon,* written in the third century C.E., as well as the Apocrypha, are primary sources for early Judaism, and that Saadia Gaon, governed by intellect, proved himself unimaginative in his attitude on Palestine.

213. Jewish Apocryphal Literature, Solomon Zeitlin editor-in-chief, *The Third and Fourth Books of Maccabees,* edited and translated by Moses Hadas, published for the Dropsie College for Hebrew and Cognate Learning by Harper & Brothers (New York: 1953), pp. xii–248. (Cf., no. 173, 181, 227.)

214. "A Reply to a Reviewer," *Journal of Jewish Studies,* Vol. IV, No. 2 (1953), pp. 85–90. Regarding a review of the *First Book of Maccabees,* translated by Sidney Tedesche.

I Maccabees was edited after 70 C.E. by one who favored the Romans; at that time many Jews sought a rapprochment with Rome, as did R. Joshua. The sons of Tobias were priests, descendants of Simon I on the maternal side. (Cf., no. 181.)

1954

215. "The Second Day of the Holidays in the Diaspora. A Historical Study," *JQR,* Vol. XLIV, No. 3 (January 1954), pp. 183–193.

The acceptance of witnesses, even on the Sabbath, for the birth of the new moon was due to the policy of stressing the change to a lunar calendar. This is the origin of the sanctification of the new moon. Fire signals and, later, messengers were sent to inform the Jews in the Diaspora. The authority was that of the Patriarch.

When Christianity became a state religion, difficulties arose about sending apostles. Hillel II arranged the order of intercalation on a scientific basis. The religious leaders of Palestine, however, wanted the Diaspora to keep two days of the holiday, hoping that the Sanhedrin would be reestablished and the previous method of sending apostles would be restored, thus making Babylonian Jewry dependent on Palestine. Ben Meir, in the early tenth century, tried to implement Palestinian supremacy by means of the old calendar system, but Saadia opposed him. (See also no. 218.)

216. Footnote to article, "The So-Called Bar Kokhba Letter," by Ernest R. Lacheman, *JQR,* Vol. XLIV, No. 4 (April 1954), p. 286.

The Bar Kokhba letter, which begins with the prefix "from" and has a signature at its end, should not be compared to the Aramaic documents of the fifth century B.C.E. (See also no. 210.)

217. Footnote to the article, "The Benediction Over the Luminaries and the Stars," by Solomon Gandz, *JQR,* Vol. XLIV, No. 4 (April 1954), p. 305. Signed Z.

The daily benediction over the luminaries was not recited in the Temple and is not mentioned in tannaitic literature. It originated in Babylonia and has no relation to the prayers of the Essenes. (Cf., also no. 219.)

218. "The Second Day of Rosh Hashanah in Israel," *JQR,* Vol. XLIV, No. 4 (April 1954), pp. 326–329.

R. Zerahiah ha-Levi, the critic of Alfasi, states in Bezah 5a that only one day of Rosh Hashanah was observed in Palestine.

A talmudic story about a two-day observance in Usha is explained by the Amoraim as the result of a miscalculation, or as referring to a recurring event in two consecutive years.

Originally, in Jabneh and Usha, due to the necessity for waiting for calendrical testimony by witnesses, observance of Rosh Hashanah was for two days. At the end of the second century C.E., when the wars of Severus separated Babylon from Palestine, Rabbi Judah ha-Nasi introduced a one-day observance of Rosh Hashanah; in the twelfth century, however, the Diaspora influenced Palestine to observe the second day as well. (See also no. 215.)

219. "The Morning Benediction and the Readings in the Temple, *JQR,* Vol. XLIV, No. 4 (April 1954), pp. 330–336.

The Mishnah does not specifically mention יוצר אור. Apparently even the Rabbis in the third century did not know the ancient formula; hence they gave varied explanations. The benediction was introduced into liturgy because of the influence of Babylonian Jewry in reaction to Persian belief. (See also no. 217.)

A prayer is a plea; a blessing is a grateful acknowledgment. The Essenes had a prayer to the sun, but the Pharisees did not. There are only blessings for the sun, but not prayers. (Cf., no. 157.)

220. "Ceramics in the Talmudic Literature," *JQR,* Vol. XLIV, No. 4 (April 1954), pp. 343–345. Review of: כלי חרם בספרות התלמוד מאת יהושע בראנד.

Jews did not differ much from the Greeks and Romans in dress and culture, except in religious practices. The priests in the Temple wore beards and had to cover their heads; among the pagans, the priests were shaven and their heads were uncovered. The Greek Orthodox Church follows the ancient Jewish custom; the Western Church does not. Miters for popes were introduced in the ninth century.

The custom of burial in coffins is of late origin. In ancient days only shrouds were used. There is no talmudic mention of eating at graves. It is an idolatrous practice already inveighed against in Jubilees 22:17.

221. "The Antiquity of the Hebrew Scrolls and the Piltdown Hoax. A Parallel," *JQR,* Vol. XLV, No. 1 (July 1954), pp. 1–29.

Proof from Midrash Tannaim and Targum Sheni about the ancient mode of writing letters is not admissable as supporting evidence, because these texts are medieval.

It was not the practice in the Hellenistic-Roman period to begin a letter with the prefix "from" (the sender). (See also nos. 210, 216.)

At no time were two men simultaneously called "Rabban" (our Master). After the period of the Zugot there was only one head of the Sanhedrin.

The letter of Rabbi Judah to Antoninus is not a historical document; it is only a recorded story. "Antoninus" could only be Marcus Aurelius.

The Jews never called the Christians "Galileans." The nickname was first used by Julian the Apostate. Hence this cannot be used to show that the Bar Kokhba letter is early and authentic.

A Fragment of Exodus, recently found, has vowel points. Vowels were not introduced until the sixth or seventh century C.E. (See no. 187.)

The deceptions of Firkovitch and of Shapira, the concept that the Slavonic Josephus was a translation of an Aramaic and Greek draft written by Josephus, (cf., no. 37), as well as the "Piltdown Man" hoax are examples of scholarly misinterpretations.

222. "Jewish Symbols in the Graeco-Roman Period," *JQR,* Vol. XLV, No. 1 (July 1954), pp. 66–73. Review of: *Jewish Symbols in the Graeco-Roman Period,* Vol. I: The Archaeological Evidence from Palestine (Bollingen Series XXXVIII), by Edwin Goodenough.

Most of the Apocryphal literature was written in Aramaic or in Hebrew in Judaea. One cannot speak of Hellenized Judaism.

II and IV Maccabees, written in Greek, stress observance of the Law. They do not contain apocalyptic notions of messianic expectations and a judgment to come. The Apocalyptists bequeathed the books of Enoch, Adam, Twelve Patriarchs, and IV Ezra. (Cf., no. 224.)

The exclusiveness of Jews was based on religious, not on racial grounds. The pagans despised the Jews and hated the Christians because of their introduction of the concept of the universality of God, as opposed to their own national gods. The Stoics were especially resentful. (See no. 205.)

There was no such person as Trypho. Justin, himself, developed his concepts and dialogues.

The Greeks exerted a great influence on Diaspora Jews. To resist Hellenism, Philo and IV Maccabees express views which are different from normative Judaean concepts.

The development of Christianity stemmed from Diaspora Jews.

The Rabbis opposed the translation of the Mishnah and halakhot into a foreign tongue, because they felt that every Jew should know Hebrew. They were disappointed with the LXX.

There was a Bet Din in Rome. The story of Theudas in Rome, who sought to offer a paschal lamb, deals with the period after Bar Kokhba when such sacrifices had ceased in Palestine. But Rabbi Judah's opposition to this prevailed.

The Patriarchs had complete authority over the leaders of the community, as is evident in the Theodosian code. (Cf., no. 206.)

Jews never bowed down before a synagogue, nor is there proof that synagogues were built to resemble pagan temples.

There were no "half-proselytes" or "half-Jews."

223. "Responsa of the Tosaphists," *JQR,* Vol. XLV, No. 1 (July 1954), pp. 73–76. Review of: תשובות בעלי התוספות, ערוכות בידי אברהם יצחק איגוס.

The principle that "the law of the government is the law" refers only to civil matters. It is not mentioned in tannaitic literature, because, in the Second Commonwealth, the Sages recognized the authority of the civil government. After 70 C.E. even civil matters became part of the Bet Din. The Jews held that the land belonged to them (it was *Eretz Yisrael*); hence in the Palestinian Talmud we have no mention of this law. Rabbenu Tam pointed out that Jewish courts also are bound to execute the laws of the government. (Cf., no. 373.)

224. "The Essenes and Messianic Expectations. A Historical Study of the Sects and Ideas During the Second Jewish Commonwealth, *JQR,* Vol. XLV, No. 2 (October 1954), pp. 83–119.

The Sadducees did not permit innovation, whereas the Pharisees regarded the Pentateuch as the basis for interpretation, and stressed the elasticity of the law.

Where Josephus has "Essenes," the early book of *Yosippon* uses the term "Hasidim" (the pious). The probability is that Josephus' term has the connotation of "oracle," "prophecy." The High Priest's *hoshen* is called *essen,* signifying *logion* (oracle). Just as Josephus coined the name "Sicarii" (because of the sect's use of the dagger) so, also, he used the designation "Essene" because of the loin cloth, signifying, like the *hoshen,* the gift of foretelling the future.

The extremist group of Hellenists caused the emergence of an opposing extreme, the Hasidim, who rejected all compromise in

Jewish life. They aided Judah against Antiochus, but when the Commonwealth was established they opposed the Hasmoneans. They held that the priesthood belonged to the family of Zadok, and that this new Hasmonean dynasty defiled the Temple; therefore, they sent no sacrifices there. They did not use oil because its use was part of the ceremony of the Temple sacrifice. (There is no connection between the Essenes and the priests of the city of Ephesus.)

Josephus lived among the Essenes and is more reliable than Philo on the subject; the latter never met any Essenes, depending only on hearsay.

To the Essenes the table was an altar and they respected their Zadokite priests, giving them the tithe. They were particular about laws of purity, performed ablutions, and were strict in the observance of the Sabbath. They were opposed to slavery and, generally, to marriage, because it involved laws of purity (with sacrifice in the Temple). Sexual relations were only for procreation. They took no oath, to avoid taking the name of God in vain. They held strong ethical beliefs, never resorted to the use of capital punishment, showed allegiance to the ruler of the state; but they did not recognize the Sanhedrin, holding their own courts and using excommunication as punishment. They lived in close-knit groups in the cities; believed in fate and in immortality of the soul, but rejected the belief in a Messiah.

Messianic expectations, in general, arose only after the Destruction. Before that, only the Apocalyptists (see also no. 222) believed that the Messiah was created before Creation. Neither Philo nor Josephus make reference to a Messiah.

After the Bar Kokhba period many explained that the Messiah of Ephraim had been killed, and that a Davidic Messiah should now be expected. Messiah is not mentioned in the entire Mishnah (there are interpolations in Tractate Berakhot).

The Assumption of Moses (composed in 140 C.E.) calls those who led the Bar Kokhba revolt "deceivers." Even after the Destruction, normative Judaism, for a century and a half, did not entertain the idea of a Messiah. It was Christianity that gave an impetus among the Jews in shaping the concept of a supernatural Messiah. (Cf., no. 151.)

The Essenes are not mentioned in tannaitic literature or the Gospels because they were individualists; they did not participate in the affairs of the Jewish people, religiously or politically. They cannot be considered an extreme wing of the Pharisees because they opposed any modification of the Law. Whereas the Apocalyptists were interested in stimulating the Jews by their prophecies, the Essenes were concerned with their individualistic prophecies, i.e., in saving the individual. They recognized the state; the Apocalyptists did not. The Essenes believed in common property. Their opposition was to the corrupting effect of money, slavery, and women.

John the Baptist was not an Essene. He was interested in baptism as the way to free men from sin. The Essenes were concerned with levitical purity. They did not believe in proselytism. (See no. 151.)

The Theraputae were not Essenes. They were Christian monks in Egypt.

The Essenes would not live in the Diaspora, for they held that the land of the Gentiles would defile. Since they did not reject the state, they also fought in the War.

They probably wrote books on angelology, immortality, and purity. Although they were martyrs for Judaism, they could not reconcile themselves to the progressive ideas of Pharisaism. (See also no. 256.)

225. Footnotes to the article "Emendation of the Dead Sea Manual of Discipline and Some Notes Concerning Habakkuk Midrash," by W. H. Brownlee, *JQR,* Vol. XLV, No. 2 (October 1954), pp. 143, 144, 149, 152, 153, 154, 155, 157, 158. All notes signed S.Z. (Cf., no. 230.)

226. "A Note on the Fiction of the 'Bar Kokhba' Letter," *JQR,* Vol. XLV, No. 2 (October 1954), pp. 174–180.

The formula "from . . . to" came into vogue possibly as a result of Arabic influence. (See also nos. 210, 216.)

The Bar Kokhba revolt was led by educated leaders. Hence the letter, with its ignorance, does not belong to that period.

227. Jewish Apocryphal Literature, Solomon Zeitlin, editor-in-chief, *The Second Book of Maccabees,* Edited by Solomon Zeitlin with Introduction and Commentary. English translation by Sidney Tedesche. Published for the Dropsie College for Hebrew and Cognate Learning by Harper & Brothers (New York: 1954), pp. xiii–271.

The primary theme of II Maccabees is the uprising for religious freedom led by Judah Makkabi.

The book is a composite work. The story of the religious martyrdom of the mother and sons was not part of the original work of Jason of Cyrene. It originated in Antioch and reflects the persecution of the Jews there.

Here one finds for the first time the expression "Judaism"—Jewish religion, in contrast to Hellenism—Hellenistic culture, and *allophylism*—pagan religion. The Epitomist, who was an Antiochan Jew, wrote with the purpose of setting forth moral ideas. Judaism in Antioch signified the religion opposed to Hellenism. The Antiochan Jews called themselves Hebrews, whereas in Judaea and Egypt they called themselves Jews, and did not use the term Judaism in a religious sense.

Mention of "Nicanor day," the day "before the day of Mordecai" is that of the Epitomist who did not know that in 161 B.C.E. there were two Adars. 13 Adar referred to the *first* Adar. The Epitomist mistakenly added "day before Mordecai." Generally Jewish festivals are not assigned to personalities. Purim may have been called Day of Mordecai only because the Antiochan Jews stemmed from Babylon.

The Epitomist abridged the work of Jason to limit it to the hero-worship of Judah. The facts, however, including that of the other brothers, had been given by Jason.

The Church called this book *Maccabees* because it deals with Judah, and derives its title from its hero. The first book was *Sefer bet Ḥashmanim*; the second was called *Maccabees* (though the Epitomist did not know the meaning of the names).

It may have been called *Second* because it had been written late, or because it was an epitome—i.e., "second."

The only reference that we have to Jason is through the Epitomist. The date of composition may have been in the period of Agrippa and Caligula, about 42 C.E. The author recounted how Jews in the time of Antiochus were ready to die to defend the holiness of the Temple, inferring the same readiness in the time of Caligula.

The first to mention II Maccabees is Clement of Alexandria at the end of the second century. IV Maccabees is also an Antiochan work, written in the time of Caligula. The fact that these books were written in Antioch illustrates that the culture that existed there was unlike that of Egypt.

The book was written in Greek, is free of Hebraisms, but reveals the Epitomist's Hebrew education. He was a pious Jew, but his biblical passages are from the LXX.

Since the system of the Seleucidan era was not used in Egypt, a letter to the Jews with this dating could not have been written in that country.

The letter of 188 A.S. (125 B.C.E.) was written to glorify the Temple. Hence the story is introduced about Jeremiah's fire coming from heaven. (See also no. 252.) To this was appended the letter of 169 A.S. (144 B.C.E.) telling of the tribulations under Antiochus.

The Second Book stressed the idea of reward by resurrection; the Fourth Book, that of ransom. Torture was to atone for one's sins.

The Epitomist is the first to call Judaea "the Holy Land." He gives historical details not found in I Maccabees. The story of the struggle and civil war is from Jason of Cyrene. It is the only authentic historic document of that period. The philosophical and religious aspects were added by the Epitomist. These stress ministrations of angels, importance of dreams, belief in visions, *lex talionis* (measure for measure) and the concept of bodily resurrection, as well as the religious practice of praying for the dead.

The Jews of Antioch were more zealous in their observances than those in Judaea, but more primitive. II Maccabees shows the influence of Antiochan Jewry on later Judaism.

Messiah is not mentioned because normative Judaism did not as yet anticipate the coming of a Messiah (see no. 224). II Maccabees also reveals the enormous influences that Antiochan Jews had on the development of Christianity. The Church Fathers often mentioned II Maccabees because of the story of martyrdom.

228. הימים האחרונים של בית שני, *Gilyonot,* Vol. XXXI, Nos. 8–10 (Ab-Elul 5714–1954), pp. 108–113.

The Pharisees cannot be compared to present day *Neture Karta.* The former were not opposed to the state, but only to the tactics of Alexander Jannai.

Both the Sicarii and the Apocalyptic groups believed in the concept, "no lordship of man over man." The first carried this out by means of force, the second by eschatological beliefs. It is also wrong to regard Sicarii and Zealots as identical. (See also nos. 4 and 7.)

The provisional government was ostensibly aristocratic and pro-

Roman; the Zealots were democratic opponents, led by Eleazar ben Simon.

Internal warfare developed among the Zealots; they accused John of Gishchala of seeking to become a despot and called Simon bar Giora to battle him. Bar Giora was an extreme democrat who was closer to the Sicarii and did not support Eleazar ben Simon.

All factions were idealists, but the internal warfare of the parties caused havoc in the nation.

1955

229. Footnotes to article: "Emendations of the Dead Sea Manual of Discipline and Some Notes Concerning the Habakkuk Midrash," by. W. H. Brownlee (continued, see no. 225), *JQR,* Vol. XLV, No. 3 (January 1955), pp. 202, 203–204, 205–206, 207, 208, 209, 211, 214, 215, 216, 217. All notes signed S.Z. (Cf., no. 230.)

230. Additional Remarks. *JQR,* Vol. XLV, No. 3 (January 1955), pp. 218–229. See nos. 225, 229. Reply to W. H. Brownlee's "Emendations of the Dead Sea Manual of Discipline and Some Notes Concerning Habakkuk Midrash."

The author of the *Pesher Habakkuk* was semiliterate; the Hebrew in the book is replete with grammatical errors and misspellings.

The Karaites made reference to many sects, but never to the Essenes. Such an omission would have been impossible had they been influenced by the Essenes.

During the early Middle Ages there were many messianic and ascetic sects, e.g., Mourners of Zion; their writings are similar to those now being found. Many still unpublished medieval MSS. (from Egypt, dealing with purity and impurity, discovered by Harkavy and now in libraries in Russia) should be examined for comparison.

The discovery of the Book of Kohelet disproves an early Essene provenance. These ascetics disdained life and believed in the immortality of the soul, that is, in ideas contrary to Ecclesiastes (see no. 24). The Essenes accepted only the Pentateuch. Moreover, Kohelet was canonized late—in Jabneh.

The "Servant of the Lord" or "his suffering" are not mentioned in the Manual of Discipline.

231. "The Interpretation of the Fourth Gospel," *JQR,* Vol. XLV, No. 3 (January 1955), pp. 270–273. Review of: *The Interpretation of the Fourth Gospel,* by C. H. Dodd.

John 8:16, "but I and He who sent me," are not the same words as Rabbi Judah's in Mishnah Sukkah 4.5—*ani wa'ho*. The Mishnah is *Ana Yahweh,* "We beseech, O God." The John text should be "but *I* and the Father that sent me."

The term *Shem ha-mephorash* did not come into use until the late third century. It is not mentioned in the Palestinian Talmud and may be an interpolation in the Mishnah.

The word "Torah," during the Second Commonwealth, applied only to the Pentateuch. Only in the third century did some Rabbis apply it to the whole Bible. The MSS. of Sanh. 91 do not have the words מנין לתחית המתים מן התורה. (See also no. 268.)

The term "Messiah" became a technical term only with the Apocalyptists (cf., nos. 37, 224).

232. "The Sources of the Synoptic Gospels," *JQR,* Vol. XLV, No. 3 (January 1955), pp. 268–270. Review of: *The Sources of the Synoptic Gospels,* by Wilfred L. Knox, edited by H. Chadwick, Vol. 1, "St. Mark."

Jesus was never called "Rabbi." Those crucified with Jesus were designated as "robbers" (*lestai*), not thieves.

233. "Mishneh or Mishnah?" *JQR,* Vol. XLV, No. 3 (Janury 1955), pp. 274–276. Reply to Bernard Bamberger.

"Mishneh" means "study" and also "law" (halakhah). It has no plural form. The term applied to every section as well as to the complete text, as with the term "Torah." In the Roman codes, the correct understanding of the word Mishneh is given, perhaps furnished by the Jews.

The term "Mekhilta" was coined by the Geonim. The entire collection of Pentateuchal commentary is Midrash Torah (see no. 208), and was called, fully, "Sifre." As a code, Mishneh appears only in Amoraic literature, when referring to its source.

234. "The Scrolls and History," *The Jerusalem Post,* Friday, February 18, 1955, p. 8.

The description in the War Scroll stating that the priests in battle stood a distance away, not to be defiled by the slain (i.e., not to profane the oil of their anointment), shows that the text is late, since the notion of such priestly defilement came only after the Destruction. (Cf., no. 255.)

The term "Togar" for Turkey is also late.

235. "Jewish Learning in America," *JQR,* Vol. XLV, No. 4 (April 1955), pp. 582–616.

History shows that it takes centuries to produce native scholars. A foundation of talmudic study in Poland, like that in Spain, was laid by immigrants. Russia developed as a center during the nineteenth century, but the traditional method of talmudic study had been pursued, as in the medieval age, for a long time before. There was no scientific or historical study of Bible or Talmud in Russian; in fact, there was opposition to it. Baron David Günzburg, a great patron of learning, set up an Academy for Jewish Studies that lasted only a few years.

The foundation of Jewish learning in America may be traced to Isaac Leeser. In time various educational institutions arose. These are here evaluated.

The opposition to Dr. Bernard Revel's notion of synthesis in Yeshiva College caused the growth of many Yeshivot of the traditional type. These Yeshivot, comparable to the Yeshivot of Europe of the past century, will exert a great influence on American Jewish life, for the students have a profound knowledge of the Talmud. However, they also display great fanaticism.

Problems such as riding on the Sabbath, amendments of *Ketubah,* and mixed pews cannot be decided by committees. A responsum must be written to amend any halakhah; this can be done only by those who know and respect the law. Learned Rabbinics is the substance of Judaism.

Secular forces are now dominant; the cohesive force, however, is still religion. All institutions of higher Jewish learning should be supported by the Jewish communities, through research scholarships and fellowships. Philanthropy and anti-Semitism do not promote Judaism. Torah learning is its quintessence.

235a. לפולמוס המגילות הגנוזות, זמנים, יום ו׳, י״ז מנ״א, תשט״ו.

A summary of the main points of contention against the antiquity of the Scrolls, based on the lateness of certain usages of expression or ideas.

1. "The defilement of the priestly oil" cannot apply to Second Temple practice.
2. The crossing out of words and additions on top were not used.
3. Hyphens were introduced only in the medieval period.
4. In the Second Temple era "Kohen ha-gadol" was the accepted title; *Kohen ha-rosh,* used in the Scrolls, is only biblical phraseology. (See also no. 167.)
5. The scribe copied names of biblical peoples who did not exist in the Second Temple era. "Togar" is also a late rendition.
6. *Asshur* in the Scrolls does not refer to Rome or to Syria.
7. How can an uncommon Persian phrase "nahshir" appear in an inter-Testamental text?
8. The author used Targum Jonathan profusely. The word עתודים (future) is karaitic usage.
9. The names of the four angels are copied from Midrash Rabbah.
10. "Essenes" is not recorded in the Scrolls. Though they were pacifists, some individuals among them even became generals.
11. The fictional stories in Eldad ha-Dani and *Sefer ha-Yashar* are similar to the descriptions in the War Scroll.
12. The medieval chronicler utilized fantasy and the popular number "seven' in his narratives.
13. The fact that biblical phrases are in the Scrolls does not invest them with antiquity. Medieval authors often simply copied biblical language.

236. יום שני של ראש-השנה, *Hadoar,* Vol. XXXV, No. 37 (September 9, 1955), p. 713. Hebrew reprint. (Cf., no. 218.)

237. "The Propaganda of the Hebrew Scrolls and the Falsification of History," *JQR,* Vol. XLVI, No. 1 (July 1955), pp. 1–39, VII pl.; Vol. XLVI, No. 2 (October 1955), pp. 116–180, III pl. (Cf., no. 255.)

238. *Maimonides, a Biography,* second edition, Bloch Publishing Co. (New York: 1955), 234 pp., illus. (Cf., nos. 56, 57.)

239. *Who Crucified Jesus?* (third edition), Harper & Brothers (New York: 1955), pp. xxii–250. (Cf., also nos. 105, 156.)

Introduction to third edition: The Nazis knew they had to destroy Judaism before they could abolish Christianity. Since the Jews were already regarded as "children of the devil," the German people helped to destroy them.

Judaphobia began in the ancient Diaspora because Jews held to the belief in a universal God, contrary to the deity concepts of other nations. In the Hellenistic Diaspora Jews were killed because they opposed the national gods.

In early days, Christians were regarded as heretics (*minim*). Later it was recognized that Christians were not idol worshipers, but that they also believed in the universality of God.

Justin Martyr was the first to bring the charge that Jews crucified Jesus. The Apostolic Fathers never attributed the Crucifixion to them.

Goodwill organizations and anti-defamation societies cannot eradicate anti-Semitism. The Jews have been defamed too long. The blood of the Jewish martyrs in the Diaspora was the seed of the Christian Church. The reintroduction of the Apostles' Creed into the Church and its schools would help eradicate anti-Semitism.

1956

240. "The Propaganda of the Hebrew Scrolls and the Falsification of History," (continued from *JQR,* XLVI, No. 2, 1955), *JQR,* Vol. XLVI, No. 3 (January 1956), pp. 209–258. (Cf., no. 255.)

241. סדר של פסח (פרק מתוך מחקר היסטורי על החתימה הראשונה של הליטורגיה העברית), *Hadoar,* Vol. XXXVI, No. 21 (March 23, 1956), pp. 414, 415.

The Seder is strictly concerned with intimate family observance, unlike the celebration of other festivals. The three questions in Yerushalmi Pesaḥim are basic, referring to redemption. The one added in the Babli about *maror,* signifying enslavement, came after the Destruction. The three questions have their origin in the Torah: 1) matzah, 2) roast, and 3) dipping, reminiscent of the blood. The Rabbis invalidated the sprinkling of blood (still practiced by the Samaritans). The *ḥaroset,* nevertheless, is symbolic of this. Because Passover and circumcision symbolize Jewish freedom, one who was uncircumcized could not take part in the paschal lamb. The first two questions (dippings, roast) deal with physical emancipation. The idea of the Amora Samuel that the physical redemption is the prime aspect caused the rearrangement of the recital; hence *matzah* came first in the "four questions." (Cf., no. 159, 283.)

242. "Antiquity of Scrolls Disputed," to the Editor of *The New York Times,* March 30, 1956.

In refuting the antiquity of the Scrolls, the purpose is to stress that they are not of the pre-Christian period, nor of the first century of the Christian Era; hence they have no value for the early history of Christianity or Judaism.

242a. "Dead Sea Scrolls No Value for Judaism or Early Christianity," *Long Island Jewish Press,* March 1956, p. 10. (See also nos. 245a, 255.)

The Scrolls were written between the seventh and twelfth centuries of our era by semiliterate Jews, followers of men who claimed to be messiahs. This is based on internal evidence, the spelling of Hebrew words, and expressions and signs which came into usage in a later period. It has been proved that the carbon-14 test has not been thoroughly reliable, since other tests produced variant dates.

243. "Cave Scroll Dating," to the Editor of *Commentary,* Vol. XXI (March 1956), p. 282.

Is there any indication in the photostat of the Bar Kokhba letter for dating the "deliverance of Israel through Simon ben Kosbah, Prince of Israel"?

244. Note to: "The Idea of a Second Coming of Moses," by N. Wieder, *JQR,* Vol. XLVI, No. 4 (April 1956), pp. 364–366.

The idea of a "second coming of Moses" was not known to the Jews in the first centuries of our era.

The expression *doresh ha-Torah* in the Zadokite Fragment is based on Targum Jonathan Gen. 49:10.

245. "The Dead Sea Scrolls," to the Editor of *Commentary,* Vol. XXI, (April 1956), p. 383.

Only the context, not the paleography, of the Bar Kokhba Fragments can give an idea of authenticity and antiquity.

245a. "How Significant are the Scrolls?" *The American Zionist,* April 1956, p. 16. A condensation of a lecture given at the New York Public Library. (See 235a, 242a.)

246. "The Dead Sea Scrolls," *JQR,* Vol. XLVI, No. 4 (April 1956), pp. 389–400. A discussion of some of the writings on the Dead Sea Scrolls: Millar Burrows, *The Dead Sea Scrolls;* Edmund Wilson, *The Scrolls from the Dead Sea;* Yigael Yadin, *The War Between the Sons of Light and the Sons of Darkness;* and others.

It is erroneous to interpret *rabbim* in the Scrolls as a plural of "rabbi." Only after the Destruction did the sages bear the title "rabbi." *Rabbim* is not a synonym of "ḥaberim"; *b'rabim* in talmudic literature means "publicly."

In the War Scroll, the author copied the biblical list of nations and the strategy of the Byzantine army.

The term *midbar yerushalaim* is found in medieval, messianic literature.

247. "The Battle of the Dead Sea Scrolls. Dr. Zeitlin Replies to Yeivin's Claims; Challenges Antiquity Director's Facts, *The Jewish News,* Detroit, July 13, 1956, Vol. XXIX, No. 19. (See also no. 255.)

Authoritative scholars have not established the fact that the first Scrolls were found in Cave I. Muhamed al-Dib revealed himself only four years after the discovery. Archaeology must be discounted as a factor in determining the dating. The ideas and laws set forth in the Scrolls are in direct contradiction to those held and promulgated by the Essenes (see no. 224). There is no proof that the scriptorium was of the pre-Christian era. Arabic coins and MSS belonging to the ninth century and Greek MSS commentaries on the Gospels have also been found.

As late as the fourth century C.E., the Jews used the old Hebrew script, but the *matres lectionis* were introduced in the second century C.E. on the authority of Rabbi Akiba (see nos. 168, 187, 194, 255).

The archaeologists themselves did not see the Scrolls in the jars or in their original state, wrapped in linen. Can it not be that the bones found in the caves are of the time of the persecution of Heraclius, about 628 C.E.?

The term קץ האחרון was coined after the time of Bar Kokhba. The early Christians were not aware of the Essenes.

248. "A Jewish News Exclusive: Günzburg Library and Hebrew in Russia. Dr. Zeitlin Describes Status of Archives," *The Jewish News,* Detroit, Vol. XXIX, No. 21 (July 27, 1956), p. 1.

The Günzburg Library, as far as is known, has not been split up. It is in boxes (for it was destined for Jerusalem). When catalogued it will be a boon to scholarship.

249. "The Dead Sea Scrolls: A Travesty on Scholarship," *JQR,* Vol. XLVII, No. 1 (July 1956), pp. 1–56 + 2 pl. (See also no. 255.)

Alexander Jannai is not mentioned in the Scrolls as crucifying a "teacher of righteousness"; therefore no comparison can be made with Josephus' record of Alexander Jannai crucifying the Pharisees.

The phrase pertaining to two Messiahs, Aaronide and Davidic in the Zadokite Fragment and in the Manual of Discipline, is based primarily on Pesikta Rabbati.

Supernatural powers were never claimed for Bar Kokhba, even if he was called a Messiah.

The word, טבילה, baptism, is not in the Scrolls. רחץ therein means only washing off physical impurity. In the Gospels, baptism is for cleansing from sin. There is no mention in the Scrolls of baptism in the name of the "teacher of righteousness."

Josephus and Hippolytus, in their accounts of the Essenes, never used the theological word "baptism," which is different from the Essenic washing of the body.

The Eucharist may be traced to the Last Supper, which was a *Seder.* This institution, associated with the blood and body of Jesus, has no connection with the Scrolls or with the Essenes who recited blessings before and after the meal, as other Jews did as well.

There are references to "false prophets" in the Gospels. Surely, if there were an Essene "teacher of righteousness" who, as assumed, influenced Christianity, both he and the Essenes would have been mentioned.

There is nothing in the Scrolls indicating that a "teacher of righteousness" was assassinated by a wicked priest, and that his followers expected his "return." The text about the Messiah reappearing may well be a reference to Yudghan. His followers believed he would reappear, even after he had been killed. (See also no. 255.)

There is no letter in the Talmud beginning with the phrase "from." (Cf. nos. 210, 216, 226.) Simon ben Shetaḥ's letter in the Talmud is apocryphal.

The so-called Lamech Scroll uses the name *Salem*—which is Jerusalem. This usage is a copy of the Midrash and Targum.

The Copper Scroll's listing of hidden treasure is a repetition of tales told by medieval storytellers. The question is: why did a Jew write on a copper scroll?

Demetrius, mentioned in *Pesher Nahum,* is only a reference to an ancient personality and event. Similarly, medieval commentators on Daniel referred to Vespasian and Constantine. Alexander Jannai is not mentioned in *Pesher Nahum.* Neither is the word *thraki,* referring to cruelties. The phrase "Lion of wrath" may refer to Antiochus Epiphanes who hanged many who remained loyal to Jewish law.

The expression "to hang men alive" is from a late minor Midrash telling the story of Judith. (Cf., also no. 267.)

250. Untitled article. Begins: "I believe . . ." *JQR,* Vol. XLVII, No. 2 (October 1956), pp. 182–183. Comments to an article by Oskar K. Rabinowicz, entitled "The Shapira Forgery Mystery."

Information about the Shapira forgeries can be obtained by referring back to the *Jewish Chronicle* of London, August 4, 1883.

251. "Revealing Data on the So-Called Discovery of the Dead Sea Scrolls," *JQR,* Vol. XLVII, No. 2 (October 1956), pp. 183–187. Review of J. M. Allegro, *The Dead Sea Scrolls.* (See no. 255.)

Who is the original owner: Kando, Firaz, or another Arab? Why didn't the Jordanian government demand the return of the Scrolls when displayed in Washington, D.C.? Is there a possibility that it already had proof that the Scrolls were not discovered in Ain Feshka?

252. "Are Judaism and Christianity Fossil Religions?" *JQR,* Vol. XLVII No. 2 (October 1956), pp. 187–195. Review of: *A Study of History,* by Professor Arnold J. Toynbee.

The Gospels trace Jesus' genealogy from David. Hence it is wrong to say that Jesus was born of Galilean Gentiles who were forced to accept Judaism.

The statement in the Gospels about "fighting God" cannot be attributed to Rabban Gamaliel; it was only a Greek concept.

The men who were crucified with Jesus were *lestai,* members of the Fourth Philosophy; Jesus was an Apocalyptist, (cf., no. 7).

The Synoptic Gospels accuse Jews only of the rejection of Jesus, but not of the crucifixion. The Gospel of John, which has the accusation, was written by early Christians to ingratiate themselves with Rome. In the Bar Kokhba period the Judaean Christians were Fifth Columnists for the Romans.

Judaism did not become sterile after the rejection of Jesus, as witness the great literature and accomplishments of the Jews. It is absurd to use the term "fossil" in connection with the Jewish people and Judaism. (See no. 304.)

Judaism is the parent of Christianity; the Synagogue is the mother of the Church. Christianity developed fully in the Diaspora, accepting much of Hellenism.

The Gospels contain many aspects of Judaism. Were Judaism a "fossil," then, according to Toynbee, the phrase should also be applied to Christianity; on the contrary, both have great vitality.

253. "Recent Literature on the Dead Sea Scrolls," *JQR,* Vol. XLVII, No. 2 (October 1956), pp. 196–214 + 3 pl. Review of: *The Qumran Community, Its History and Scrolls,* by Charles J. Fritsch; *The Dead Sea Scrolls and the Originality of Christ,* by Father Geoffrey Graystone; *The Meaning of the Dead Sea Scrolls,* by Rev. A. Powell Davies; *The Dead Sea Scriptures in English Translation,* by Dr. Theodor H. Gaster.

The description of the mode of life in the Manual of Discipline parallels that of the early monks as described by Jerome (fourth century).

The Sanhedrin never delegated its authority to pagans to carry out verdicts of justice.

The term *kittim* was not used in a loose form, and never had the connotation of "barbarians." As found in Maccabees, Josephus, and Yosippon it refers to the Greeks and the Romans. During the Middle Ages it was applied to those living in Italy and in the Byzantine-

Roman Empire. (See no. 167.) The term "Amalek" was then used to refer to barbarians.

254. מאי חנוכה?, *Hadoar,* Vol. XXXVII, No. 5 (November 20, 1956), p. 84.

Ḥanukkah was observed for eight days (and not seven) because it was for the purification of the Temple (not merely for dedication).

"Ḥanukkah" was the official Temple term; the populace called it Festival of Lights, as noted by Josephus. The narrative in the Talmud about the reason for the lights came later; the practice, however, was ancient.

The Pharisees were not opposed to Ḥanukkah, but only to some of the Hasmonean rulers. There is no special Tractate Ḥanukkah because the Books of the Maccabees were not canonized, as was Megillat Esther. (Cf., nos. 72, 181.)

255. *The Dead Sea Scrolls and Modern Scholarship,* The Dropsie College for Hebrew and Cognate Learning (Philadelphia: 1956), pp. xvi–154 + 16 pl. (*The Jewish Quarterly Review,* Monograph Series, Number III). [Full reprint of nos. 239, 240, 242a, 247, 249, 251 with additions.]

The title "teacher of righteousness" has no bearing on the fact that Jesus was a teacher, and "righteousness" is mentioned frequently.

No midrashim on biblical books were written before 70 C.E. The author of *Pesher Habakkuk* used *Targum Jonathan.* The cardinal concepts of the Essenes, such as immortality, reward and punishment, and resurrection are not found in the Manual of Discipline.

The halakhot of the Manual of Discipline are like those of the Zadokite Fragment of the medieval Genizah.

Jews expected the Messiah as a result of the wars of Heraclius. The Mohammedan conquest stimulated the further expression of messianic beliefs, propounded by Abu Issa and Yudghan, and by ascetic sects, and the Mourners of Zion.

Priests in the Second Temple did not use anointed oil. Jesus is never mentioned as "anointed by oil." The law that the "blood of a slain person defiles" was enacted by the Tannaim (see no. 234).

The War Scroll author used the Midrash Rabbah of Numbers, mentioning the four angels' names inscribed on banners.

The Essenes were opposed to war and would not have composed a War Scroll. It is similar to Eldad ha-Dani's exploits and to *Sefer ha-Yashar*; these have no historical validity. The number seven plays a great part in the War Scroll, as it does in Eldad ha-Dani's fictional tales.

The letters in Maccabees bear the name of the sender "to," not "from." (Cf., no. 210.) Yosippon is based on it, with interpolations of the medieval period. The medieval works Midrash Tannaim, Targum Sheni, and *Sefer ha-Yashar* do have letters beginning with "from." It is not to be found in the literature of the Second Commonwealth.

The Karaites used a phraseology of אודכה אלי.

Jews never had the Decalogue inscribed in their phylacteries, especially because of the variants in the texts. (See also nos. 210, 387, 392.)

There are no coins of the third year; how, then, can there be a deed of the third year of Bar Kokhba? How did an obscure deed come into the cave supposedly containing significant documents?

The author of the War Scroll read the account of Eldad ha-Dani and copied early phrases from the Bible and rabbinic literature.

With the error of dating the Nash Papyrus, which is of the third or fourth century, came ultimately the error of dating the Hebrew Scrolls.

Saadia had the Book of Jubilees; Nahmanides quotes from the Wisdom of Solomon. The editor of the Zohar refers to the Book of Enoch. There is a Midrash of Noah, and one containing fragments of the Testament of the Twelve Patriarchs. There were Hebrew translated versions of Judith, Tobit, Ben Sira, and other Apocryphal books in the Middle Ages. These have now been rediscovered.

If fragments of the Bible are now found with different readings from the Masoretic text but similar to LXX, it should be known that these were common in the Talmudic days, because there are passages in the Bible for which the Rabbis had different readings. Hence, there is no proof that LXX was based on these Scroll fragments.

The Gospel of John uses terms like Passover (for Festival of Matzot), Messiah, rabbi; these evidence a late dating, past 70 C.E. There are no affinities between the Scrolls and Christianity.

The *matres lectionis* may have been used in secular writings; only in the time of R. Akiba were they introduced into the sacred writings.

Inverted "nun's" were not used in earlier sacred Torahs; so declared even R. Solomon Luria.

The sign X in the Isaiah Scroll is not a Christian sign; nor is the "taw" a sign of death, as noted in Midrash Tanhuma. There is no place in the Talmud or Midrash where the rabbis attached a Greek meaning to the sign X. It is erroneous to state that the signs had been affixed by Judaean Christians to the Isaiah Scroll. If so, they should have been near the so-called Christological passages.

The fact that some manuscripts had old script (including the Tetragrammaton) does not indicate antiquity (see also no. 264), because even as late as the fourth century Jews still used the old script (see Sanh. 97b).

Jews, during the Second Commonwealth, were not afraid to write *Ado-nai*; only in the Middle Ages did they refrain from spelling it out and replaced the letters with dots or ellipses.

Masudi applied the term *Yaḥad* to the Ananites. The words *mastema* and *irim* (angels), found in Jubilees, occur in Hebrew medieval compositions, *Midrash Noah* and the *Zohar*. The Scrolls copied these.

How can the Zadokite Fragment (if Essene) refer to the sale of slaves or birds to Gentiles, if the Essenes had no private property?

The Essenes did not leave their houses on Sabbath, whereas the Zadokite Fragment speaks of "Sabbatical 2000 cubits."

The doctrines of the *Zaddukim* (Sadducees) or of the Essenes have no affinity with laws and ideas in the Scrolls.

The first change from the old Hebrew script to the square style is ascribed to Ezra, but the *matres lectionis* and final letters (מנצפ"ך) were introduced by Rabbi Akiba. Before rendering decisions paleographists should determine the differences between the scripts of Babylonian, Palestinian, and Egyptian Jewry.

The Nash Papyrus Decalogue is a conglomeration. It does not follow the order of the Hebrew Pentateuch or LXX. It appears to be part of a Babylonian Jewish amulet, as already indicated by Jerome.

It is astonishing that scholars maintain that the medieval Scrolls will bring a reevaluation of Christianity, because a "Teacher of Righteousness" preceded Jesus! There is no mention in the Gospels of a "Teacher of Righteousness" or that there had been another Messiah before Jesus. (See also no. 284.)

Many of the biblical readings found in rabbinic literature are preferable to the Masoretic. In the *JQR* of July 1950 there is a collection of one hundred variants of Isaiah alone. (Cf., no. 176.)

Josephus never mentioned that the Essenes lived near the Dead Sea. Only Pliny, after the Destruction, remarked on it, for in his own period a remnant of the sect settled there.

Believing in fate and predestination, the Essenes kept faith with the state. According to them, no ruler attained his office save by the will of God. If the Essenes had believed in a Messiah, Josephus would have alluded to it in such a manner that the Romans would not suspect him of holding such a belief, even as he wrote in the case of the Apocalyptists, whom he calls imposters.

Messianism involved proselytism; the Essenes, being individualists, did not proselytize. (See no. 351.)

The idea of redemption—that the Messiah died for the sins of the people—was unknown to the Scrolls' authors.

"Son of God," "Son of man," "Rabbi," "resurrection," and "crucifixion"—themes stressed in John—are not found in the Scrolls.

Communal meals are common among many groups. Hence a Scroll reference to these is no proof of Christian-like practice.

It is singular that in the Scrolls the priest is superior to the Messiah. In karaitic literature *mashiah* means any anointed priest, but "priest" refers to the High Priest. Thus a karaitic affinity is again evident.

A Scroll fragment of Samuel mentions that Samuel was a Nazirite. This is based on tannaitic literature.

The Masoretic text contains the name "Rabshakeh"; the Isaiah Scroll—"Rab-Shakeh." To deduce that this comes from older texts is unacceptable, for in the Vatican there are medieval MSS of Isaiah with the reading "Rab-Shakeh."

It is wrong to maintain that the conflict between Rabban Gamaliel and Rabbi Joshua dealt with the calendar *per se*. Rather, the conflict centered about the question of authority and reliance on the testimony of witnesses.

During the Second Commonwealth the Pharisees had no societies called *Ḥaburah,* whose members were Ḥaberim.

Kohen ha-Rosh does not mean chief priest, but "the first priest."

The manifold contradictions about the Scroll discovery are still unsolved. The orthography, punctuation, and terms are medieval. The halakhot in the Scrolls could not have been enacted in the pre-Christian period. The Hebrew University was a bit hasty in purchasing these Scrolls at an exorbitant price.

1957

256. "The Dead Sea Scrolls: 1. The Lamech Scroll—A Medieval Midrash; 2. The Copper Scrolls; 3. Was Kando the Owner of the Scrolls?" *JQR,* Vol. XLVII, No. 3 (January 1957), pp. 245–268.

The Lamech Scroll records the name of Lamech's wife—Bitenos. In 1895 Harkavay wrote about medieval fragments found in Damascus in which Lamech's wife is called בתאנוש, Bitenos.

The Lamech account resembles the Apocryphal book of Noah. The story about Abraham is like that in the Book of Jubilees. Similar stories were extant in Aramaic texts even in the thirteenth century. Yet, there are distinct differences. In the Scroll there are no laws; in Jubilees the law of homicide is noted at the time of Cain, the law of tithes as having been ordained after Abraham's battle with the kings, and Shabuot was set at the time of the vow to Noah. Moreover, *Ado-nai* is rendered as "my master," *Mori*; and *Medinah* (city) applied to Damascus. In the latter part of the seventh century, Damascus was the capital of the Omayyads.

The phrase טור תורא may refer to Mt. Taurus. The rabbinic statement that when the Jews were persecuted they had to write on "the horn of the ox that they had no part in the God of Israel" is a reference to Mt. Taurus—i.e., publicly proclaiming their apostasy. Later rabbinic literature rendered it as "horn of an ox."

It has been conceded that the Copper Scroll was written by a semiliterate, perhaps a crank.

257. Untitled Article begins: "The Calendar used . . .," *JQR,* Vol. XLVII, No. 3 (January 1957), pp. 294–295. Comments to article "The Dating of the Last Supper," by Norman Walker.

Paraskeue in the Hellenistic world refers to the eve of (the day before the) Sabbath as well as to the eve of holidays; it began with the dawn of that day. (See no. 348.)

258. "Law and Society," *JQR,* Vol. XLVII, No. 3 (January 1957), pp. 304–308. Review of: משפט וחברה מאת א. ויתקין, הוצאת דביר, תל-אביב.

The religious leaders of Israel should have the foresight of the Sages of the Second Commonwealh and utilize the halakhot, through amendment and legal fiction, for further development and for adjustment to life, as did the Pharisees.

259. "The Tosefta," *JQR,* Vol. XLVII, No. 4 (April 1957), pp. 382–399. Review of: Saul Lieberman's *The Tosefta According to Codex Vienna, with Variants from Codex Erfurt, Geniza Mss. and Editio Princeps (Venice:* 1521) *Together with References to Parallel Passages in Talmudic Literature.*

The origin of the Tosefta and its relationship to the Mishnah and the Baraitot is still unsolved. Many instances can be collected demonstrating the original reading as in *Prosbol, ba'sar taavah* (flesh of desire), laws of *hefker,* crops of the fourth year, the nine periods of gifts of wood by the priests, recital of blessing over the sun, etc. The historical background and internal evidence, and not mere comparison of texts, must always be utilized in determining a reading.

260. Communication to the editor of *American Historical Review,* Vol. 6, No. 3 (April 1957). Rejoinder to Prof. Albright's review of October 1956.

The verbal terms and the halakhot in the Scrolls are like those that were composed after the Destruction of the Second Temple. Parentheses, ellipses, and connecting lines for the script, and crossing out lines were not known to Jews in the pre-Christian period. (See no. 264.)

261. "The Titles High Priest and the Nasi of the Sanhedrin," *JQR,* Vol. XLVIII, No. 1 (July 1957), pp. 1–5.

The term "Nasi" in the Bible was applied to secular leaders. Why then was it applied to the religious head of the Sanhedrin? Its origin may be discovered in the last chapters of Ezekiel, where the High Priest was designated as Nasi because he was both the sole ruler of the State and had sole religious authority as well. In the Second Temple the High Priest was called Kohen ha-Gadol (in the First Temple, Kohen ha-Rosh), while in Persian days he may have been called *Kahana Rabba,* which is a translation of *Nasi.*

262. "The Dead Sea Scrolls; Fantasies and Mistranslations," *JQR,* Vol. XLVIII, No. 1 (July 1957), pp. 71–85. Reviews of: *The Essenes* *and Christianity* by Duncan Howlett; and discussions of contributions in current periodical literature relating to the Scrolls; also comments on remarks by scholars at the Dropsie College Symposium; it reviews, also, Krister Stendahl's *The Scrolls and the New Testament.*

The terms "Gentile" and "tax collector" are not to be found in the Manual of Discipline, suggesting any comparison to Matthew 18:17. The allusion to *Urim v'Tumim* (Deut. 33:8) is best explained by referring to the Targum, unlike the rendition of LXX.

The Aramaic texts in Daniel and Ezra, that of Megillat Taanit (excluding the late scholia), and the Aramaic parts in Midrash Lamentations and the Palestinian Talmud do not have mixtures of Hebrew and non-Hebrew words. These are of an early period. Genesis Apocryphon (Lamech Scroll), however, has a mixture of languages, similar to the karaitic writings.

In Targum Jonathan *medinah* is "city." In early texts *ir* is city; *medinah* is province. מקנה is "cattle"; נכסין is "property," "chattel." The Genesis Apocryphon renders *mikneh* as *nikhsin,* showing the lateness of its usage, based on Targum Jonathan.

Where in the Bible we find "bread and wine," the Scroll, following the Palestinian Targum, uses "food and drink." (See also no. 270.)

262a. "The Dead Sea Scrolls," Akten des Vierundzwanzigsten internationalen orientalisten-Kongresses, München, 28 August bis 4 September 1957, herausgegeben von Herbert Franke, Deutsche Morgenländische Gesellschaft e. V., Sektion III: Altes Testament/ Biblische Archäologie und Judaica; Vorsitz: H. H. Rowley (Manchester), pp. 198–200.

Abridged version of paper read at the Congress reviewing and stressing the arguments against the antiquity of the Scrolls. An appeal to scholars to refute openly and in scholarly fashion: "truth cannot be killed by silence. . . . Conscience will not be silenced." (See also no. 269.)

263. "The Book of 'Jubilees' and the Pentateuch," *JQR,* Vol. XLVIII, No. 2 (October 1957), pp. 218–235. (See also nos. 77, 132, 255, 256, 290.)

The original title of Jubilees may have been *Torat Moshe,* like the Pentateuch. In the Book of Jubilees there is no mention of *Omer* or seven-week counting. In Judaea, Shabuot was called *Azarta* and in the Diaspora "Pentecost." The origin of Sukkot in Jubilees is attributed to Abraham, and is not based on the Exodus.

All laws in reference to circumcision, idolatry, intermarriage, nakedness, and association with Gentiles are already to be found in the Bible and are not the result of Hellenistic contact. Jubilees is more chauvinistic than even the book of Nehemiah.

The phrase, "until this day," is used frequently in the Bible, and also in Jubilees; hence, the use of such a phrase cannot be employed to determine any specific date. (Cf., no. 209.)

In the Hasmonean period there was no conflict on the subject of the calendar. It became an issue only at the beginning of the Persian period, when Jubilees was written.

Jubilees changes the order of the festivals. It also made the fifth year the year of release.

After the Restoration the Pentateuch was canonized; there was no idol worship in Judaea.

Jubilees was written in opposition to the Pentateuch. According to the Torah, Moses received the Ten Commandments, and the laws were given to the people later. According to Jubilees, all the laws were written at the time of Creation, and were given to Moses by the Angel of the Presence.

There is no reference to Jerusalem in the Pentateuch; Jubilees speaks of the Temple to be built on Mt. Zion.

The Pentateuch forbids marriage alignments with the seven nations; Jubilees opposes intermarriage with any foreign people.

The festivals, according to Jubilees, were celebrated on Sunday. There is no reference to a Messiah in Jubilees, whereas in the Scrolls there are such references.

Though rejected, Jubilees influenced later rabbinic literature—apocalyptic and midrashic, even as did Ben Sira. Saadia had a Hebrew or Aramaic copy of Jubilees. (Cf., no. 255.)

264. "How Ancient are the Hebrew Scrolls from the Dead Sea?" *Judaism,* Vol. VI (Winter Issue 1957), pp. 55–58.

A restatement of the salient points:

The Scrolls were discovered by Bedouins, not by archaeologists. The style of writing indicates illiteracy, and the time of composition to be during the Middle Ages.

Scriptio plena was introduced by the school of Rabbi Akiba. (See no. 247.)

Moreh ha-zedek came into vogue in the Middle Ages.

Covenant of Abraham is due to Paul's attack on circumcision. The Scrolls are products of karaitic writings and *Targum Jonathan.*

In a later period the Tetragrammaton was no longer used; hence *El* is found in the Scrolls. Paleography is not a criterion for dating. The carbon-14 tests were made on the linen, not on the Scrolls.

265. האסנים (האסיים). [מתוך מחקר היסטורי על הכתות בישראל בימי בית שני.] ב-„ספר הדואר" למלאות לו 35 שנה. תשי"ז—1957, דפים 48—52.

"Essene" in Greek refers to those called "Hasidim" in Hebrew. Azariah dei Rossi was the first to use the Hebrew term אסיים. The Essenes reacted against the Hellenization and the decrees of Antiochus (168 B.C.E.); they opposed priests who were not of the Zadok family, and hence did not send offerings to the Temple.

Philo never saw the Essenes. John was not an Essene. The Essenes were not the same as the Therepeutae who lived in Egypt. The Essenes regarded the Diaspora as unholy; they felt that nomocracy was wrong, for they believed in a theocracy. Pharisaic views, not Essenic, penetrated into Jewish thought. Because of their asceticism and exclusive beliefs (unlike the progressiveness of the Pharisees), the Essenes disappeared. (See also no. 224.)

266. Jewish Apocryphal Literature. Solomon Zeitlin, editor-in-chief, *The Book of Wisdom.* An English Translation with Introduction and Commentary by Joseph Reider. Published for the Dropsie College for Hebrew and Cognate Learning by Harper & Brothers (New York: 1957), pp. x–233.

267. "The Phrase יתלה אנשים חיים," *Journal of Jewish Studies,* VIII, Nos. 1 & 2 (1957), pp. 117–118.

This phrase, describing a fact, does not occur in early Hebrew literature. Mention of it in the midrashic *Sifre* is of late origin. (See also no. 249.)

1958

268. "The Idolatry of the Dead Sea Scrolls," *JQR,* Vol. XLVIII, No. 3 (January 1958), pp. 243–278. (See no. 267.)

Muhamed al-Dib said that the discovery was in the 1945, that he broke *all* the jars and used a scroll for sandal straps.

Sixth of Gorpiaeus in 65 C.E. was the third Tishri (in 66, it was 14 Tishri). Menaḥem had won the victory over the Romans by then.

If Menaḥem, a Sicarius, had tried to introduce a new calendar, Josephus would have assailed him even as he did the Zealots for choosing a High Priest by lot, thereby profaning the Jewish religion.

The word *Perushim* in the talmudic passages of Sotah has only the connotation of "separatists," (cf., no. 305). The Pharisees did not believe in bodily resurrection; they did believe in the immortality of the soul (cf., no. 62). The term תחית המתים may apply to the soul. In Yerushalmi Peah 16b there is no mention of the phrase מן התורה (cf., no. 231). Josephus likewise does not mention bodily resurrection—only the resurrection of the soul.

Yadin's theory that Paul or Barnabas wrote the Epistle to the Hebrews to the Qumran Community is preposterous.

269. קונגרס המזרחנים והמגילות הגנוזות, *Haaretz,* Tel Aviv, January 16, 1958.

At the Congress in Munich, 1957, it was stressed that only knowledge of rabbinic and karaitic literature can yield an understanding of the Scrolls. Unfortunately, many scholars cannot read these literatures with facility. (See no. 262a.)

270. "Dating the Genesis Apocryphon," *JBL,* Vol. LXXVII, No. 1 (March 1958), pp. 75–76.

The author of the *Genesis Apocryphon,* like Targum Jonathan, has the word אנתתא exactly eleven times. The Scroll is a late rabbinic interpretation of Genesis 12.

271. "Dating the Dead Sea Scrolls," letter to *The New York Times,* April 6, 1958.

Hyphens, parentheses, etc., in the Scrolls, as well as the use of medieval Hebrew words, and references to late Jewish laws indicate clearly that the Scrolls were not written in the pre-Christian period. (See also no. 264.)

272. "The Manuscript of the Tractate Abodah Zarah and Creative Scholarship," *JQR,* Vol. XLVIII, No. 4 (April 1958), pp. 391–

397. Review of: מסכת עבודה זרה, כתב־יד בית המדרש לרבנים בניו יורק, הוכן לדפוס בצירוף מבוא והערות בידי שרגא בהר"ר קלמן זצ"ל אברמסון.

The MSS dated 1290 was first used by Dr. Zeitlin in his dissertation *Megillat Taanit* (1917). (See no. 16.) In it he expresses the view that the Mishnah was written down even before the time of Rabbi Judah; this MSS, produced in Spain, accords with Maimonides' opinion that the halakhot were, in fact, written down.

According to Rashi, to find the exact year of a Sabbatical cycle add one year to that in the era of the Destruction. According to the MSS, following the Geonim and accepted by R. Tam, one must subtract two years or add five years to the era (of the Greeks). Based on chronology, Rashi's reading is the correct one.

273. "The Phrase תולים אותו חי," *JQR,* Vol. XLVIII, No. 4 (April 1958), pp. 398–399. Reply to Dr. Wieder's "Rejoinder" in the *Journal of Jewish Studies,* Vol. VII, Nos. 1 & 2 (1957).

A *baraita* in Sanh. 46 notes that governments hanged a criminal alive and then put him to death, whereas the Jewish law demanded that he be put to death and then hanged. The clause "they shall hang up alive" is found only in the Sifre and is a later interpretation of the *baraita.* (See also nos. 249, 267.)

274. A correction (3 lines) to the article: "The Idolatry of the Dead Sea Scrolls," on p. 257. *JQR,* Vol. XLVIII, No. 4 (April 1958), p. 399. (See no. 269.)

Judah, the father of Menahem, was the founder of the Fourth Philosophy, i.e., the leader of the Sicarii.

275. "The Medieval Mind and the Theological Speculation on the Dead Sea Scrolls," *JQR,* Vol. XLIX, No. 1 (July 1958), pp. 1–34.

Christian scholars, following a theological perspective, maintain that the Scrolls will reveal the true causes of the rise of Christianity. Others believe that the Scrolls will support the doctrines of the New Testament. Jewish scholars never regarded the Scrolls as of historical value to Judaism.

During the Second Commonwealth, *ha-Shem* referred to the Divine name; in the medieval period it referred to God, Himself. (Cf., no. 203.)

The Jews in Egypt in the Ptolemaic period wrote Aramaic or Greek, but not Hebrew.

Professor Trevers now states that on February 22, 1948, he joined together Columns VII and VIII of the Manual of Discipline.

In the Genesis Apocryphon we find the word דרמשק for Damascus. This is exactly the style of Targum Jonathan.

276. "Personal Status in Israel," *JQR*, Vol. XLIX, No. 2 (October 1958), pp. 122–132. Review of: המעמד האישי בישראל מאת פרופ׳ משה זילברג, ירושלים תשי"ח.

The religious courts of Israel are authorized to deal with matters of personal status: marriage, divorce, inheritance, etc. Often there is open collusion with the civil courts. Many instances are given here showing the conflict between religious and national law.

According to old halakhot, a transaction, to be valid, does not require witnesses; they are necessary only when there is a conflict or denial by one of the parties. The Mishnah in Kiddushin does not mention the necessity for witnesses to validate a marriage. The Amoraim, however, declared that to legalize a marriage, the testimony of witnesses is required. (See no. 303.)

Jewish law cannot be compared with the canon law of Christianity which is a religion of many peoples and races. Jewish law is the creation of the genius of one people.

The question "Who is a Jew?" belongs to the domain of spiritual leaders. (Cf., no. 288.)

After 70 C.E., according to the halakhah, a mere declaration of the acceptance of Judaism was not sufficient.

277. "The Sabbatians and the Plague of Mysticism," *JQR*, Vol. XLIX, No. 2 (October 1958), pp. 145–155. Review of: שבתי צבי והתנועה השבתאית בימי חייו, מאת גרשם שלום.

It is an oversimplification to claim that the Lurian Kabbala was the main cause of the creation and spread of the Sabbataian movement. There were many causes: the Thirty Years' War, the belief in a "second coming," and a reaction by the Marranos who had been brought up as Catholics and now sought a new Messiah. The Marranos, psychologically driven, vindictively, demonstrated their hostility to Christianity by flocking to the banner of the new Messiah.

The movement was not as popular in Poland as in the Levantine states. The Chmielnicki pogroms, however, spurred the acceptance of Shabbatai Zevi. (Cf., no. 58.) The Puritan movement, and idealism, too, may have been added factors. Shabbatai Zevi's lewd life influenced him to institute the practice of calling women to the Torah.

Nathan, "his prophet," was a genius in promoting the movement. The rabbis of that time had failed to guide the people, but instead had followed the masses. Consequently many Jews lost faith in the rabbis as their spiritual leaders.

Mysticism is a threat to Judaism which intrinsically is, and should always be, based on knowledge and learning.

278. Untitled article. *Begins*: "Dr. Baumgarten's note both amused and disappointed me . . ." *JQR,* Vol. XLIX, No. 2 (October 1958), pp. 160–161. Comments to article, "1QSa 1.11—Age of Testimony or Responsibility?" by Joseph M. Baumgarten.

Mar Zutra of Babylonia (fifth century) held that one who did not attain the age of twenty was not qualified to be a witness in real-estate transactions. The author of the Manual of Discipline most likely heard of this halakhah and adopted it, though incorrectly.

279. "The Masora and the Dead Sea Scrolls," *JQR,* Vol. XLIX, No. 2 (October 1958), pp. 161–163. Comments to article by Dr. Robert Gordis in *Tarbiz,* Vol. 27, No. 4, entitled:

The Masorah was not established during the Second Commonwealth. The inverted "nun" was introduced only during the Middle Ages. (Cf., also no. 255.)

The Sages from Ezra to 70 C.E. were known as Soferim. After the Destruction they were called Rabbanim. The Isaiah Scroll is worthless to someone who wishes to probe the Masoretic text.

280. Jewish Apocryphal Literature, Solomon Zeitlin, editor-in-chief; *The Book of Tobit,* An English Translation with Introduction and Commentary by Frank Zimmermann. Published for the Dropsie College for Hebrew and Cognate Learning by Harper & Brothers (New York: 1958), pp. xii–190.

281. ישו הנצרי „מלך היהודים", זמנו, משפטו וצליבתו. עברית: ד"ר יוסף בר-לב, הוצאת ספרים מ. ניומן בע"מ, ירושלים תל-אביב, תשי"ט. Hebrew edition of "Who Crucified Jesus?" (Cf., nos. 105, 156, 239.)

1959

282. "The Dead Sea Scrolls," *The Jewish Spectator* (January 1959), Vol. XXIX, pp. 26–27. (Correspondence.)

The discovery (not the Scrolls per se) is a hoax. The assignment of the Scrolls to the pre-Christian era is theologically motivated.

The hyphen (*makif*) was introduced into Hebrew literature in the seventh century.

282a. "Different Slant," *The Christian Century* (January 7, 1959). Reply to W. F. Albright's "Return to Biblical Theology" in issue of November 19, 1958.

Normative Judaism arose and was shaped before the Herodian period, hence long before the compilation of the Mishnah.

Though there were dissenting views, the Sadducees followed the laws prescribed by the Pharisees.

The laws in the Scrolls are not Essenic, but were enacted long after the Destruction.

283. "Historical Studies of the Hebrew Liturgy," *JQR*, Vol. XLIX, No. 3 (January 1959), pp. 169–178.

The Pentateuch never mentioned a command to eat *maror* (bitter herbs) separately on the first night of Passover (as it does in the case of the command of sprinkling blood and that of eating unleavened bread). The Palestinian Talmud does not even include *maror* in its questions. Hillel ate it together with the paschal lamb and unleavened bread. Rabban Gamaliel of Jabneh introduced the practice of eating *maror* separately. He wished to delete the question of "dipping," since it was not applicable, but he was not succeessful. (Cf., nos. 159, 241.)

זכר למקדש כהלל cannot refer to Hillel's Temple practice, for then all three items were eaten together. Perhaps כהלל refers to the Amora Hillel who declared that one commandment can cancel out another. Hence eating the two, *matzah* and *maror*, together is permissible, contrary to the opinion of the Sages. Hillel's practice was adopted without the recital of a blessing.

The phrase in the New Moon liturgy . . . חברים כל ישראל should be rendered "Haberim (Sanhedrin members) [and] all Israel: the

New Moon is herewith proclaimed." The concluding words "let us say Amen" belong to the previous phrase "of in-gathering of the dispersed."

284. "More Literature on the Dead Sea Scrolls—More Pseudo-Scholarship," *JQR,* Vol. XLIX, No.3 (January 1959), pp. 221–238. Comments on periodical literature about the Dead Sea Scrolls and the following books: *The Lost Years of Jesus Revealed,* by Charles F. Potter; *The Excavation at Qumran,* by J. Van Der Ploeg; *The People of the Dead Sea Scrolls in Text and Pictures,* by J. M. Allegro; *L'Énigme des manuscrits de la Mer Morte,* by H. E. del Medico; and *The Historical Background of the Dead Sea Scrolls,* by Cecil Roth.

Both agnostics and fundamentalists maintain a pre-Christian dating for the Scrolls. Agnostics use the Scrolls to explore the fallacy of the cardinal principles of Christianity, and the theologians seek to find analogies to uphold the doctrines. The Scrolls thus have become a two-edged sword.

Nowhere in the Scrolls is the "Teacher of Righteousness" mentioned as a prophet or as "an intermediary" between God and his followers.

A Greek document bearing the name, Commodus, has been found. He was emperor from 180 to 192 C.E. How could such a document appear among Essene writings?

The Day of Atonement in 65 or 66 C.E. did not occur on a Saturday; hence a *Pesher Habakkuk* allusion to an event then has no meaning.

Hadassi, the Karaite, mentions a sect that maintained that the first day of Passover must be on a Thursday and the Day of Atonement on Sabbath. This is possible only if the Book of Jubilees were followed. This work was still extant in the Middle Ages. One cannot associate "Teacher of Righteousness" with "rebellious elder." The latter referred only to a member of the Sanhedrin who opposed its decisions.

285. "Dear Editor:" *The Chicago Jewish Forum,* Vol. XVII, No. 3 (Spring 1959), p. 172. Remarks about an article in the *Chicago Jewish Forum,* "Scholars on the Dead Sea Scrolls," by N. Mezvinsky. Also correspondence on Professor Monsoor's views on the Scrolls concerning the Shapira forgery.

286. "To the Editor," *Judaism,* Vol. VIII, No. 2 (Spring 1959), pp. 177–178. Remarks about Dr. Cecil Roth's article "The Zealots—A Jewish Religious Sect," which appeared in *Judaism,* Winter, 1959.

"Zealot" as a sect is first mentioned in *Wars* 2:22 (see no. 299). In the Bar Kokhba period the Judaean Christians were suspected of being spies for the Roman government.

287. "To the Editor," *Judaism,* Vol. VIII, No. 3 (Summer 1959), pp. 277–278. Remarks about Cecil Roth's rejoinder to a letter in *Judaism,* Spring 1959.

Josephus never used the word "Zealot" in *Antiquities* as a sect. It is often used only as an adjective.

There is a vast difference in meaning between the words "Gentile" and "uncircumcized."

288. "Who is a Jew? A Halakhic-Historic Study," *JQR,* Vol. XLIX, No. 4 (April 1959), pp. 241–270.

The question was raised with the Law of Return enacted when the State of Israel was established, namely that any Jew can become an Israeli citizen. Whether the term "Jew" applied to religion or nation first arose when the Jews were politically emancipated after the French Revolution.

Throughout the Middle Ages the Church looked upon the Jews as an ethnic group, and upon its religion also as ethnic—not universal. Jews, however, never asked themselves the question, because one born into or who embraced Judaism was a Jew.

Till the Restoration in 540 B.C.E., the term "Judaean" had a tribal connotation. During the Second Commonwealth those who lived in Judaea were called "Judaeans," but those in the Diaspora were "Hebrews." Circumcision then was not a *sine qua non* for proselytes, as is evident in the story of Hillel, and also in the story (related by Josephus) about the conversion of Izates. Only after the Destruction did circumcision become a requisite, as did baptism.

After the Destruction, the Jews called themselves "Israelites" to combat the contentions of the Christians. The term "Judaism" was used for the religion.

The Romans regarded the Jews as a religious community, and the *fiscus Judaicus* was a religious tax to emphasize Jupiter's victory over them.

When Christianity became the religion of Rome, the Church began to regard Judaism as an ethnic religion, not a *religio licita* any more, as did the Roman State. The Christians argued that Judaism had to be curbed because it was a "superstition." Jews, however, did not surrender their idea of a universal religion; Christianity then did not allow Jews to proselytize.

The unity of Jews is based on religion, and Judaism cannot be renounced; even atheists are considered to be a part of the Jewish community (cf., Kid. 36a).

In the Law of Return the view of the religious leaders carried weight. According to the ancient halakhah, the marriage between a Jew and a non-Jewish woman is not recognized. The children of such a union are not Jews, unless the mother accepted Judaism prior to her marriage. (Cf., no. 294.)

The term "Jew" on an identity card applies to those born into or professing Judaism. To have "Jew" alongside "Israeli" may lead to difficulties for the Jews in the Diaspora; there are Christian Israelis, too.

The religious leaders have no right to exclude any Jew. The bond between Jews in the Diaspora and those in Israel is strong. If Israel becomes an ordinary Levantine state, even if democratic, it will have no influence on Judaism and humanity.

289. "The Account of the Essenes in Josephus and the *Philosophumena*," *JQR*, Vol. XLIX, No. 4 (April 1959), pp. 292–300. Comments on an article in *HUCA*, Vol. 29 (1958), pp. 273 ff., "The Description of the Essenes in Josephus and the *Philosophumena*," by Prof. Morton Smith.

Josephus' passages on the Essenes were not copied from another source. By using the word *theosebeia* for religion, the author of *Philosophumena* (P.), Hippolytus, reveals that it was a text by a Christian author who copied passages, adding and deleting much. He gave a description of the Messiah whose advent the Jews anticipated in 371 C.E. and he used Hegesippus of the second century, a convert to Christianity who lived during the Bar Kokhba period of animosity. The Christians of the period sought to ingratiate themselves with Rome and disassociate from the Jews.

The word "Sicarii," coined by Josephus, is found in P. This too proves that its author was acquainted with Josephus, through Hegesippus.

Megillat Taanit does not list 15 Shebat as a day of no fasting.

It is absurd to speak of a "pre-Mishnaic" period for a text. Only a talmudist can determine the layers of the text.

290. "The Beginning of the Day in the Calendar of Jubilees," *JBL,* Vol. LXXVIII, No. 2 (June 1959), pp. 153–156.

The text in Jubilees 49: "By night, on the evening of the 15th," referring to the paschal offering, should correctly read: "by night on the eve (before) the 15th." *Erev* means before. (See no. 257.)

291. "Paul, the Apostle to the Gentiles," *JQR,* Vol. L, No. 1 (July 1959), pp. 89–90. Review of: *The Genius of Paul,* by Samuel Sandmel.

The Synoptic Gospels were written in Aramaic, as is revealed by the usage of the terms *geburah,* "right hand of power" (see no. 307), and "end of Sabbath" referring to Saturday night or Sunday (see no. 200). Moreover, unlike John, the genealogy of Jesus and the halakhic controversies that are recorded in the Synoptic Gospels are evidence that they were written for Jewish Christians.

It is wrong to state that Paul considered himself a Jew. He was interested in destroying Judaism, in preaching to and proselytizing among the Gentiles, and in creating a new religion based on the resurrection of Jesus. He was opposed to the Torah as well as to the Oral Law.

Jesus said that he did not come to destroy the Torah; Paul held that one should not uphold the "oldness of the letter." Jesus preached that the apostles should go to the lost sheep of Israel; Paul, however, was an apostle to the Gentiles. Paul substituted faith for Torah, and wanted Judaism to be superseded by this new religion and for the Jews to assimilate with the Gentiles. The Jews were right to regard Paul as an enemy of their people.

292. "To the Editor," *Tradition,* Vol. II, No. 1 (Fall 1959), pp. 175–187. Regarding the Dead Sea Scrolls.

A full analysis is presented of all the problems of the Scrolls, with rejoinders to many of the accepted arguments. The Scrolls cannot be of the Essenes because the sect came to the shores of the Dead Sea only after the Destruction of the Second Temple. The caves were a Genizah of the sectarians and Mourners of Zion during the Persian-Byzantine Wars and later, i.e., after the conquest of Palestine by the Arabs.

There is no Iranian vocabulary used in the Scrolls; any such Iranian influence was on Babylonian Jewry, much later.

1960

293. "Queen Salome and King Jannaeus Alexander. A Chapter in the History of the Second Jewish Commonwealth," *JQR,* Vol. LI No. 1 (July 1960), pp. 1–33.

John Hyrcanus had consolidated the country and unified the people but a rift soon took place with the Pharisees as he drew closer to the Sadducees. His son Aristobulus changed the Commonwealth to a monarchy, widening the breach. Inspired by his wife, Salome, he killed Antigonus, his brother. Judah the Essene may have known about the conspiracy of murder in Straton's tower, but disguised it as a prophecy. Salome later married Alexander Jannai while he was still an ordinary priest, before he assumed the throne and high priesthood. She was a sister of Simon ben Shetaḥ, but she failed to change Jannai's attitude toward the Pharisees. Jannai had been reared in Galilee and was suspicious of the Judaeans. The Pharisees opposed his wars and regarded him only as a secular ruler.

In those days, Cleopatra II, on the advice of the Alexandrian Jews, aided Jannai against her son Ptolemy. She gained control of Acco, but did not annex Judaea, in order not to arouse the antagonism of her Jewish subjects. Jannai was more Hellenistic than Judaean, and he used mercenaries, which meant heavy taxation. Popular animosity was displayed when he was pelted with ethrogim in the Temple. Jannai met defeat at the hands of the Nabateans. The Pharisees called in Demetrius II against Jannai because they disliked his monarchical rule; perhaps many felt there should be a return to a theocracy. Jannai lost to Demetrius of Syria, whereupon the Pharisees evinced a change of heart upon the realization of the consequences of the defeat. Nevertheless, Jannai vented his anger by crucifying six thousand Pharisees. He was then called *Thrakidos,* the Thracian, referring to his ferocious acts. He died a sick man and advised his wife Salome to yield to the Pharisees.

In Jannai's day, the Sadducees, who had opposed proselytism and were interested in ethnicism, now, for political reasons, adopted a policy of expansion and forced conversion. These conquered peoples were regarded by the Sadducees as second-class citizens.

The civil war of Jannai was basically a struggle between Pharisees and Sadducees who had become involved in politics. Herod's tyranny brought forth the Apocalyptic movement with its belief in a supernatural Messiah.

Though Salome was a pious woman, she was driven by desire for power. Her reign is generally regarded favorably, although it was successful only for her own time. She was well disposed to the Pharisees, but did not seek to settle the rift between the groups, rather encouraging the Pharisees to become more political, and avenge themselves on the Sadducees. Hence, as soon as she died, actual civil war broke out. Jannai's lack of diplomacy and Salome's viciousness thus brought on tragic consequences.

294. "The Offspring of Intermarriage," *JQR,* Vol. LI, No. 2 (October 1960), pp. 135–140.

The words in the Mishnah "She is believed," pertain to the ruling in regard to the offspring of a woman who had relations with a Kohen, that her child would be considered as of a priestly family. The law that a mother is the deciding factor in the status of her child was enacted, in fact, for political and religious reasons during the time of Nehemiah. The Samaritans insisted that the Temple be built on Mt. Gerizim. In order to have proper Zadokite priests, Sanballat, a Samaritan, gave his daughter in marriage to the grandson of the Judaean High Priest, so that his own grandson would be the rightful priest. To prevent this, and to ensure that the Temple would be in Jerusalem, it was enacted concerning the offspring of a mixed marriage that, where the mother is not a Jewess, the child is not Jewish. (Cf., no. 288.) Sanballat's daughter was a Samaritan; hence, even though the father was a High Priest, the child was not to be considered of priestly descent.

Another instance of the Rabbis' enacting a rule to protect the Temple in Jerusalem was the decree that land outside of Judaea be regarded as defiled. Thus, a shrine like the Onias Temple in Egypt was not acceptable.

295. "Recent Literature on the Dead Sea Scrolls: The Sicarii and the Zealots," *JQR,* Vol. LI, No. 2 (October 1960), pp. 156–169. Reviews of: *Ten Years of Discovery in the Wilderness of Judaea* by J. T. Milik; *The Dead Sea Community* by Kurt Schubert; *The Language and Linguistic Background of the Isaiah Scroll* by Eduard Yechezkel Kutsher; and a discussion of current periodical literature. To be continued. (Cf., no. 299.)

296. "Josephus and the Essenes: A Rejoinder," *Journal of Semitic Studies,* Vol. V, No. 4 (October 1960), p. 386.

The word *Zelotos* in *War* II, 444 means *studiosos,* zealous (an adjective); in 564: *affectantem,* "by disposition." Zealots as a noun (a party) is used for the first time in II, 2:22.1 (651).

297. "Zealots in the Jewish War," *Judaism,* Vol IX, No. 1 (Winter 1960), p. 81. Re: Mr. Isaiah Kitowsky's communication in *Judaism*, Vol. VIII, No. 4.

Generally, Josephus uses the term "zealot" in the connotation of "imitation, spirit and nature."

1961

298. "The Temple and Worship. A Study of the Development of Judaism. A Chapter in the History of the Second Jewish Commonwealth." *JQR,* Vol. LI, No. 3 (January 1961), pp. 209–241.

A detailed description is given of the Temple environs, functionaries, services, the priestly obligations and renumerations, and the daily procedure of public and private sacrifices.

The High Priest worshiped with covered head, unlike pagan priests. He wore a golden plate on his forehead inscribed only with the Tetragrammaton.

The Second Temple was called the *Bet ha-Mikdash,* "Holy House," in contrast to the First Temple, "House of God."

The absence of Cherubim, Urim and Tumim, and holy ointment in the Second Temple was due to the fact that the Jews were no longer henotheists, or even monotheists, but universalists. Emphasis was laid on the event of the Exodus as the spiritual basis of Judaism. There was now a new relationship between God and man: instead of *Tefillah,* "argument," it became "prayer." (Cf., no. 157.) Prophecy ceased because of the canonization of the Pentateuch.

The Bet ha-Midrash was an early academy for advanced study of the Pentateuch to legislate halakhot and to establish the common law as statutory law. Hence the word *dat* (*nomos,* law) became the accepted term for the Jewish religion. Laws introduced by the Soferim were meant to adjust and adapt religion to life.

299. "Recent Literature on the Dead Sea Scrolls, Socratic Irony," (continued from *JQR,* Vol. LI, 1960), *JQR,* Vol. LI, No. 3 (January 1961), pp. 254–261. (See no. 295.) Further comments on books and articles already reviewed and reviews of: E. F. Sutcliffe, *The Monks of Qumran;* A. Dupont-Sommer, *Les Écrits esseniens découverts près de la Mer Morte;* Kovalov and Kublanov, *Publication on the Dead Sea Scrolls* (in Russian); A. Powell Davies, *The Meaning of the Dead Sea Scrolls*; and T. H. Gaster, *The Dead Sea Scriptures.*

The term Galilean, as a designation for Christian, does not occur in the early Church Fathers. (See also no. 221.)

There are papyri letters of the fifth century C.E. that begin with the word "from," similar to the Bar Kokhba letter, thus indicating its late date of composition.

The Pharisees were in existence long before the appearance of the Hasidim (Essenes).

Daniel 7:25 refers to Antiochus IV's aim to change the festivals, not the calendar.

Josephus mentions the Zealots for the first time when he speaks of the establishment of the provisional government, and for the last time in the account of the capture of Jerusalem.

The Sicarii are mentioned during the time of Felix, 54 C.E., and also 73 C.E. Josephus traces them back to the period of the revolt in the time of the census of Quirinus.

The term "Zealot," as a sect, never occurs in *Antiquities.* (Cf., nos. 286, 287.) Josephus uses the term "Zealot" in *War* fifty times as a proper name, even after Menahem the Sicarius was assassinated. The

Zealots participated in the War; the Sicarii did not. Hence the Zealots cannot be associated with Menahem the Sicarius.

Josephus was the first to use the Latin *sicarii* as "robbers." Later it was used by Greek writers in Greek literature. It is found thus in Acts and in tannaitic literature.

300. "La Reine Salomé et le Roi Alexandre Jannée," *Evidences,* twelfth year, No. 87 (Paris: Janvier–Février 1961), pp. 37–42. (See no. 293.)

301. "The Fiction of the Bar Kokhba Letters," *JQR,* Vol. LI, No. 4 (April 1961), pp. 265–274.

The expression ערב שמיטה instead of ערב שביעית in the Scroll is very late. The date 130–131 C.E. for the Scroll (as a Sabbatical year) is chronologically incorrect.

The term רהומה, referring to the Romans, is not found in rabbinic literature. It occurs only in north Syrian inscription chronology, and was never used by the Romans or Jews.

The name בר כוכבא and בר כשבא—spelled in various ways—indicates that it is not genuine.

302. "Some Reflections on the Text of the Pentateuch," *JQR,* Vol. LI, No. 4 (April 1961), pp. 321–331. (See also no. 306.)

The examination of the ten places where there are dotted words in the Pentateuch, denoting errors, shows that these phrases were not in the original Pentateuchal text, but were inserted later.

Other examples of error are cited, as Exodus 34:25, where the reading חג הפסח is incorrect, since we already have זבח.

With the introduction of the *matres lectionis* and punctuation, many errors crept in, as in the word ערכך (Lev. 27:2).

This essay is also a criticism of many renderings in the new JPS translation, as ים המלח rendered as Dead Sea. Readings found in the rabbinic literature should be collated, and care taken in the instances of faulty vocalizations.

303. "Family Life in Israel," *JQR,* Vol. LI, No. 4 (April 1961), pp. 335–339. Review of: דיני משפחה מאת ד"ר בנציון שרשבסקי, ירושלים, ראובן מס, תשי"ח.

Historically, the necessity for witnesses was not in order to validate or legalize marriage, but to serve as proof against those who later might deny the marriage. (Cf., no. 276.)

The giving of the ring to a bride by the groom is never referred to in the Talmud. It was a custom of great antiquity among the Hellenes and Romans.

Originally the expression was כדת משה ויהודאי referring to Pentateuchal and Judaean customs. It was changed to כדת משה וישראל to counteract the Christians' claim that they were the true Israelites.

A minor cannot marry through the directive of his father, because intention by the groom is necessary.

According to Ezekiel, a Kohen can marry only a virgin of Israel. Rabbi Simon permitted marriage to the daughter of a proselyte. (See also no. 80.)

304. "Jewish Rights in Eretz Israel (Palestine)," *JQR,* Vol. LII, No. 1 (July 1961), pp. 12–34.

This is a refutation of the assertions of Professor Arnold Toynbee that Jews have no rights to Palestine.

Palestine as a whole was not the Holy Land to the early Christians. They were interested only in holy places, those connected with Jesus' birth, and they spoke only of a heavenly Jerusalem. Pope Urban II, in 1095, was the first to call the land *Terra Sancta.* In the religion of Islam, the focus is on Mecca, rather than on Jerusalem. To the Jews, as long ago as in the days of II Maccabees, Judaea was the Holy Land. (See no. 227.)

A historical survey proves that, with the changing rulers of Palestine, the Jews never left the area they called Land of Israel; they never renounced title to it, nor was there ever a period when there were no Jews there. The Palestinian Arabs never ruled Palestine; it had only been conquered by Arabs who came from the desert.

Military conquest alone, without legal annexation, is not valid. The rights of the Arabs were based on possession, but not on title. The statute of limitations does not apply to peoples whose countries were taken away by force, so long as they have not relinquished their legitimate rights. (See also no. 152.)

Though Toynbee retracted his description of Judaism as a fossil religion, he displays, in general, a lack of knowledge of Judaism, and he distorts its history. (See no. 252.)

305. "The Pharisees. A Historical Study," *JQR,* Vol. LII, No. 2 (October 1961), pp. 97–129.

"Pharisees" was an epithet applied to them by their adversaries, the Sadducees. At the time of the canonization of the Pentateuch differences arose pertaining to the halakhot, old unwritten laws, perhaps older than those in the written Pentateuch. The Sadducees maintained that only the laws in the Pentateuch are binding, not the oral law and customs. Sadducees would not punish one for nonobservance of the unwritten laws. The Pharisees felt that the unwritten laws were on a par with the written, and they further derived new laws from them.

The Sadducees believed in an ethnic God; the Pharisees, in a universal God. In the Pentateuch, the expression *"Adonai Yahweh"* does not occur.

The Pharisees molded Judaism and made it a living law, in consonance with actual life. (See no. 63.)

306. "Some Reflections on the Text of the Pentateuch," *JQR,* Vol. LII, No. 2 (October 1961), p. 130. Comment to article; unsigned. (Cf., also no. 302.)

In Deut. 1:32, "night" precedes "day," but in the parallel account, in Num. 14:14, "day" precedes "night." (See no. 137.)

Exodus 34:5 should be rendered: "And Yahweh passed before him and Yahweh proclaimed, 'Yahweh, God merciful and gracious.'" This agrees with the interpretations of the LXX, Targum Yerushalmi, Saadia, and Rabbenu Nissim.

307. "The Prophet from Nazareth," *JQR,* Vol. LII, No. 2 (October 1961), pp. 187–189. Review of: *The Prophet from Nazareth* by Morton Scott Enslin.

An understanding of New Testament terms will afford a better comprehension: "son of man" in the Gospels is based on a mistranslation of the Aramaic (it simply means "man"); "Right hand of Power" is simply *geburah,* a name for God.

Tannaitic literature and Josephus show that Jews had the right to impose capital punishment, before 70 C.E., even on foreigners who entered the Temple precincts.

308. Introduction: „על הספר", הקדמה ל„סנהדרין הגדולה" תולדותיו ופעולותיו של ב"ד הגדול בימי הבית השני, מאת שמחה בנימין הוניג, תורגם מאנגלית ע"י ד"ר ישראל אלדד, הוצאת מוסד הרב קוק, ירושלים תשכ"א.

The Great Sanhedrin that arose in the Second Commonwealth had vast jurisdiction over all aspects of life throughout Jewry until its abolition in the fifth century. This is noted in the Theodosian Code (*c.* 429 C.E.); its authority in calendation is also found in the talmudic records of the fourth century. For the restoration of the Sanhedrin, so vital today, one must first know its background and history.

1962

309. "The Need for a New Code," *JQR,* Vol. LII, No. 3 (January 1962), pp. 193–215.

Many early laws are now obsolete because of historical or social change. Rabbi Judah, the compiler of the Mishnah, in his codification presented some of R. Meir's views anonymously in order to make these laws acceptable, as opposed to the opinions of other Sages. The views of Rabbi Judah in the Tosefta belong to an earlier period.

There are layers, even in a section of the Mishnah, dating back to earlier compilations. Mishnah is second to the Torah. Rabbi Judah wanted the Mishnah to be an elastic code; hence he also recorded minority views.

Maimonides' Code and Caro's Code are static. Both were criticized by R. Solomon Luria as having been built on a foundation of errors.

Many features of Talmudic law, such as *Prosbol* and *ha'arama,* are here analyzed, emphasizing the difference between them. One is a *takkanah,* a modification of law, and the other is a loophole used by an individual.

The concept of *hefker Bet Din,* a court's declaring property *res nullius,* came into being after 70 C.E. The term שעבוד הגוף does not occur in the Talmud because, after the Restoration, the Sages abolished the right of a creditor over the person of a debtor, (see no. 325). Neither does the term ברירה occur in tannaitic literature; it was introduced by the Babylonian Amoraim who injected their interpretations into the tannaitic halakhot.

One must recognize the principle of intention, (cf., nos. 11, 26), as introduced by Hillel, in modifying many pentateuchal laws, as well as in the statutes not recorded in the Pentateuch but introduced by the Sages. Among these are possession, partnership, agency, and testamentary succession.

The Palestinian Talmud should be considered as a factor in any codification, and a codifier must be aware of the reasons for the enactment of the law.

The need is for a corpus of halakhot based on historical development, and not on a dogmatic approach. The corpus of the Second Commonwealth halakhah should become the basis for the Code of the Third Commonwealth. It must be in the spirit that laws are made for man to promote his progress. (See nos. 191, 193, 346.)

310. "The Hidden Years of Jesus of Nazareth," *JQR,* Vol. LII, No. 3 (January 1962), pp. 279–281. Review of: *Jesus of Nazareth. The Hidden Years,* by Robert Aron.

The early life of Jesus is still unknown. The practice of opening a door for Eliyahu, and the Star of David as a Jewish symbol, are features that were introduced in the Middle Ages. The custom of Bar Mitzvah or wearing a *Talit Katan* are also of a late period. *Kaddish* had not been composed in Judaea in the time of Jesus.

311. "La Palestine est-elle Eretz Israel? Arnold Toynbee—Salomon Zeitlin," *Evidences,* thirteenth year, No. 91 (Paris: Janvier 1962), pp. 36–42. French translation of the Toynbee-Zeitlin debate (cf., no. 304).

312. "The Fallacy of the Antiquity of the Hebrew Scrolls Once More Exposed," *JQR,* Vol. LII, No. 4 (April 1962), pp. 346–366. Review of: *Discoveries in the Judaean Desert II. Les Grottes de Murabba'at,* by P. Benoit, J. T. Milik, and R. de Vaux; *The Judaean Desert Caves: Archaeological Survey,* 1960, by Yigael Yadin; *The Essene Writings from Qumran,* by A. Dupont-Sommer; also comments on periodical literature.

The carbon-14 test applied to the textiles of Murabba'at yield a date *ca.* 546–566 C.E. This invalidates the claims of antiquity.

A newly found document notes the second year of Nero's reign as a Sabbatical year. The explanation is that Nero became emperor in October, 54. The Sabbatical year began September, 54. Nero's second year was counted from January 1, 55. Hence, it is the second year which was Sabbatical.

There is no dualism in the *Assumption of Moses*. The legend about the body of Moses is in the Midrash, not in the *Assumption,* composed after 70 C.E. Origen copied from the Midrash. The *anno mundi* reckoning came into use only after 70 C.E.

The belief in immortality and reward and punishment after death are not found in the Scrolls, although the Essenes believed in these concepts.

During the Second Commonwealth foreign pagan slaves owned by the Jews were not obligated to be circumcized. This law was introduced much later.

The War Scroll is similar to the ninth or tenth-century *Shilte Gibborim,* describing tactics of warfare.

Could not the skeletons found in Qumran be of the period of Heraclius?

313. "Correspondence. Arnold Toynbee and Solomon Zeitlin," *JQR,* Vol. LII, No. 4 (April 1962), pp. 367–381. Concerning the article, "Jewish Rights in Eretz Israel." (See no. 304.)

In reply to Toynbee's thesis that "human rights (of Arabs) override historical claims (of Jews)," one must remember that the United Nations has as yet "been unable to draft and define the principle of human rights in a manner acceptable to all members." It cannot be said that "Israel is occupying territory not belonging to her," if Israel has been recognized as a state by the U.N.

Jews did not expel Arabs; the Arabs fled on orders of the Arab League. Israel has given equal citizenship to the Arabs who remained.

There is evidence of a great population of Jews in Palestine in the time of Heraclius, which was greatly reduced by the activities of the Crusades. Jews had sovereignty in Palestine under the Patriarchs until 415 C.E. when Theodosius I removed Gamaliel VI, and have always looked forward to the Restoration. That privilege should not be denied by the world.

314. *Jewish Rights in Palestine* by Arnold J. Toynbee. *Jewish Rights in Eretz Israel* (*Palestine*) by Solomon Zeitlin. Correspondence, from *JQR,* Vol. LII, Nos. 1 & 4 (1961 and 1962), pp. 49. (Reprint of nos. 304, 313.)

315. "The Hallel. A Historical Study of the Canonization of the Hebrew Liturgy," *JQR,* Vol. LIII, No. 1 (July 1962), pp. 22–29. (See also no. 157.)

Hallel is much older than the Hasmonean period, perhaps even than the Persian, when the sanctuary was still called "House of God." "House of David" is not mentioned therein; "Fearers of God" may refer to non-Jews who feared Yahweh.

The *Hallel* was first recited in the Temple. After 70 C.E. it was made part of the liturgy of the Synagogue. Its recitation on the first day of Passover took the place of the custom of reciting it at the time of slaughtering the sacrifice: it was also recited in the Temple on the eight days of Hanukkah. The recital of a section of *Hallel* (Psalms 113 and 114) before grace on Passover was according to the school of Hillel. Those who could not recite the *Hallel* at their table went to the Synagogues. The recital was a form of community singing; it was not to be abridged. In Judaea the full *Hallel* was always recited. In Babylon, the *Hallel* for the New Moon and the other six days of Passover was introduced, but in an abridged form. The recital of a blessing even for the full *Hallel* was introduced after the talmudic period; there is no reference to it in the Talmud.

Full *Hallel* is only for those days specified in the Palestinian Talmud; an abridged *Hallel* is a Babylonian custom. Since there was no blessing for the abridged *Hallel* there should be no objection to its recital on 5 Iyar, the Independence Day of Israel.

316. "The Trial of Jesus," *JQR,* Vol. LIII, No. 1 (July 1962), pp. 77–88. Review of: *The Trial of Jesus* by Josef Blinzler.

There are no references to Jesus in the Palestinian Talmud, and it is strange that such are found in the Babylonian where there were no Judaean Christians! All references to Jesus in Hebrew literature are of a late, medieval period and have no value as basic historical sources of Jesus' time. (See also no. 356.)

The notion that the Crucifixion was on a Wednesday, following a solar calendar, is erroneous, for Jews could not have followed a sectarian calendar for any Temple service.

The divergence between the Synoptic Gospels and John is only theological. It cannot be said that Jesus was condemned for blasphemy because he used a substitution title (*geburah*=Power); such a use of a name for God was not considered blasphemous. (Cf., no. 307.)

There is no reference in rabbinic literature to any source that intimated that the Jews practiced the custom of granting amnesty to a prisoner on Passover.

It is erroneous to say that the Sanhedrin which tried Jesus was Sadducean; the latter had to follow Pharisaic law, as indicated by Josephus. That the Court met on Friday is impossible; indeed, Augustus Caesar even decreed that Jews should not be compelled to come to Roman courts on Friday after 3 P.M. (See no. 348.)

Evidence cannot be drawn from Megillat Taanit, for there are no references in it to the victories of Pharisees over Sadducees, (cf., no. 70).

The Sanhedrin of the Jesus trial was one that was especially summoned; it was not a regular session of the court. Crucifixion was a Roman method of execution. The Roman practice was to publish on the cross the reason for the execution. Jesus was crucified as a political offender by Roman authorities; the Romans never interfered in the religious laws of other peoples. (See no. 105.)

Reproofs directed against *Perushim* in the Talmud refer only to individuals who separated themselves from mundane life to demonstrate their piety; these have no bearing on Pharisees in general.

No scholar held the title "Rabbi" during the Second Commonwealth; hence, it cannot be applied to Jesus.

317. "The Dead Sea Scrolls," *Proceedings of the XXVth International Congress of Orientalists, Moscow, 9–16 August* 12, 1960, Vol. I (Moscow: 1962), pp. 350–352. Abridged version of paper read at the Congress. (Cf., no. 235a.)

The paper was introduced in Russian with personal reminiscences by Professor S. Zeitlin, who said, "Russia was the country of my early Jewish studies, providing the foundation and tools to deal authoritatively with the Scrolls. It was also the place of my probing the Slavonic Josephus manuscripts, proving its medieval provenance. This opinion has now been widely accepted."

"As a non-conformist pertaining to the Scrolls, my opinions are based on the terms, words, laws, mode of writing, the form of the Bar Kokhba letters, the inaccuracies concerning the discovery, etc., etc. My arguments against the antiquity of the Hebrew Scrolls have never been refuted."

318. "Korban," *JQR,* Vol. LIII, No. 2 (October 1962), pp. 160–163.

The biblical term *korban,* "sacrifice," meant also "vow" in the time of the Second Commonwealth. At a later time it was applied also to prayer. LXX renders it as "gift." The word in Mark means "vow." The words "that is, a gift" were added later by a scribe, following LXX. The translation of *korban* as "oblation" has a christological connotation, (cf., no. 380).

319. "There Was No Synagogue in the Temple," *JQR,* Vol. LIII, No. 2 (October 1962), pp. 168–169.

Mishnah Middot, Josephus, and the architectural plan of the Temple do not reveal any synagogue in the Temple. Scholars wrongly relied on a later addition in the Palestinian Talmud.

The version about the *Bet ha-shoebah* festivity in the Tosefta is the original. (See no. 202.)

Rosh knesset in Yoma means "head of assembly"—not "head of the synagogue."

320. "Bouleuterion and Parhedrion," *JQR,* Vol. LIII, No. 2 (October 1962), pp. 169–170.

The term *Parhedrion* may be derived from *paredros,* "assessors." Originially, the council chamber was known as *bouleuterion*; later it was called, satirically, *parhedrion,* for the High Priests were coadjutors, lieutenants of the Roman authorities.

321. "Zealots and Sicarii," *JBL,* Vol. LXXXI, Part IV (December 1962), pp. 395–398. Review of: Martin Hengel's *Die Zeloten.*

The Sicarii (Fourth Philosophy party), founded by Judas the Galilean in 6 C.E., are not mentioned in the writings of Josephus dealing with 65–70 C.E. since they did not participate in the War against the Romans. They appeared in the historical arena again only in 72 C.E. (Cf., also no. 299.)

The Zealots were not a messianic movement. Abba Sikra is called Resh Biryana; this is an explanatory clause.

322. *Studies and Essays in Honor of Abraham A. Neuman,* Edited by Meir Ben-Horin, Bernard D. Weinryb, Solomon Zeitlin. E. J. Brill (Leiden: 1962), pp. xiii–649. Introduction by Solomon Zeitlin, pp. vii–xiii.

Early Jewish historiography consisted of chronicles. Since facts alone do not make history, the function of the historian is to explain, give the causes, and trace the influences of events. History is both a science and an art, requiring technical knowledge and vision.

323. "Johanan the High Priest's Abrogations and Decrees," *Studies and Essays in Honor of Abraham A. Neuman* (Leiden, 1962), pp. 569–579.

This is a historic analysis of Mishnah Masser Sheni 5:15. From the period of the Restoration, the tax-burden was heavy on the "Am ha-aretz," landed folk and farmers, who supported the priests and the state. With the Ptolemaic rule, a third, middle class developed, consisting of artisans, traders, military and working people, and land tenants. This class expanded with the Commonwealth of the Hasmoneans to include the seafaring, and others. John Hyrcanus, after conquering much territory, settled Judaeans there as tenants of the state. (Cf., no. 39.)

According to the Pentateuch the owners of the land had to make a confession when they brought the first fruits. John Hyrcanus abolished the confession in connection with the tithe because the land belonged to the state.

The farmers resented the burden of taxation which fell upon them and not on the urban population; they did not give the tithe to the Levites. Therefore, John Hyrcanus abolished the ceremonial ritual. Since the economic condition of the Levites was impaired, he "decreed on the demoi," the common people, that they give the tithe.

The term *demoi* does not mean "doubt." It is used only in the context of agrarian matters, and refers to the "produce of the people." The mode of identification is a shortened characteristic language usage, common in early tradition, as in "formula of the *ketubah*" or "declaratory note, *Pros-Boule* before the Court."

Resentment developed between the farmers and the urban population, particularly those scrupulous about levitical purity who suspected the farmers of not observing the levitical laws. This latter group was known as *ḥaberim*—associates for levitical purity. Thus, social strife arose.

Basically, the term *ḥaber* is used only in opposition to *am ha-aretz*—farmer. After the Destruction, new meanings were given—*am ha-aretz* meant "ignorant" and *ḥaber*, "learned."

During the Seleucidan period the priest's prayer was Psalm 44, an appeal to God, as it were, to be aroused and redeem His people. With the Hasmonean stability of the state, John Hyrcanus abolished this recital. This is the reference in the Mishnah "He abolished the 'Awakeners.'" The practice was to "beat with hammers," a symbolic implementation, to awaken. The Mishnah therefore refers also to the abolition of the "knockers" associated with the "awakeners," (מעוררין).

324. *The Rise and Fall of the Judaean State. A Political, Social and Religious History of the Second Commonwealth, Volume I.* 332–37 B.C.E., The Jewish Publication Society (Philadelphia: 1962), pp. xxi + (1) + 528. (See also no. 362.)

This volume, the culmination of fifty years of research, crystallizes in a popular form the newest in Jewish historical study. It demonstrates that the history of the Second Temple era is derived basically from the sources of halakhah and not merely from Aggadah and nonrabbinic sources, although Josephus, Philo, Apocrypha, Gospels and classical writers are essential.

To understand the Second Commonwealth one must see it in terms of the daily life of the people, their struggles—economic, political, social, sectarian—and also their relationship to the outside world—the Greek and Roman environment.

Volume One is devoted to the *Rise.* It discusses the Return from the Exile, Judaism confronting Hellenism, the emergence of the independent Hasmonean state, the social and religious development of the early centuries just before the Common Era, and the kingdom of the last Hasmoneans till the rise of Herod.

New insights are perceived, for example, that the conflicts of the Pharisees and Sadducees were not concerned merely with interpretation of verses, or written law versus oral law, but rather with concepts of ethnicism versus universalism.

The ancient Judaeans were not impressed by the beauty of the images of the Greeks and Romans. Jews were not opposed to art, they objected only to images representing human beings. Though there had been mutual influences of linguistic and of a literary-intellectual nature, fundamental Judaism was not influenced by Hellenism. The Judaean teachers emphasized that the survival of the Judaeans lay only through their religion.

The study includes the religious divisions of the time, the Bet Din, the Calendar, Festivals and Holy Days, the Temple, Religious Faith and Practice, the literature of the biblical and Apocryphal books, and Judaean society and economy. It is well annotated with continuous reference to the manifold articles in *JQR* and other scholarly journals, wherein the full details, research, and proof are given.

Especially significant is that the inter-Testamental period is not hampered by the usual emphasis on Judaism as "the forerunner of Christianity," and it demonstrates that to understand even Greek and Roman civilization one must utilize rabbinic sources.

1963

325. "Slavery During the Second Commonwealth and the Tannaitic Period," *JQR,* Vol. LIII, No. 3 (January 1963), pp. 185–218.

The Jewish Sages taught that slaves were human beings and were to be accorded humane treatment, but they did not advocate the abolition of slavery. In the Bible slavery is bondage limited by time.

In the Second Commonwealth, as recorded by Josephus, if a thief could not pay the fine, he was sold into slavery. Later talmudic law limited the period of enslavement to covering the amount stolen. Josephus also records that the plaintiff had the right to enslave the thief; it was a private wrong, like that of injury or bodily mutilation. The maimed person had the right to apply the law of *talio.* This was abolished later, through the use of a legal fiction, on the basis of size, color, etc., of each eye.

The law of enslaving debtors became obsolete when the Jubilee year was eliminated. A creditor then had the right only to the property, not to the person of a debtor.

The law that a slave sold into a foreign land becomes free was to counteract the effect of Herod's "housebreakers' " law. Thus it became imperative for Jews to ransom Jewish slaves. (See also no. 350.)

326. "Josippon," *JQR,* Vol. LIII, No. 4 (April 1963), pp. 277–297.

The date of its composition is in the third or the early part of the fourth century C.E., before the redaction of the Talmud. Hegesippus, during the fourth century, made use of *Yosippon.* The Mantua edition is the closest to the *Ur-Yosippon*; many additions not in the

Ur-Yosippon were made later. The author was acquainted with the story of the martyrdom of Eleazar and of the mother and her seven sons, as narrated in II and IV Maccabees. Hence it cannot be said that *Yosippon* was composed during the Crusades and reflects that martyrology. The story of the coronation of Otto is likewise a later addition.

Most of the letters in *Yosippon* are copies of Josephus, with the name of the sender first (without the preposition "from"). Only later were letters used with "from" preceding the name of the sender.

The author of *Yosippon* had the original text of Josephus and was acquainted with Greek and with some works of the Church Fathers. He also knew the Pliny narrative of the caesarian birth of Julius Caesar. The author did not record the late talmudic story of the Hanukkah miracle, but only the Maccabean version.

327. "Herod, A Malevolent Maniac," *JQR,* Vol. LIV, No. 1 (July 1963), pp. 1–27.

Herod was a Jew, a descendant of Idumean proselytes; however, Idumea is employed only as a geographic term. According to the Pharisees, anyone who accepted Judaism was the spiritual descendant of the Patriarchs.

After the battle of Actium, Herod went to Octavian Caesar in fear, not because of his previous friendship with Antony, but because of the difficulty of the internal situation in Judaea. Generally, Roman rulers welcomed traitors who renounced their allegiance to their rivals.

The accounts in Josephus that the 6000 Pharisees had to pay a fine because they would not take the oath of allegiance refers to the Apocalyptic Pharisees, who stressed the ideas of a supernatural Messiah, foreknowledge, and Divine intervention. This group differed from the Fourth Philosophy (Sicarii) who believed in the use of arms. The Quietist Pharisees, however, who followed Pollion (Hillel), showed their loyalty and did not have to take the oath.

The Essenes, too, were absolved from taking the oath of allegiance because they would not take the name of God in vain. They also held that anyone who became a ruler obtained his position through the will of God. Hence Herod respected their views.

The writings of Josephus reveal that Herod was paranoiac. He believed that he was destined by God to rule. The Judaeans hated and feared him; the Jews of the Diaspora admired him since, through his friendship with Caesar, they received many benefits. They were known as Herodians.

328. "Mumar and Meshumad," *JQR,* Vol. LIV, No. 1 (July 1963) pp. 84–86.

The original talmudic texts had the word *meshumad* instead of *mumar.* In the Second Commonwealth a Jew who embraced another religion was called *mumar,* "changed." This was also the designation for one who accepted Judaism.

The term *ger,* proselyte (biblically, a stranger) came into use after the Destruction; *mumar* was then applied to a Jew who willingly became an apostate. A Jew who was forced under threat of death to adopt another religion was called a *meshumad.* Later, the term was used for any apostate because, generally, they were informers; *meshumad* then gained the connotation of "one deserving extinction." Still later, the appellation was applied to any Jew who transgressed laws or who was immoral.

Christian censors, who were generally apostates, altered the texts to read *mumar,* though the Palestinian Talmud has the original correct reading of *meshumad.*

329. "A Reply," *JQR,* Vol. LIII, No. 4 (April 1963), pp. 345–349. Replies to Hershel Shanks' article, "Is the Title 'Rabbi' Anachronistic in the Gospels?"

Internal evidence, not the *Epistle of Sherira,* is the source of the information that the term "Rabbi" was not used in the Second Commonwealth period. "Rabban" means "our nasi" and is not derived from the biblical "rav" (great, considerable).

The Gospel of John, written in the middle of the second century, contains the term "rabbi" which was already then in use, but had to be explained as "teacher" for the benefit of the Gentiles. (See no. 232.)

330. "The Expression *BeTalmud* in the Scrolls Militates Against the Views of the Protagonists of Their Antiquity," *JQR,* Vol. LIV, No. 2 (October 1963), pp. 89–98.

B'Talmud, in the Scrolls, does not refer to the Pharisees. Only after the completion of the Talmud (*c.* 500 C.E.) could such a term be used. (See no. 342.)

331. "Hillel and the Hermeneutic Rules," *JQR,* Vol. LIV, No. 2 (October 1963), pp. 161–173.

Examining the texts of the Palestinian and Babylonian Talmud, and the Tosefta pertaining to Hillel's arguments about the paschal lamb on the Sabbath, one will note variations. The logic of *kal v'homer* (inference from minor to major) is found in the Bible; it is not Hellenistic. Hillel did not invent the principle.

Gezerah shavah is "a comparison with the equal subject"; it is not a result of Greek terminology (*syncrisis*). The principle of analogy had already been used by Simon b. Shetaḥ, although the term is late. *Gezerah* is the translation for *hok* (statute).

Originally, inference by analogy of equal laws applied both to equal rules and verbal congruity. Later the analogy of equal halakhah and expression was called *gezerah shavah.* The analogy of equal subject was later called *hikish*; the principles, however, existed long before.

Hillel, in his use of these hermeneutic rules, aimed to apply them to the unwritten laws and make the custom of slaughtering the paschal lamb on the Sabbath a statutory law. This event occurred on the fourteenth of Nisan, a Sabbath, 31 B.C.E. It was an intercalated year (having two Adars), so that Passover should occur in the spring.

332. "The Fallacy of the Antiquity of the Hebrew Scrolls Once More Exposed," *The Gates of Zion,* Vol. 18, No. 1 (October, Tishri 5724, 1963), pp. 8–10. To be continued. Reprinted from *JQR.* (See no. 312.)

333. *In the Time of Harvest. Essays in Honor of Abba Hillel Silver on the Occasion of His* 70*th Birthday,* editor, Daniel Jeremy Silver; Board of Editors: Solomon B. Freehof, Emanuel Neumann, Daniel Jeremy Silver, Solomon Zeitlin; The Macmillan Company (New York); Collier-Macmillan Ltd. (London), 1963.

334. "The Origin of the Idea of the Messiah" (see previous number). *In the Time of Harvest* (1963), pp. 447–459.

The expectation of a Messiah made Jewish survival possible, but the messianic movement also brought much suffering and degradation, like that caused by Shabbatai Zevi.

The term *mashiah* means "anointed," and applied to one appointed by God. Thus the priests were anointed, as were also Saul, David, and even Cyrus. It was always an adjective "anointed of Yahweh." In the Second Commonwealth priests and kings were not anointed.

There is no indication in the Bible of a personal—natural or supernatural—Messiah. Since the Church Fathers interpreted biblical passages as referring to Jesus as the *Christos,* the Rabbis interpreted these very same passages as referring to the Jewish *mashiah.* The expectation of a millenium—of peace and no war—is not the expectation of a personal Messiah. We must differentiate between the concepts of a millenium and a Messiah. The word *mashiah* does not occur in the Apocryphal literature; the idea of a supernatural Messiah is found in the apocalyptic literature written after the time of Herod. The normative Pharisees believed in the coming of a Messiah, but differed from the Apocalyptists in that they held that he would not be supernatural or the product of a miracle. The terms "son of David" and "King Mashiah" are synonymous.

After the collapse of the Bar Kokhba rebellion, the belief in a supernatural Messiah gained adherents, as well as the expectation that he would rebuild the Temple and establish the Jewish State. This, however, did not become an article of faith. Rabbi Judah ha-Nasi does not refer (in Mishnah Sanhedrin 10:1) to the coming of the Messiah, in connection with the dogmas of Revelation and Resurrection. In time, however, the belief in a supernatural Messiah gained popularity and became one of the cornerstones of Jewish survival.

335. "Talmud," *Encyclopedia Britannica,* Vol. 21 (1963), pp. 768–770 (7 columns). (Same volume number and pagination in 1964 edition.) Also bibliography to article, on p. 770.

The Jews had unwritten as well as written laws. There are many references to customs not found in the Pentateuch, such as the requirement of a deed, and witnesses in the transfer of real property (cf. Jeremiah 32:25), and enslavement by a creditor. The unwritten laws were perhaps older than some contained in the Pentateuch. Many nations felt that the unwritten (common) law was superior to the written (cf. the opinion of Aristotle).

The breach between the Pharisees and Sadducees was created because of the insistence of the Sadducees that the unwritten laws were less binding than the pentateuchal laws. Transgressors against the unwritten laws could not be punished like those who violated Torah laws. The Pharisees maintained that the pentateuchal laws could be embellished and amended by the Soferim (scribes) to conform to changing conditions, as in the case of the rules of levitical purity, the washing of hands, rules about carrying on the Sabbath, ritualistic slaughter, etc.

The oral tradition expresses the spirit of the law. Thus, civil legislation was interpreted in rules of torts, laws of partnership, the idea of testament and rights of seizure of the property, not the person, of a debtor. The use of promissory notes modified the pentateuchal law of the Sabbatical year. *Lex talionis* was abolished.

The Sages sought to turn the halakhot into statutory laws in order to be able to derive new laws. This gave rise to different schools of thought—the conservative Shammaites and the liberal Hillelites. To establish a legal system of interpretation, Hillel applied three hermeneutic devices which were later amplified. (Cf., no. 331.)

After the Bar Kokhba rebellion the Sages decided to collect the halakhot. Some felt that the collection should be made according to the biblical sequence of text: this is the *Midrash Mikra*—Mekhilta, Sifra and Sifre; others preferred to arrange the halakhot according to subject matter. The latter prevailed, becoming the Mishnah, *deuterosis,* compiled by Rabbi Judah ha-Nasi. The halakhic decisions in the Mishnah became binding.

An analysis of the six orders of the Mishnah shows that the texts were compiled at different times, representing different sequences. Being a code, it lacked *haggadot* and ignored messianic and eschatological ideas.

The opinions of the minority are included in the Talmud so that in the future the Rabbis could find support for new laws and enactments.

Unlike the Pentateuch which was considered divine, or the Roman code derived from secular authority, the Rabbis considered that the authority of the Mishnah derived basically from their own interpretation and knowledge.

There is a controversy about the actual writing down of the Mishnah. Internal evidence shows that not only the Mishnah was written down, but that many halakhot had been put into writing long before R. Judah's time. The interdict was not to put into writing any customs or oral laws not yet made statutory.

Rabbi Judah did not include laws that had become obsolete. Many of these are in the Tosefta, containing eschatological notions. The word *Gehinnom* is not in the Mishnah.

Other halakhot are found in the *Baraitot*—"outside" texts. Both Tosefta and Baraitot are as important as the Mishnah itself for the history of the religious and social life of the Jews. In the Mishnah as a code, the laws are presented in legal form; in the Tosefta, some laws are illustrated by parables.

The Mishnah attained canonical authority soon after its completion. The Sages who expounded the Mishnah were the Amoraim. Their work is the Gemara, which constitutes both a commentary on and interpretation of the Mishnah.

There is a Palestinian Talmud from which many tractates are missing. The reason for the omission is not known. Perhaps these were lost. The Palestinian academies were in Tiberias, Caesarea, and Acco. By the end of the fourth century these ceased to exist, and the Palestinian Talmud came to an abrupt end.

In Babylonia, in Sura and Pumbedita, great yeshivot arose.

The Babylonian Talmud was completed by Rabina (*ca.* 499 C.E.). The Saboraim ("reflectors") of the sixth and seventh centuries explained the terminology and added interpretations. Sometimes, because of lack of manuscripts, it is difficult to recognize the differences between Amoraim and Saboraim. The work of the Saboraim was carried on by the Geonim. The Babylonian Talmud became the standard authority.

Some of the halakhot in the Talmud are academic and even casuistic. The Palestinian Talmud reveals a marked influence of Roman law, whereas the Babylonian Talmud contains Parthian customs.

There are many *haggadot* dealing with theological and historical problems in the Talmud. Babylonian superstitions also figure prominently, but the rabbis deplored superstition and dream interpretation. The Geonim conceded that *Haggadah* was not authoritative.

The Palestinian Talmud has no mention of Christianity. That which is contained in the Babylonian Talmud is only the result of hearsay.

The Church Fathers attacked the Mishnah. In the sixth century, Justinian prohibited its reading. In the Middle Ages the Christians frequently burned the Talmud and censored its teachings. The Karaites and the Enlightenment were antagonistic to it. In modern yeshivot Talmud is still the major subject of study as a portion of sacred tradition.

The best commentary is that of Rashi. A critical edition of the Talmud is still urgently needed; it is a dense forest, and one needs expert guidance in its study.

1964

336. "The Fallacy of the Antiquity of the Hebrew Scrolls Once More Exposed," II (continued from October 1963 issue), *The Gates of Zion,* Vol. 18, No. 2 (January 1964), pp. 2–4. Reprint. (Cf., no. 312.)

337. "The Tefillah, The Shemoneh Esreh: A Historical Study of the First Canonization of the Hebrew Liturgy," *JQR,* LIV, No. 3 (January 1964), pp. 208–249.

In very early times appeals to God were made in terms of bargaining (*tefillah*), arguing and vow (*neder*), or in terms of conditional promise. Later connotations developed and *tefillah* became praying, begging (*preces*), and *neder,* a vow without stipulation. (See no. 157.)

There were no standard formal prayers, except perhaps that of the High Priest on the Day of Atonement. A supplicant, before offering his personal plea, would make his confession and give praise.

When Judaea was subject to sovereign states, sacrifices had to be offered for their rulers. When Rome subjugated Judaea, sacrifices were offered for Caesar; after 70 C.E., it was suggested that prayers be offered for the peace of the Roman Empire; we find mention of this by R. Ḥaninah, Baruch I, and Clement of the first century.

In the *Maamadot* in Judaea the Pentateuch was read. This is the origin of the Synagogue Assembly (*knesset*) which, originally, was not a place of prayer, but of instruction. (Cf., no. 38.)

The *tefillah* as arranged in Jabneh originally consisted of seventeen blessings. The eighteenth prayer "against apostates," was added soon after, also in Jabneh. The prayer for "the stem of David" was added about one hundred years later, becoming the nineteenth; it was originally included in the prayer for the restoration of Jerusalem. There is no mention of Messiah in the *tefillah.*

The fifty-first chapter of the Hebrew Ben Sira contains certain allusions to *Shemoneh Esreh,* but this is a medieval translation from the Syriac. The doxology of the *Shemoneh Esreh* is echoed by the Church Father, Clement.

Rosh Hashanah became recognized as a Day of Judgment after the period of Jabneh, hence the inclusion then of *Malkhuyot, Zikhronot, Shofrot* prayers.

338. "The Fallacy of the Antiquity of the Hebrew Scrolls Once More Exposed," *The Freethinker,* Vol. LXXXIV, No. 11 (London: Friday, March 13, 1964), pp. 83 and 86. Reprint. (Cf., no. 312.)

339. "The Sadducees and the Belief in Angels," *JBL,* Vol. LXXXIII, Part I, March 1964, pp. 67–71.

According to the Pentateuch and Prophets, Yahweh is the ethnic God of the descendants of the Patriarchs and of those who left Egypt, i.e., the God of the Judaeans alone. The Pentateuch does not recognize conversion and this ethnic concept was maintained by the Sadducees. There is no concept of universalism in the Pentateuch; this concept appears only vaguely in some passages in the later Prophets.

In the Pentateuch we do have instances of angels (emissaries) who appear in human form to commune with individuals. In the prophetic books, angels are pictured as supernatural, as inflicting a plague on David, and as smiting the hosts of Sennacherib. The prophets were the emissaries of God. With the Restoration, prophecy ceased. The Bible became the source of God's word. The Sadducees adhered only to the written law: they did not believe in angels, because with the advent of prophecy, the function of angels—divine emissaries—ceased. The Pharisees believed in a direct communion with God, for Israel exclusively, but they also believed in angels as being appointed for other nations.

In Judaean apocryphal literature there is no mention of angels. In the Diaspora literature which was influenced by the Persians, we do find references to angels, but in tannaitic literature, which is Pharisaic, the belief in angels is almost ignored.

340. "Prof. Zeitlin Answers a Critic on Scrolls," *The National Jewish Post and Opinion,* Vol. XIX, No. 30 (Friday, April 3, 1964), p. 4.

Yadin's interview which indicated that some of the material from Masada was of the Byzantine period could mean that a number of people took refuge then in the fortress, and dwelt there for some time.

There were no houses of worship in Judaea in the Second Commonwealth period. Whence a synagogue in Masada?

341. "The Takkanot of Rabban Johanan ben Zakkai," *JQR,* Vol. LIV, No. 4 (April 1964), pp. 288–310.

The Temple was destroyed on Sunday the ninth of Ab, 70 C.E. In 71, Rosh Hashanah was on a Sabbath. Rabban Johanan ben Zakkai held that the Bet Din of Jabneh took the place of the Temple for worship, and he suggested blowing the shofar there. So, also, the first day of Sukkot was on a Saturday and Rabban Johanan introduced a *takkanah* that the lulab should be carried on all seven days, as was the custom in the Temple. He also introduced the *takkanah* that witnesses for the new moon could be received during the entire day, since sacrifices were no longer offered; also, as previously done in the Temple, priests should not wear sandals while offering their blessing. He abolished the custom of a proselyte bringing a sacrifice; and decreed that the new harvest may be eaten immediately on the sixteenth of Nisan. (The erroneous change to "forbidden" is saboraic.)

The different debates recorded between Rabban Johanan ben Zakkai and the Sadducees have no historical basis. The matter of inheritance by a daughter is a question of testamentary succession by a *diatheke* (will), and was introduced by the Pharisees long before Rabban Johanan ben Zakkai's era. (Cf., no. 367.)

The determination of the day of the Festival of Weeks is only a question of the time of the Omer. This was discussed early, at the time of the change of the calendar. Long before Hillel, it was already established that the Omer be brought on the sixteenth of Nisan.

The Festival of Shabuot was associated with the Sinaitic Revelation only in the time of Usha, because the sacrificial aspect of the first fruits had already been discontinued. Shabuot had no fixed date until the fourth century C.E. when the present calendar was formulated.

342. "Asher BeTalmud," *JQR,* Vol. LIV, No. 4 (April 1964), pp. 340–341.

The word Mishneh, in the sense of halakhah, came into usage after the Destruction. The expression *asher b'Talmud* in the Scrolls could not have occurred in the literature of the Second Commonwealth. (Cf., no. 330.)

343. י״ח דבר („שמנה עשר דברים גזרו בו ביום״). This is a Hebrew translation of the article "Les Dix-huit Mesures." (Cf., no. 1.) Contained in the *Bitzaron* volume issued in honor of Professor Zeitlin: SOLOMON ZEITLIN JUBILEE ISSUE—Upon the Completion of Half a Century of Scholarly Activities, *Bitzaron,* Vol. L, No. 5 (244) Iyar-Sivan, 5724 (April, 1964).

Other articles included in this issue are: "Tribute to Solomon Zeitlin," by Zalman Shazar; "In Appreciation," by Abraham A. Neuman; "Zeitlin the Scholar and His Works," by Sidney B. Hoenig; "Zeitlin's Contribution to Our Understanding of the Second Commonwealth," by Ellis Rivkin; and "Solomon Zeitlin—A Personal Tribute," by Maxwell Whiteman.

344. "I. The Date of the Birth and the Crucifixion of Jesus; II. The Crucifixion, a Libelous Accusation Against the Jews," *JQR,* Vol. LV, No. 1 (July 1964), pp. 1–22. (See also no. 41.)

The date of the birth of Jesus was unknown to the Church Fathers, which accounts for the conflicting dates. They did not know because Jews did not record birthdays which was a Roman custom. The exact year of the Crucifixion is unknown. It is known that it took place on a Friday, but whether on the eve of Passover or on the first day is the subject of a discrepancy between John and the Synoptic Gospels.

Jesus was born as a Jew sometime between 6 B.C.E. and 6 C.E., and was crucified as a political offender by the Romans between 30 and 35 C.E.

The Church Father, Justin Martyr, was the first to lay the blame for the Crucifixion on the Jews. In the Apostles' Creed it is not stated that the Jews crucified Jesus, and this fact should be reinstated in the liturgy of the Church and its schools. The Church must emphasize that in reality the Jews are not historically guilty of the Crucifixion. The Christian world must atone for its guilt towards the Jewish people in using the story of the Crucifixion as a pretext for persecuting the Jews throughout the ages. (See no. 356.)

345. *Who Crucified Jesus?* Harper and Brothers (New York, 1964). Introduction to Fourth Edition: "The Crucifixion of Jesus, a Libelous Accusation Against the Jews." (Cf., nos. 105, 156, 239; See also no. 344.)

The Gospels and Apostolic Fathers did not place the onus for the Crucifixion on the Jews. The accusation was brought forth by the early Christians in order to show that Judaism was no longer the true religion.

One must recognize a distinction between theology and historical facts in connection with the Crucifixion. The Gospels are not historical books. They present only theological concepts.

Jesus was crucified with an inscription "King of Jews" on the cross. This was pursuant to the Roman custom, which gave the reason for the execution.

The Jews need not apologize to the Christians. The spiritual leaders of that time were not guilty. Jews do not wish to convert Christians, nor to be converted to Christianity.

The unjustifiable stigma should be removed from the schema.

346. תשובה כהלכה, *Hadoar* (13 Elul 5724-August 21, 1964), No. 35 pp. 634–635. Re: A New Code. Reply to article of M. Minkovitz.

The dogmatic method of Talmud study belongs to the halakhist; the critical method to the historian.

The rule that descent is traced from the mother is due to the fact that Sanballat the Samaritan married off his daughter to Manasseh the brother of Jaddua, the grandson of Eliashev (Neb. 13:28), hoping to make his son-in-law the new High Priest in Gerizim and, thus, assure his grandson of the priesthood as a descendant of Zadok. This naturally would endanger the priesthood in Jerusalem. (See no. 294.) Hence the rule was passed that descent is to be reckoned only from the mother. Proselytism was introduced later.

One must recognize the historic dating of the development of halakhot before giving judgment upon any particular ordinance or practice. (Cf., no. 309.)

347. "History, Historians, and the Dead Sea Scrolls," *JQR*, Vol. LV, No. 2 (October 1964), pp. 97–116.

Again it is emphasized that the Scrolls are medieval compositions. Archaeological evidence must be eliminated because the Scrolls were brought to light by the Bedouins. The carbon-14 test is not a criterion, for it has not shown to be reliable even when applied to the woolen wrappings.

The term Zealots used to describe a group does not occur in *Antiquities* because Josephus concluded this book with events preceding the outbreak of the Revolt, and the Zealots had not yet come into existence. "Sicarii" (the followers of the Fourth Philosophy) is found in *War* and in Book XX of *Antiquities,* for they came into being in 6 C.E.

It is impossible to say that *Moreh Zedek* refers to Jesus, for the term was coined by the Karaites; nor can one regard the Scrolls as having been written by Jewish Christians during the second century, for there is no reference in them to Jesus or to the doctrine of resurrection, which were the foundations of the early Church.

The fact that the Zadokite Fragment, (cf., no. 201), contains a phrase about entering into the "Covenant of Abraham," meaning circumcision, militates against the view that it was written by Jewish Christians influenced by the writings of the Church Fathers.

If these are Christian scrolls, why has a modern "Shrine of the Scrolls" been set up by Jews in Israel?

348. "The Edict of Augustus Caesar in Relation to the Judaeans of Asia," *JQR,* Vol. LV, No. 2 (October 1964), pp. 160–163.

The edict, issued at the intervention of Herod in 8 B.C.E., records for the municipalities of Asia that Jews cannot be forced to appear in court on the Sabbath or on the afternoon of Friday (*paraskeue*), the day of preparation. This expression was coined by Judaeans who lived in the Hellenistic Diaspora, and is found in the Gospels, but not in rabbinic or in Judaean-Hellenistic literature.

Sabbaton is a place of assembly and is explained in the edict as *andron* (a place where men gather). It is not an ark.

348a. I. "The Dates of the Birth and the Crucifixion of Jesus"; II. "The Crucifixion, A Libelous Accusation Against the Jews." Reprint (see no. 344). *The Freethinker,* Vol. LXXXIV, No. 51 (London: Friday, December 18, 1964), p. 401 ff.

1965

348b. *Ibid.* (continued). *The Freethinker,* Vol. LXXXV, No. 1 (Friday, January 8, 1965), p. 11 ff.

348c. *Ibid.* (continued). *The Freethinker*, Vol. LXXXV, No. 2 (Friday, January 15, 1965).

349. "The Duration of Jesus' Ministry," *JQR,* Vol. LV, No. 3 (January 1965), pp. 181–200.

There is no direct statement in the Gospels as to the length of Jesus' ministry, since these books were not directed toward the recording of simple historical facts. The early Church Fathers argued this point and were at variance, as well, as to the dating of the year of Jesus' crucifixion (see no. 344).

The execution of John the Baptist was due to political reasons. It is not definite that Jesus was baptized by John, nor even that Jesus baptized people. His disciples did. There are indications of enmity between the disciples of John and Jesus.

Jesus was crucified on a Friday (the day of Adam's creation); the dates and the day put the accent on theology rather than on history.

According to John, Jesus began his ministry late in 29 (when he first met John the Baptist), and continued until the spring of 34—a little more than three years. In the Gospels, the reckoning is from the death of John the Baptist (end of 33 or beginning of 34) till the Crucifixion—i.e., only a few months.

In 34 C.E. the Festival of Unleavened Bread did not fall on a Friday or a Saturday. Only if 34 was an intercalated year (with two Adars), could Passover fall on a Saturday (according to the Synoptists), but that year was a Sabbatical year and there could have been no intercalation unless there was a drought and the crops had not ripened.

350. "Mar Samuel and Manumission of Slaves," *JQR,* Vol. LV, No. 3 (January 1965), pp. 267–269. (See also no. 325.)

The Amora Samuel held that a master could free his slave. The report by Rav Judah in the name of Samuel, that one who frees a pagan slave violates a pentateuchal precept, is not Samuel's statement. The phrase "you must always enslave him" in the text of Rabbi Ishmael (who held that one had the option to sell) is saboraic.

351. "Proselytes and Proselytism during the Second Commonwealth and Early Tannaitic Literature," *Harry Austryn Wolfson Jubilee Volume,* American Academy for Jewish Research, 1965.

Contrary to the Book of Deuteronomy which forbids conversion, the Books of Ruth and Judith, which were written under the influence of the Pharisees, favor it. The phrase *mityahadim* in Esther means "pretended to be Judaeans." The Book of Esther was composed before the concept of universalism had taken hold.

Conversion became possible when theocracy was abolished and nomocracy became the norm for Judaism.

The term *ger* in the sense of "convert" does not occur in early tannaitic literature. There is no proof to be drawn from the folk tale about Hillel. The term "convert" is not found in Josephus, the Apocryphal literature, or in Philo. *"Proselytos"* in the LXX is simply a translation of *ger*, a sojourner, or newcomer into a foreign land.

A convert needed only to accept the God of Israel as the God of the universe. In time, circumcision became a *sine qua non*—in order to observe the laws. The institution of baptism for proselytes was introduced after 65 C.E., when pagans were considered ritually unclean like a *zab*. Prior to that, they were not subject to the laws of purity and impurity; hence, baptism is not mentioned in Apocryphal literature and in Josephus when referring to conversion. Sacrifice by a convert was required because through its offering, he was no longer considered a *zab*.

Jews were zealous to make proselytes, and many among the Romans joined them. The observance of Jewish customs had become widespread among the pagans. There were also non-Jews in the Diaspora who revered the God of Israel, (יראי ה'); these persons followed Judaean customs, but did not become converts.

There were no semi-proselytes. A *ger toshav* was a foreigner who lived in Judaea, accepting the Noahide laws, *jus gentium*.

The Sadducees did not regard the proselyte as the equal of a native Jew. The Sages did not agree with them. (Cf., no. 328.)

352. "Who is a Jew? A Halakhic-Historical Study," in *Jewish Identity, Modern Responsa on the Registration of Children of Mixed Marriages. David Ben-Gurion's Query to Leaders of World Jewry.* A Documentary Compilation by Baruch Litvin, edited by Sidney B. Hoenig (New York: 1965), pp. 365–391. Reprint. (Cf., no. 288.)

353. "Masada and the Sicarii, the Occupants of Masada," *JQR*, Vol. LV, No. 4 (April 1965), pp. 299–317.

Masada means "fortress." It was a place of refuge for David in the time of Saul, for Jonathan, the Hasmonean, who fled the Syrians, and for Herod seeking refuge from the Parthians and when he was in fear of Cleopatra. In 65 C.E. Menahem, the Sicarius, appropriated

Herod's armory at Masada which the Romans then held. Eleazar, Menahem's successor, escaped to Masada after Menahem was killed. The Sicarii remained there until 72. During the war they were inactive. When attacked by Silva they did not resist, but committed suicide. Josephus, nevertheless, recorded that they gave up their lives for liberty.

The coins found in Masada include Byzantine ones, thus revealing that people lived in Masada during the Middle Ages. Many buildings there were also completed during the Byzantine period, and Jews found refuge there in the time of Heraclius.

The Masada "Synagogue" and "Mikveh" are misnomers. There were no special houses of worship in Judaea during the Second Commonwealth, and there was then no fixed halakhah regarding *mikveh.*

The jars inscribed with letters "taw" and "tet" may be those which the Sicarii plundered. There is no proof of true Sicarii religiosity. (See also nos. 357, 364, 383, 400.)

354. "Did Agrippa Write a Letter to Gaius Caligula?" *JQR,* Vol. LVI, No. 1 (July 1965), pp. 22–31.

There is no historic evidence that Agrippa actually wrote a letter to Gaius, although he intervened for the Judaeans. The letter, as recorded by Philo, is only in accord with his own presentation of Judaean theology. The speech of Agrippa at a banquet, as presented by Josephus, was written by the historian in the spirit of Greek historiography—putting the authors' words into the mouth of his heroes.

355. "There Was No Court of Gentiles in the Temple Area," *JQR,* Vol. LVI, No. 1 (July 1965), p. 88.

Neither Josephus, Mishnah Middot, nor the stone inscription prohibiting non-Jews from entering the latticed portion of the Temple, mention a "Court of Gentiles."

356. "The Ecumenical Council Vatican II and the Jews," *JQR,* Vol. LVI, No. 2 (October 1965), pp. 93–111.

The teaching that Jews crucified Jesus (deicide) accelerated anti-Semitism. There are no historical sources for any Jewish responsibility in this event. The Apostolic Fathers mention only that Jesus was crucified under Pontius Pilate. The Josephus text was interpolated by Eusebius. (See no. 37.) The Palestinian Talmud makes no mention of Jesus. (See also no. 316.) The passages of the Babylonian Talmud are of the third century and have no historical value for this incident. The Gospels contradict each other about the Crucifixion, but agree that the High Priests plotted. The accusation was reaffirmed by some popes. Some of them, however, showed their good will; others declared that Jews must be persecuted, but not annihilated.

When emancipation came, Jews were still blamed for the Crucifixion. Emancipation was a political action, not a religious one. The doctrine of deicide can also be said to have contributed to the killing of the six million Jews in the Nazi holocaust.

There is a contradiction in the schema. If Jesus went to his death freely—to ransom men from sin—how can even a few Jews be accused of the Crucifixion?

It was wrong for the Jews to lobby for the emendation of the schema theology. Basically, it is not the Jews who have to atone, but the Christians, for their libelous accusations.

Dialogues are contrary to the history of true Judaism; the medieval disputations were imposed through force. Both Jews and Christians need enlightenment on the historical background of the "Parting of the Ways." (See no. 345.)

356a. "Who Crucified Jesus?" *Jewish Spectator,* Vol. XXX, No. 8 (October 1965), pp. 7–13. Part of a chapter of the fourth edition of the book. (See no. 345.)

1966

357. "The Ben Sira Scroll from Masada," *JQR,* Vol. LVI, No. 3 (January 1966), pp. 185–190.

The Hebrew text of the Masada Ben Sira Scroll is a copy of the Syriac translation, and is of the Middle Ages. The words *shutaf* (partnership) and *tagar* (local merchant) are not of the early Second Commonwealth period. They were terms introduced into rabbinic literature only after the Destruction.

358. "The Semikhah Controversy between the Schools of Shammai and Hillel," *JQR,* Vol. LVI, No. 3 (January 1966), pp. 240–244.

The "laying on of hands" upon animal sacrifices was believed to be a "transfer of sins." Since no sin offerings were offered on the Sabbath and holidays, the School of Shammai forbade such practice then, even if peace offerings were brought. The School of Hillel regarded the practice as being only symbolic. To encourage pilgrimages to the Temple, they later gave sanction to such practices. This controversy dates from the time of Herod. It has no bearing on the Semikhah controversy—the "tradition" of the Zugot. (Cf., no. 2.)

359. "Were There Three Torah Scrolls in the Azarah?" *JQR,* Vol. LVI, No. 4 (April 1966), pp. 269–272.

The story about the three Torahs with different readings is not historical fact. The Temple had only one official text. Aramaic or Greek renditions may have crept in later (e.g., Exodus 24:5, 11–זטוטי). [See Meg. 9a.]

To establish the notion of a correct biblical text, and to give authority to the *matres lectionis* (hé, yod, waw), the Sages in the third century recorded this aggadah about the variations in the spellings of words.

360. "The Judaean Calendar During the Second Commonwealth and the Scrolls," *JQR,* Vol. LVII, No. 1 (July 1966), pp. 28–45.

During the Second Commonwealth the first day of Passover and the Day of Atonement could and did occur on Fridays. *Adu* and *Badu* came into vogue only after the fourth century. In ancient days the Festival of Weeks did not have a fixed date. Sometimes it was on the fifth, sixth, or seventh of Sivan. This depended on intercalation (see nos. 13, 28, 341).

Zemanim, in Daniel and in Jewish liturgy, means festivals.

The Zadokite Fragment reveals the use of a lunar-solar calendar in its stressing of observance of Friday night.

The theory of two parallel calendars in Judaea during the Second Commonwealth has no basis.

There was no law, before the Destruction, that a Judaean entering a heathen home was defiled for seven days.

361. "The Maimonidean Controversy," *JQR*, Vol. LVII, No. 2 (October 1966), pp. 154–158.

As a result of the Albigensian Crusade there was a reaction against liberalism. Jews of southern France feared that heretical views would bring retaliation from the Church. Hence, Maimonides' Aristotelian views in *Moreh Nebukhim* caused apprehension and controversy.

The *Mishneh Torah* was also criticized because many felt that Maimonides, by not quoting sources, sought to set aside the Talmud. During Maimonides' lifetime, Samuel ben Ali, in Egypt, opposed him because Maimonides upheld the institution of the Exilarchate, whereas Samuel ben Ali sought his own spiritual prestige. He therefore accused Maimonides of heretical belief and nonobservance, of denying the belief in resurrection and of misinterpreting the laws of Sabbath. (See nos. 56, 57, 71.)

1967

362. *The Rise and Fall of the Judaean State, A Political, Social, and Religious History of the Second Commonwealth, Vol. II,* 37 B.C.E.–66 C.E., The Jewish Publication Society of America (Philadelphia: 5727-1967), xiii + 465 pages. (See no. 324.)

This second volume deals with the turbulent period of Herod, the procurators, and the events leading to the Destruction; it ends with the conclave of 65 C.E. when the Eighteen *Gezerot* were enacted to strengthen the religious and national aspects of the state (see no. 1). Included is a vivid picture of Hillel, his influence on the growth of Judaism, the new trends in religion, and Hillel's personality as a counterpoise to the tyranny of Herod. Significant is the discussion of the hermeneutic rules, the principle of intention, the enactments of Hillel, and his control of leadership.

The origins and sources of Christianity from both the Jewish and non-Jewish viewpoints, with all their implications and influences, are evaluated together with a portrayal of Jesus and his relationship to Judaism in this age of crisis.

Discussing the physical background of Judaean life, the volume also contains a description of the character of the land, the population, the economic resources of Judaea, its natural products, etc. We read of the treatment of slaves—Judaean and Gentile—the liberalizing of the slave laws and the activities of the craftsmen and artisans in the land.

In the chapters on social and communal life there is a full account of the organized town, the charitable institutions, the dwellings, the home furnishings, dress, food, etc. Associated with this analysis is the probing of marriage customs, the foundation of the home, parental authority, and the various customs of the Sabbaths and holidays, of personal joys and sorrows.

The triumph of Pharisaism is described, as well as the relationship of Judaism to its neighbors, the life of the Jew in the Diaspora, and the new religious groupings that arose in the first century. Added to this is a keen appraisal of the literature, education, religion, prayer and worship, the canon, etc.

An appendix contains the text of Megillat Taanit, the dialogues between the Sadducees and Pharisees as recorded in the Talmud, the descriptions of the sects as given in Josephus, and the text of the so-called Christ passage, analyzed, together with the opinions of Pliny and the early Church Fathers.

The chronological table of the High Priests as well as a summary of the key figures and events in that century, with the notation of the Sabbatical cycles and the genealogical table of Herod's family are a further amplification for the student of the history of the period. The comprehensive notes refer back to the original sources, primary and secondary, substantiating the scholarly research.

363. "Paul's Journeys to Jerusalem," *JQR,* Vol. LVII, No. 3 (January 1967), pp. 171–178.

In the Epistle to the Galatians, written by Paul, it is recorded that he made two journeys to Jerusalem. Acts records four visits; this is not historical because of the anachronisms. Acts no doubt consists of two composite halves, each author having recorded two journeys.

The term "Christian" was coined in Antioch, perhaps as an opprobrium because the idea of an anointed Messiah was incomprehensible to the pagans. The followers of Jesus were first called "disciples" or "brethren."

Paul was converted in 44–45 C.E. His first visit to Jerusalem was in 48. His second was in 58–59, when he was arrested.

364. "The Sicarii and Masada," *JQR,* Vol. LVII, No. 3 (April 1967) pp. 251–270.

Josephus was the first to use the term "Sicarii," since he was prejudiced against them. The Talmud later used the term to signify "assassins."

The Sicarii did not fight against the Romans during the War, even in Masada. Their belief in "no lordship of man over man," meant opposition to any form of government in Judaea. To them, God was the only ruler. After the war they continued to propagate their ideology in Egypt, for they would not call Caesar "master."

In Masada, by committing suicide, they delivered the fortress to the Romans. In their fanaticism they did harm to the Judaean state. Josephus and the Talmud place the onus of the destruction of State and Temple upon them. They cannot be considered devout Jews for they were guilty of crimes of murder and plunder.

Texts of Leviticus with "open" and "closed" sections were found at Masada. This scribal practice was introduced long after the Destruction of the Temple.

The Hebrew Scrolls of Masada belong to the time of Heraclius (*ca.* 630). The skeletons may be of the Byzantine monks and Judaeans who took refuge there during the Parthian Wars. (See nos. 312, 353.)

364a. "A Chronological Error on a Stamp of Israel," *Judaica Philatelic Journal,* Vol. III, No. 4 (June, 1967), pp. 375–76. (See no. 178.)

365. *The Seventy-fifth Anniversary Volume, JQR* (1967).

1. Foreword, pp. ix–xi by S. Zeitlin, Editor.

This volume also marks the sixtieth anniversary of the founding of Dropsie College in 1907—the same year Baron David Günzburg opened the Academy in St. Petersburg. The high purpose of both institutions was to develop scholars. The legacy of Moses A. Dropsie has been preserved in America, and that of the Academy of St. Petersburg is evident in the scholarship of such dignitaries as the present President of Israel, Zalman Shazar.

366. 2. "Seventy-five Years of the Jewish Quarterly Review," *ibid.,* pp. 60–68.

JQR was founded in England in 1888 by Israel Abrahams and Claude Montefiore to promote scholarship. Its first article was by Heinrich Graetz, "The Significance of Judaism for the Present and the Future." In October 1907 this (old) series was suspended. It had encouraged the Genizah discoveries by Solomon Schechter and the Geonic Responsa of Louis Ginzberg. In 1908, Dropsie College, under

Cyrus Adler, began the new series. During the World Wars, when other scholarly publications were suspended, *JQR* was the only continuing vehicle for scholarship. The old series had stressed theology. Under Dr. Adler's editorship (together with Dr. Max Margolis), more emphasis was placed on philology, Bible, and history. The present editorial policy (of Dr. Zeitlin) is to encourage younger scholars in all branches of Jewish learning. Scholarship does not depend on the views of the majority or on dogmatic statements. *JQR* has not shunned controversial articles on Judaism or the "Parting of the Ways." It is the only scholarly Jewish journal whose contributors are both Jewish and Christiain. (See also no. 401 and *Epilogue.*)

367. 3. "Testamentary Succession: A Study in Tannaitic Jurisprudence," *ibid.*, pp. 574–581.

According to the Pentateuch, inheritance exists only where property remains within the family. Real property could not be sold forever; it had to revert to the original owners. When the concept of a tribal society became obsolete, the Sages of the Second Commonwealth introduced the principle of testamentary succession by the making of a will. This is a Judaean ordinance, though the technical word *diatheke* had been borrowed from the Greek, even as has *prosbol.* This does not mean that the principle was borrowed from the Greeks.

A person could give his property by gift to anyone, if he was well. He could change his mind during his lifetime, so long as the property was in his possession.

Originally, a will which contradicted the Pentateuchal laws of inheritance was invalid. In the second century, Rabbi Johanan ben Beroka held that a testator could bequeath to a potential heir. The Rabbis did not approve of disinheriting children.

The *diatheke* could be written in any language, but in the conclave of 65 C.E. opposition was shown to Greek. Thus the principle of testamentary succession—bequeathing real property to a stranger by writing a will or bestowing it as a gift—was introduced in the Second Commonwealth to meet social and economic changes.

368. "Israelites, Jews in the Pauline Epistles," *JQR,* Vol. LVIII, No. 1 (July 1967), pp. 72–74.

The early Christians claimed that they were the true Israelites, hence Jews called themselves "Israel." The term assumed an ecclesiastical connotation as a community (*knesset Yisrael*). In the Pauline letters the term "Israelite" is used in a theological sense. (See no. 204.)

369. "The Word BeTalmud and the Method of Congruity of Words," *JQR,* Vol. LVIII, No. 1 (July 1967), pp. 78–80. (See also no. 330 and no. 342.)

"Talmud" is not synonymous with "gemara." "Talmud" is teaching, the interpretation of Mishnah. "Gemara" is tradition, synonymous with *kabbalah*; it is never used in talmudic texts to mean interpretation of Mishnah. Where it does occur, it is definitely a censor's change from "talmud," as found in manuscripts. Only after the completion of the Talmud did "gemara" become synonymous with "talmud."

The Pharisees never claimed to be the only authorities on interpretation of the oral tradition.

370. "The Life of Jesus (Critical Notes)," *JQR,* Vol. LVIII, No. 2 (October 1967), pp. 164–166.

The custom of bar mitzvah did not exist in the time of Jesus. It came into vogue during the Middle Ages. The listing and arrangement of the 613 *mitzvot* is of the fourth century. (See also no. 310.)

The Pharisees never called themselves "Rabbis." The title came into use after 70 C.E. The Pharisees stressed knowledge, not fasts and sacrifices. At the time of Jesus the pagans were not considered unclean.

Quotations taken from secondary sources or given by ignorant persons (like Pranaites of the Beilis trial) are inexcusable. Universities should have chairs for Rabbinics and the history of the Second Commonwealth to give Christians a true perspective of that period.

1968

371. "The Slavonic Josephus and the Dead Sea Scrolls: An Exposé of Recent Fairy Tales," *JQR,* Vol. LVIII, No. 3 (January 1968), pp. 173–203.

To understand a manuscript, and to obtain its dating, one must not depend only on its paleography, but one should also be fully cognizant of the expressions and laws mentioned therein. In the Slavonic Josephus there are many Greek words which came into vogue in the

Byzantine period. The author of the Slavonic Josephus made use of the Latin Hegessipus of the fifth century. (See no. 37.)

A parallel sensation is that of the Scrolls. Here, again, is a review of many of the arguments against the antiquity of the Scrolls, stressing that only internal evidence can be relied upon. There was no High Priest in the Second Commonwealth known as Akavia as mentioned in the Scrolls. (Cf., also no. 312.)

372. "The Need for a Systematic Jewish History" [containing also a review of the *World History of the Jewish People, Second Series: Medival Period Vol. II; The Dark Ages,* editor Cecil Roth, Rutgers University Press (1966)], *JQR,* Vol. LVIII, No. 4 (April 1968), pp. 261–273.

Heinrich Graetz, although the greatest of Jewish historians since Josephus, relied only on the literature of scholars—he did not have a profound knowledge of the original sources. S. Dubnow drew from Graetz, and also from Isaac Hirsch Weiss, who lacked historical vision, (see also no. 171). Jewish history cannot be written by one man. It is a continuous development, and must be written as a unit and can be done correctly only by the united efforts of a group of specialists in their own fields. Unlike the Cambridge History, Jewish history must be systematic and unified. The edition of the *World History of the Jewish People* demonstrates this in that articles on diverse items are not coordinated. An example are the essays on the activities and the work of Rashi.

The problems of writing Jewish history should be discussed by an international society of Jewish historians.

373. Foreword to: *Jewish Law in the Diaspora: Confrontation and Accommodation*, by Leo Landman, The Dropsie College for Hebrew and Cognate Learning (Philadelphia: 1968), pp. 11–14.

Jews were always politically loyal to their adopted countries, but cherished a great affection for Judaea, and were religiously guided by the Sanhedrin. After the Bar Kokhba revolt, Babylonia became the center of the Jews. Samuel the Amora laid down the principle that the "civil law of the state is law." This did not refer to religious laws. This principle is not found in the Palestinian Talmud because the Jews considered the Romans as ruling them by force, not by right. In

Babylonia, however, the government was accepted as the rightful political ruler. (See also no. 223.)

In the eleventh century two centers of Jewry arose: in France, following Palestinian sources, and in Spain, modeled after Babylonian custom. Spain had a centralized government, while France did not. These differences explain the variegated applications of the civil law principle. French Jewish leadership sought to limit the authority of the government over their community, hence they introduced the *Ḥerem* preventing unwelcome migrants to a community. In the Spanish Jewish community there was no such *Ḥerem* since the whole administration was controlled by one central authority. (See nos. 99, 150.)

374. "Recollections," in *Rabbinics and Research: The Scholarship of Dr. Bernard Revel,* by Sidney B. Hoenig, Yeshiva University Press, (New York: 1968), pp. 148–155.

In the early decades of this century there was great opposition in the yeshivot to critical research of Talmud. Despite the many obstacles which beset him, Dr. Revel, the founder of Yeshiva College, encouraged the pursuit of scholarship with sincerity in probing the original sources. Dr. Revel demonstrated that the Karaites were not the descendants of the Sadducees, but were influenced by the writings of Philo and that, as early as the fifth and sixth centuries, Jews were already acquainted with Philo in translation. There is also a close resemblance in approach between Maimonides and Philo, as in the explanation of the rite of circumcision.

375. *The Rise and Fall of the Judaean State,* second edition, *JPS* (May 1968), with added preface and appendix, pp. 444 a–k: "On the Pharisees." (See no. 324.)

The origin of the Pharisees belongs to the period of the canonization of the Pentateuch, when the question of the binding nature of the unwritten laws as held by the Pharisees began to confront the people. This was long before the Hasmonean period. The controversy of the Omer was one pertaining to the change of the solar calendar to a lunar-solar one, and arose at the beginning of the Second Temple era.

Josephus' first reference to the sects in *Antiquities* occurs in his discussion of the Essenes in the time of Jonathan, when he introduces the Essenes for the first time. His mention of them in *War* is in the time of Archaelus, because he then introduces the Fourth Philosophy. (See also no. 388.)

376. מצדה, *Bitzaron,* Vol. LVIII, No. 6 [272] (May/June 1968), pp. 71–78.

The subject of Masada and the Sicarii has been inflated with wild assumptions.

The Hasmoneans, in their revolt, established the Judaean state, but the Sicarii, with their philosophy of self-annihilation were responsible for its destruction.

The Temple was burned in the year 70, not 69 C.E. Eleazar ben Yair fled in 65 C.E., at the beginning of the Revolt. The Sicarii remained in Masada till 72, and did not defend it, as their brethren defended Antonia, the Temple, Jerusalem, and Machaerus. (See also nos. 353, 364, 383, 400.)

377. "Some Reflections on the Text of the Talmud," *JQR,* Vol. LIX, No. 1 (July 1968), pp. 1–8.

To edit the Talmud critically "majority rule" is not to be applied to readings in manuscripts. Sometimes one text is superior to all others. Readings in later rabbinic literature must be taken into account, yet one must be on guard for emendations that have crept in. Where there are textual variants, the internal evidence based on historical background and context must be the scientific criterion.

As an example, since the agrarian laws were not applicable in the Diaspora, Rav Judah, a disciple of Samuel, ruled that possession applied to a field held during the period of *Orlah,* i.e., the first three years of planting. Halakhah, according to Samuel, meant the custom of the country (*hilkhata de'medina*).

Similarly, since after 70 C.E. the Jews called themselves "Israelites," we must conclude that the statement employing *Yom tov l'yisrael,* a term based upon the usage in the Book of Esther, for the fifteenth of Ab and Yom Kippur, was uttered by Rabban Simon b. Gamaliel II (*ca.* 150 C.E.), who referred back to the joyous days before the Restoration. The fifteenth of Ab was the time of the approach of the sun to the autumnal equinox. The reading *Yom Kippurim* should be *Yom Purim,* and pertains to the approach of the vernal equinox. The textual change to *Yom Kippurim* came early, hence arousing discussion about the reasons for the *Yom tov.*

378. "The Blood Accusation," *JQR,* Vol. LIX, No. 1 (July 1968) pp. 76–80. Contains also an analysis of: *Blood Accusation: The Strange History of the Beilis Case,* by Maurice Samuel.

An analysis behind the scenes in the Beilis case—the lawyers, prosecution, defense personalities, the reasons for their conduct, Professors Chwolson and Kokostzof and their activity are vividly portrayed.

Jewish history in Russia must be studied. Simon Dubnow neglected the spiritual life of the Jews that had then reached its pinnacle. Many documents that shed new light have been discovered since then.

379. "Korban: A Gift," *JQR,* Vol. LIX, No. 2 (October 1968), p. 133.

The word *Korban* in the Gospels, as in tannaitic literature, often has the meaning of "vow." A gift to the Temple, however, was also called *korban*; it is also noted in Josephus. So, too, is the rendering in the limestone inscription found recently at the base of the Temple ruins. It does not have the connotation of sacrifice. (See no. 318.)

380. "The Title Rabbi in the Gospels is Anachronistic," *JQR,* Vol. LIX, No. 2 (October 1968), pp. 158–160.

During the Second Commonwealth the term "Rabbi" was not used; in no literature of that period does it occur. Usages in the Gospels, according to the manuscripts, also show its absence. (See no. 329.)

381. "The Psalm Scroll—A Rejoinder," *JQR,* Vol. LIX, No. 2 (October 1968), p. 163.

The fact that the word *tehillim* occurs in the Scrolls indicates that the fragment was written after the Destruction of the Temple.

382. "Tehillim in the Scrolls," *JQR,* Vol. LIX, No. 2 (October 1968), p. 164.

The word *tehillim* (instead of *tehillot,* referring to the collection itself) came into use only after the Psalms were canonized in 65 C.E.

383. מצדה — פרק בלתי מזהיר בתולדות היהודים, *Bitzaron,* Vol. LIX, No. 2 [275] (Kislev–Tevet 5729/November–December 1968), pp. 51–60.

There is a contrast between Masada, the retreat, and Machaerus, the fortress, first fortified by Alexander Jannai. Gabinius saw fit to capture Machaerus, but did not attack Masada. Herod also fortified Machaerus. It was finally destroyed by Bassus in 71 C.E.

Because Masada was an armory, having stores of war material, the Romans put a guard to watch it. The Sicarii captured the arms which they later used to battle their own people.

There is no record that the Sicarii fought in Masada. Josephus does not mention casualties on either side. The Sicarii only made forays against the Jews in the area, taking their property. They did not engage in any guerilla warfare. They did not aid their brethren in the War, nor did they attack the Romans; they only fought against their own. Their story is one of ignominy because their action was a self-surrender.

Masada was captured in 72 C.E. (the fourth year of Vespasian's reign). The skeletons cannot reveal any heroism.

There is no evidence of a ritual *mikveh;* Herod had only built pools. The laws of *mikvaot* belong to the post-Destruction period.

The Sicarii believed in freedom of the soul and in its immortality—the body was the prison from which the soul was to be freed. Therefore, suicide was not contrary to their belief. Josephus only obtained his information about Masada from the Roman archives and used an exaggerated image in describing Eleazar ben Yair's speech. The suicide of the Sicarii was not martyrdom; it was contrary to Jewish doctrine. One should not, therefore, praise the Sicarii. They were responsible for the downfall of Judaea, despite their idealistic striving for a utopia. (See no. 353.)

384. קורות בית שני, כרך א, הוצאת ספרים מ. ניומן בע"מ, ירושלים, תשכ"ח. Hebrew translation of Vol. I of *The Rise and Fall of the Judaean State* (1968), (Cf., no. 324.)

Research is based only on primary sources. Because the development of the sects—Pharisees and Sadducees—is interlinked with the history of the people, their narrative must always be interwoven with the various epochs, and not listed as separate items.

1969

385. "A Survey of Jewish Historiography: From the Biblical Books to the Sefer ha-Kabbalah with Special Emphasis on Josephus," *JQR,* Vol. LIX, No. 3 (January 1969), pp. 171–214. [To be continued.] (See no. 393.)

Systematic history, though tendentious, is to be found in the biblical books of Samuel, Kings, Chronicles, Ezra and Nehemiah.

I Maccabees, although favoring the Hasmoneans, describes the internal conflicts, and is the only definite contemporary source besides Polybius. II Maccabees is important for the authentic history before the Hasmonean period. Historical kernels may be found in Susanna and Judith, Bel and the Dragon; Philo's *Embassy to Gaius* has no historical value. Megillat Taanit is the only early Jewish source for events during the Second Temple era.

Josephus was the greatest Jewish historian, though not an objective one; his purpose was propaganda, his viewpoint colored by his admiration for the power of Rome and his wish to deter revolt. He was not commissioned to write his *War,* but he had access to Roman records. Many of Josephus' speeches are only imaginative, like that of Eleazar ben Yair; others are historical, as his own and that of Titus, but these are not exact. In recording events of the War, Josephus was accurate, as corroborated by the Talmud.

Severus' (Tacitus') statement that "Titus ordered the Temple to be burnt" is incorrect. Josephus is right, for the Romans did not persecute the Jewish religion then. It is true that Josephus was not impartial in his account of the war. He opposed it, basically; yet he describes the ideals of the rebels honestly. His *Jewish War,* written with skill, is comparable to the great histories of the Greeks and Romans.

386. "Jesus and the Last Supper," in *The Passover Haggadah,* Shocken Books (New York: 1969). Reprint. (See nos. 159, 186, 189.)

387. קמיע ולא תפלין, *Bitzaron,* LIX, No. 4 [277], (Nisan 5729-March 1969), pp. 147–149, 167.

According to the Talmud, Tefillin contain four *parshiot.* The Scroll bought by Professor Y. Yadin has seven sections, which include the Decalogue. The reading of the Decalogue had been discontinued because of the views of the sectarians, "who might say that the Decalogue alone is Sinaitic." This reason is a late addition to the talmudic text. The real reason for the discontinuation is due to the discrepancies in the versions of the Decalogue as found in Exodus and Deuteronomy.

What Yadin purchased is only an amulet, based on the Deuteronomic text, containing the phrase "to lengthen thy days" and "it shall be good for you," phrases used as in an amulet. So too the Exodus phrase, "night of watching," implies prophylactic aspects. The early Jewish Christians called Tefillin, *"phylacteries"* for they believed in its protective qualities. The Sadducees and Essenes did not wear Tefillin. The word is not found in the Pentateuch. The Talmud never mentions that the Tefillin contain the Decalogue. (Cf., also nos. 210, 392.)

388. "The Origin of the Pharisees Reaffirmed," *JQR*, Vol. LIX, No. 4 (April 1969), pp. 255–267.

The Pharisees could not have arisen in the Hasmonean period. Their origin is traced to the era immediately after the Restoration, at the time of the canonization of the Pentateuch. (See nos. 305, 375.)

The word השם means God (not the Name). בשם means "in the name of God (Adonai)." The insistence that Yahweh be pronounced Adonai—signifying universalism of God—was a feature introduced shortly after the Restoration.

To counteract the Christians who greeted others in the name of Jesus, the Rabbis decreed that one may give greetings (pronounce) in the Name of God. The writing of Yahweh in the old paleographic script is not sacred. Such sanctity an only be attached to Assyrian square script. (See also no. 203.)

Those who insisted on full-body immersion for purity objected on the ground that the Name of God was recited by persons after merely washing their hands. This controversy in Mishnah Yadaim is an offshoot of the conflicts on laws of purity of the first century C.E. (See no. 1.)

389. "The Excavations in the Old City of Jerusalem," *JQR,* Vol. LIX, No. 4 (April 1969), pp. 337–340.

The discovery by Professor B. Mazar of a limestone of the Herodian period with an inscription of the word קרבנ (medial nun at the end of the word) is additional proof that the final letters were introduced into the Bible after 70 C.E. (See no. 380.)

The final letters in the Qumran Tefillin militate against Yadin's theory that they are of the Second Commonwealth. The scribe of those Tefillin used the masoretic text, but probably was a heretic of the Karaitic period, for he broke up the writing of the Tetragrammaton contrary to the law and spirit of Judaism. Moreover, the Ten Commandments were never part of the traditional Tefillin. (Cf., no. 387.)

390. "Allegations of Prof. W. F. Albright Refuted by Dr. S. Zeitlin," *The Jewish Post and Opinion* (Friday, April 11, 1969). A response to Professor Albright's remarks about Professor Zeitlin's challenge of the date of the Dead Sea Scrolls in the *Jerusalem Post Weekly,* Monday, March 31, 1969, p. 10. (Cf., no. 391.)

391. "Professor Zeitlin's reply to Professor Albright's Charges." Article in the *Jerusalem Post Weekly* (Monday, May 5, 1969), p. 15.

The scholars who propagate the view that the Scrolls are of the period of the Second Jewish Commonwealth are falsifying Jewish history. They are challenged to refute the proofs submitted against the antiquity of the Scrolls, point by point, and in a scholarly fashion.

392. תפילה או קמיע של מין מתקופת הקראים, *Bitzaron,* Vol. LX, No. 5 [278], (April 1969), pp. 3–5.

The new Qumran Tefillin are neither of the type of Rashi or R. Tam (geonic) in their sequence of the biblical portions. There are final letters therein; these were not common in the ancient period. Here even the Tetragrammaton is divided up into two lines, contrary to halakhah. These "finds" were written by a heretic, and do not belong to the Second Temple era. (See also nos. 210, 387, 389.)

393. "A Survey of Jewish Historiography: From the Biblical Books to the Sefer ha-Kabbalah with Special Emphasis on Josephus," *JQR,* Vol. LX, No. 1 (July 1969), pp. 37–68. Continued from *JQR,* LIX, 3. (See no. 385.)

Josephus' *War,* first written in 73, presents the official report as recorded for the provisional government. His *Life,* published in

93 C.E., reveals the truth, that he was sent on a peace mission to Galilee. In it are recounted his relations with John of Gischala. The purpose of the *Life* was to refute the report of the war in Galilee by Justus of Tiberias. It is not an autobiography, but an *apologia pro vita sua.*

The contradictions between the two works are explained, giving an analysis of the differences between John of Gischala, the autocratic leader, and Simon, son of Giora, the leader of the faction opposed to the Zealots. This historical interpretation is that the provisional government had fallen due to the loss of Jotapata, Josephus' defection, and John's activity. Though John at first had joined the Zealots, he later broke with them and committed atrocities.

The ideological differences between the three leaders—John, Simon, and Eleazar—brought about the ultimate destruction. In the eyes of the Judaeans who fought the War, Josephus was a traitor; to those who opposed the War, Josephus' action of surrender was not to be condemned.

394. "The Dead Sea Scrolls: Journalists and Dilettanti," *JQR,* Vol. LX, No. 1 (July 1969), pp. 75–79. Review of: *The Dead Sea Scrolls* 1947–1969 by Edmund Wilson.

It is erroneous to maintain that orthodox theology sways the reasoning of those opposing the antiquity of the Scrolls. The masoretic text of the Bible is not "unquestionable" for it contains many errors in readings, and is also at variance with tannaitic literature and the Septuagint. Scholars have not yet answered the challenge that many terms, physical signs, and expressions in the Scrolls came into vogue only during the Middle Ages, and that halakhot contained in them are of a period after 70 C.E.

"Teacher of Righteousness" does not occur in the Mishnah, Talmud, Philo, New Testament, and Church Fathers. It was coined in the Middle Ages by the Karaites who claimed that they were the Righteous Teachers.

The arguments against the antiquity of the Scrolls are based solidly on internal evidence.

395. "The Five Megilloth," *JQR,* Vol. LX, No. 1 (July 1969), pp. 80–82. Review of: H. L. Ginzberg's *The Five Megilloth* and *Jonah: A New Translation, JPS,* (Philadelphia: 1969).

Ruth is read on Shabuot in commemoration of the death of David. Song of Songs had already been included in the canon in 65 C.E.

Lamentations is recited on the anniversary of the burning of the Temple (9 Ab), not on the anniversary of the capture of Jerusalem. In 587 B.C.E. Jerusalem was taken on 10 Tebet (II Kings 25:1–4). In 70, it was captured 26 September (8 Gorpiaeus).

Kohelet was rejected at the conclave in 65 C.E., but accepted in 90 C.E., in Jabneh. Kohelet is a proper name, and Ecclesiastes is an incorrect rendering.

There are more references in the Talmud to Hanukkah than to Purim, for the Scroll of Esther was not canonized until 140 C.E., and some Babylonian sages were opposed to the canonization even later. Probably because Esther was canonized later, a fringe group of Karaites rejected it; hence it is not found among the Qumran Scrolls discoveries.

The story of Jonah is similar to that of Andromeda recorded by Strabo in *Geography* 16.28.

396. "Studies in Talmudic Jurisprudence: Possession, Pignus and Hypothec," *JQR,* Vol. LX, No. 2 (October 1969), pp. 89–111.

Knowledge of Jewish law includes an understanding of the different codes—Pentateuch, Mishnah and Gemara—with an evaluation of the distinguishing features of each in rendering decisions. One should not group together talmudic laws of Palestine and of Babylon, or Responsa of different countries and eras. Each reflects diverse religious and social conditions or changes.

A. According to the Pentateuch, property was acquired through purchase or inheritance. Acquisition by *usucapio* (possession by use) for a determined period (חזקה) is not recorded therein. Such manner of acquisition is based on *halakhot,* the unwritten laws of an early period; such mode of possession entails not merely retention or occupation of property, but requires features of *bona fide* and *justa causa.* To be valid for claiming ownership, possession of real property must be within three complete years of use. Hence, during the period of *Orlah, usucapio* was not considered a means of valid possession. But in the Diaspora, where the law of *orlah* was not applicable, possession of an orchard during the three years of *orlah* was recognized as *bona fide.* Moreover, in order that ownership be acquired by usucaption the article must be susceptible of being held *in domino.* This excluded therefore a craftsman, guardian, robber, etc.

B. *Pignus* (משכון) is pawn or pledge for a loan which is to be returned when the debt is paid. The Pentateuch does not refer to a pledge given at the time of the transaction of a loan nor does it refer to a deposit (earnest money). It refers only to "security," ערבון, עבט (Deut. 24:19) and describes the situation where the creditor seeks to seize the security because the loan was not paid. (Cf., no. 121.)

The Talmud, recording the laws of *pignus,* indicates the responsibility of the creditor and demonstrates that the Sages had different conceptions thereof. Some held *pignus* was a security for the payment of the debt; if the security was lost, but not through the creditor's negligence, he could collect his debt. Others held that the *mashkon* was an exchange for the loan and the mortgagee or creditor is a paid guardian, responsible for any loss. If the *mashkon* was lost, the mortgagee lost his loan.

C. *Hypothec* is the Greek for pledge. While *pignus* refers to the object being placed in the possession of the creditor, hypothec designates that the object remained in the possession of the debtor. The creditor has the right to seize this property only if the loan was not paid. Only real property could be set as hypothec. Later another type of hypothec was set, namely, that if there was no specification in writing, the creditor could seize any other real property.

The different principles underlying these aspects of Talmudic jurisprudence demonstrate the historical, sociological, and economic backgrounds of the legal institutions of property possession.

397. Prolegomenon to Gerald Friedlander's *The Jewish Sources of the Sermon on the Mount,* Ktav Publishing House, New York, (November 1969).

Here is a review of the problems of the historical Jesus, the trial before the State Synedrion (not the Bet Din ha-Gadol) and the Sermon itself which has been regarded as the manifesto of Christianity, the charter of its ethical teachings. Friedlander's book is a catechism of apologetics aiming to prove the superiority of Pharisaic teachings over the Sermon. It is uncritical, for its disregards the historical background of the citations. Rabban Johanan ben Zakkai never had a controversy with the Sadducees about the Festival of Weeks or about laws pertaining to inheritance. (See no. 341.)

The Sermon on the Mount itself is a conglomeration, with contradictions. As recorded in Matthew and Luke it is a product of the first part of the second century. In its analysis, comparison should be made with the parallel teachings of the Sages. There is also need to explain the Beatitudes (אשרי) and the mode of observance of the Torah and Prophets by the followers of Jesus.

Contrary to the nonrealistic sentiments in the Sermon, the Rabbis taught, realistically, the discipline of *teshubah*. In the matter of divorce the Sermon followed the conservative school of Shammai. The admonition "not to swear" was also widespread among the Sages. (Cf., no. 74.)

Jesus' words "love your enemy" are neither biblical nor realistic, in contradistinction to Hillel's principle "not to harm a fellow man."

The many inconsistencies in the New Testament show that the passages are not from the same writer. Jesus' conduct at Capernaum is contrary to his own teachings.

The Synoptic Gospels refer to synagogues only as a place of assembly or as a house of study, rather than to one of prayer. Jesus only taught at Capernaum. He prayed in the open, not in a synagogue building; the reference to prayer in a synagogue in the Sermon on the Mount is a later interpolation. Prayer at first was aloud, even as Jesus cried aloud. The Rabbis instituted silent prayer. (See no. 157.)

The Apostolic Fathers had no knowledge of the Lord's Prayer.

Terms like "Gehenna," "synagogue," "Mammon" came into use much later.

The dialogue between Trypho and Justin Martyr is not actual; it is only a composition of repetitious arguments.

Goyim in the Talmud refers to pagans, not to Christians.

Jews do not seek to engage in polemics or dialogue. The basic need is to present the accurate historical background of Judaism at the time of the "Parting of the Ways."

1970

398. "Judaism and Professors of Religion," *JQR*, Vol. LX, No. 3 (January 1970), pp. 187–196.

The notion that Jesus was an Essene (as expressed by Professor Flusser) is erroneous, as is his bizarre translation of Abot 1.10: "Love manual work and hate rabbinism."

There is no reference in rabbinic literature to a custom of releasing a Jewish prisoner on Passover. During the Second Temple era *topos*, "place," was applied to the Temple. After the Destruction, the term *Makom*, "place," became a cipher for God. The term "power" in the Gospels is only a translation of *geburah*, another cipher for God. (See no. 74.)

It is vital that one distinguish between those portions in the Talmud which are historical and those which are legendary. Historical research should not be based on theological and christological interpretations.

Support for different views about Jesus when taken from Martin Buber and Sigmund Freud bear no historical value. Incorporating Christian thoughts in Jewish theology distorts Judaism, as is also the attempt to show a relationship beween "Christ, Hasidim, and Gnosis" [sic].

The newly created faculties in universities, as well as Jewish-Christian dialogues, only display the present poverty of Jewish historical knowledge.

398a. "A Note," *JQR*, Vol. LX, No. 3 (January 1970), pp. 229–230.

JQR welcomes all views regarding the Scrolls but insists that historical discipline be used. There has been thus far no substantiation that the Scrolls are Essene, nor has there been refutation of the strong arguments that they are Karaitic.

399. "The Origin of the term Edom for Rome and the Roman Church," *JQR*, Vol. LX, No. 3 (January 1970), pp. 262–263.

The use of the term "Edom" for Rome was introduced at the time that the Church forbade the observance of Easter on the 14th of Nisan. It did not allow the Sanhedrin to meet to fix the calendar, but this was done surreptitiously. The Rabbis intercalated the month of Ab, though usually Adar was intercalated. To conceal their action, they used a code (in Sanh. 12a), based on the verse in Jer. 49:17: "and Edom shall be a desolation."

400. שוב: על הסיקריקין ומצדה, *Bitzaron*, Vol. LXI, No. 3 [283], Shevat–Adar 5730 (Jan.–Feb. 1970), pp. 100–105.

The Sicarii were misguided idealists; they did not defend Masada. With unabated zeal against any rule they brought the downfall of

Judaea, not being concerned with its independence. They did not battle, as did those in Gamala. Their suicide does not portray heroism. (See no. 353.)

There was no High Priest named "Akavia" in the Second Temple era. כהנא רבא was a medieval title.

Josephus presents a definite list of High Priests who served from Herod's period till the Destruction. In the Talmud, the term כהן גדול is often applied in a haggadic fashion, as to R. Eleazar ben Ḥarsum (Yoma 35a) or to Issachar of Kfar Barkai (Keritot 28b), or to R. Ishmael ben Elisha (Echah Rabba 4:4). All of these men were not "High Priests."

Only those specifically called High Priests in the books of Josephus served in that capacity. He often uses their Greek, not Hebrew names, such as Hyrcanus. (He is Johanan, the High Priest, in the Talmud.) The title "High Priest" was not given to a member of the high priestly family or to the "segan," the deputy of the high priesthood.

401. "Eighty Years of the *Jewish Quarterly Review,*" *JQR,* Vol. LX, No. 4 (April 1970), pp. 271–274. (See also no. 366.)

A review of the nature, perspectives and policies of *JQR* in promoting genuine scholarship. (See reprint given *infra* in *Postscript.*)

402. קורות בית שני, כרך ב׳, הוצאת ספרים מ. ניומן בע״מ, ירושלים, סיון תש״ל, Hebrew translation of Volume II of *The Rise and Fall of the Judaean State.* (See nos. 362, 384.)

403. התפתחות הלוח העברי (סקירה כללית). *Hadoar,* Vol. XLIX, No. 38 (2201), 9 Tishri 5731 (October 9, 1970), pp. 710–712.

A survey of the development of the Jewish calendar and its changes in various eras, presented as a rebuttal to the strictures against the article of S. B. Hoenig in *Hadoar,* Vol. XL, No. 24 (2187), May 8, 1970 (2 Iyar 5730), pp. 410–411.

The calendar of the First Temple was a solar one, the day beginning at dawn. The Sabbath may have started in the evening as did the Day of Atonement. The Book of Jubilees, however, records the Sabbath as beginning at sunrise.

There was no separate year of Jubilee in the First Temple era; with the change of the calendar the Jubilee year could no more be counted.

The comments of Ibn Ezra and Rashban on the Jewish reckoning of the start of the 24-hour period of the day, as related to the texts of the observance of the Sabbath,and cognate tannaitic and amoraic material in the Tractates Pesaḥim and Rosh Ha-shanah, are analyzed. Further light is cast on the nature of the Jubilee year and its dissolution, demonstrating that in biblical days the Jubilee year was incorporated into the last *Shemittah* year of the seven *Septennial* cycles.

Interpretation of biblical texts according to their actual meaning does not clash with the *halakhah* and mode of practice set by the Rabbis in later generations. During the Second Temple era and later, the Jewish calendar became a lunar-solar one. The day begins with the evening before. (Cf. nos. 28, 35, 114, 137, 154, 257, 290, 306.)

404. תשובתו בצדו, *Bitzaron,* Vol. LXII, Tishri 5731 (October 1970), No. 1 (287), pp. 25–29. Reply to H. Orlan's historical notions written in *Hadoar* and *Bitzaron.*

Josephus gives the precise periods of the High Priests in their office. Those high Priests bearing the title "Rabbi" are legendary and not authentic; the title came into vogue only after the Destruction.

Though the Talmud mentions Joshua ben Gamala as High Priest in the time of Alexander Jannai, the exact reference is to Agrippa II. The Talmud often uses the name "Alexander Jannai" to designate a Second Temple monarch.

The story of R. Ishmael ben Elisha as High Priest is legendary. (As for the term often being applied in a haggadic fashion, see no. 400.)

Josephus mentions six High Priests appointed by Agrippa II. Issachar of Kfar Barkai is not listed.

Joshua ben Sappha was not a High Priest. He was only the son (*filius*) of one of the High Priests, as indicated in the Latin text of Josephus prepared before the 10th century and which is superior in many ways to our oldest extant Josephus text in Greek rendition (late 10th century).

Josephus was very particular about his use of the term High Priest and did not apply it to any person who did not actually hold that office.

The title "Rabbi" was given to Ḥaninah (*segan ha-kohanim*), the Deputy of the priests, and to Zadok because they flourished also *after* the year 70 C.E. In fact, in the entire literature of the Second Commonwealth—the writings of Josephus, the Apocrypha, Philo, and early tannaitic literature before the Destruction—the title "Rabbi" is nowhere to be found. The title is anachronistic in the Gospels (the Gospels of Mark and Matthew having been written about 70 C.E., the Gospel of Luke later, while that of John still later, after 100 C.E.).

The Sicarii in Masada were not heroes; theirs is an inglorious chapter in Jewish annals.

ADDITIONAL WRITINGS, SOON TO APPEAR

405. שמיטת קרקעות וכספים בזמן בית שני ותקופת התנאים. *Brit Ivrit Olamit* Volume, Jerusalem.

406. *The Book of Judith,* edited from the Greek by Morton S. Enslin and dedicated to the memory of Abba Hillel Silver. Introduction by Professor S. Zeitlin.

This is the seventh volume in the Dropsie University *Jewish Apocryphal Literature Series,* of which S. Zeitlin is Editor-in-Chief (see no. 181).

POSTSCRIPT

POSTSCRIPT

EIGHTY YEARS OF THE *JEWISH QUARTERLY REVIEW*

(Reprint from *JQR,* Vol. LX, No. 4 (April 1970) pp. 271–274.)

By SOLOMON ZEITLIN

Dropsie University

This number concludes the eightieth year of the *Jewish Quarterly Review.* It was inaugurated in England by I. Abrahams and C. G. Montefiore, who were the editors. This number concludes the sixtieth year of its publication by Dropsie College. The first number of the New Series of the *Quarterly* appeared in July, 1910, under the editorship of Cyrus Adler, President of the College, and Solomon Schechter, President of the Jewish Theological Seminary. After the death of Schechter, in 1915, Cyrus Adler became sole editor of the *Quarterly.* The silent editor of the *Quarterly* was Prof. Max L. Margolis.

The *Jewish Quarterly Review* is the oldest Jewish scholarly magazine which continues to appear regularly four times a year. It has served as a vehicle for scholars, Jewish and Christian, to present the fruit of their researches in the fields of Judaism and the beginnings of Christianity,—Bible, Intertestamental Literature, Rabbinics, History, Philosophy, Philology, Mediaeval literature.

When the *Jewish Quarterly Review* was established in America there were scholarly quarterlies being published in Europe. In Germany there was the *Monatsschrift für Geschichte und Wissenschaft des Judentums,* and in France the *Revue des Études Juives.*

When the *Quarterly* was inaugurated in America there were three schools of Jewish learning in America, Dropsie College, the Hebrew Union College and the Jewish Theological Seminary. The first volumes of the New Series of the *Quarterly* were written by members of the faculties of these institutions. At that time there were chairs in Semitics in different universities. Many scholars of the Semitic departments contributed articles to the *Quarterly,*—to mention a few,—H. Wolfson, G. F. Moore, C. Torrey, J. A. Montgomery, E. Goodenough, R. Pfeiffer and many other distinguished scholars. There were also contributions from many distinguished scholars from Europe. When the Yeshiva University was organized members of the faculty contributed articles. It was the principle of the editorship to publish articles on their merit alone, regardless of the religious affiliation of the contributors and their theological thinking.

When Dr. Adler died in April 1940 I assumed the responsibility of the editorship of the *Quarterly*. (After the passing of Prof. Margolis in 1932 I became silent editor.)

This issue concludes thirty years of my editorship of the *Quarterly.* (My association with the *Quarterly* began in April, 1917.) They were challenging years. During the thirty years of my editorship I endeavored to maintain its high standard of scholarship. The *Quarterly* appeared four times a year. It is true that during the past ten years it did not appear regularly, being always delayed. This was due to the fact that it is published in Holland and there were difficulties in communication and transportation.

With this issue I relieve myself of the honor and the great privilege of being Editor of the *Jewish Quarterly Review.* I believe I have been a devoted servant of true scholarship. I take this occasion to express my appreciation and gratitude to the contributors who sent their articles to the *Quarterly* which enriched scholarship. I wish to thank the host of readers, some of whom did not always agree with my views, but from their correspondence I became aware that they impatiently awaited the publication of the *Quarterly.* I wish also to express my gratitude to Dr. Abraham A. Neuman for his assistance and encouragement. Henceforth the editorship will be in the hands of spirited men deeply devoted to scholarship.

The members of the Board of Editors are the following scholars: Irving A. Agus, Robert Gordis, Solomon Grayzel, Sidney B. Hoenig, Abraham I. Katsh, Leon Nemoy, Harry M. Orlinsky, Ellis Rivkin, and Esra Shereshevsky, who is to be Managing Editor. I have consented to be Chairman of the Board. With the exception of two, the members of the Board are former students of mine. I am confident that they will continue the long tradition of the *Quarterly,* its high standard in scholarship and its integrity.

In accepting articles for the *Quarterly* the editors must judge them on their merits. The contributions must have a distinct point of view although it may not be the generally accepted view. The ideas expressed in the *Quarterly* cannot always flow with the stream but may run counter to the current. The publication of controversial articles should not be shunned since such articles stimulate both scholars and intelligent laymen. In accepting articles care must be exercised to see that the contributors have utilized the sources upon which they have based their views. Articles based on translations and second hand literature and encyclopedias should not find a place in the *Quarterly.* Such articles would lower the scholarly standing of the *Jewish Quarterly Review.* The editors must be on their guard as custodians of genuine scholarship.

As mentioned previously, the thirty years of my editorship of the *Quarterly* were challenging. My elder colleagues, Jews and Christians, gave me great encouragement and readily contributed articles which enriched scholarship. The *Quarterly* is the only Jewish scholarly journal whose contributors are Jews and Christians. My aim was that the *Quarterly* should attract young men to engage in scholarship and that it should serve as a medium to give expression to their thoughts and publish the results of their researches. I feel that my aim was fulfilled to a great extent. Some young men, under my guidance, published in the *Quarterly* the results of their researches which were contributions to scholarship. This was gratifying to me.

There were disillusionments. In the last twenty years many colleges, theological seminaries and universities established departments and chairs for the study of Judaism for which their boards of directors and the presidents should be congratulated. Many young people were attracted to these courses. Ph.D. theses multiplied. We must note that some professors called to occupy the Chairs for the study of Judaism were not well equipped. Certain young Ph.D.'s sent chapters of their theses to the *Quarterly.* It was disheartening to note the superficiality and the lack of knowledge displayed, particularly in the fields of rabbinics and history. We ascribe this to the fact that the professors were not well versed in these literatures and the students did not receive the proper guidance.

Some of my reviews were quite severe in tone. Instead of analyzing the contributions which the authors made I have had to record flagrant errors, which were due to the authors' lack of knowledge and the usage of second hand literature and encyclopedias. In my criticism I followed the axiom: *Amicus Plato sed magis amica veritas.* I did not hesitate to criticize the works of known personalities whom I ordinarily respected. I am firmly of the opinion that works which are superficial and show lack of knowledge of the sources are dangerous to genuine scholarship. Intelligent laymen may be deceived by such works.

My strong criticism of the views propagated that the Dead Sea Scrolls are of the pre-Christian period was not directed against any scholar. I am strongly of the opinion that the scholars who propagated the view that the Scrolls are of the period of the Second Jewish Commonwealth, the glorification of the Sicarii, and the findings in Masada, are distorting and falsifying Jewish history.

The *Jewish Quarterly Review* has been a citadel for true scholarship and it is my hope that it will continue to serve as a beacon for enlightenment and growth of genuine scholarship.

CITATIONS

THE DROPSIE COLLEGE
FOR HEBREW AND COGNATE LEARNING
PHILADELPHIA

C I T A T I O N

SOLOMON ZEITLIN, Professor of Rabbinic Literature in this College; colleague and friend.

You are an illustrious son of this College which conferred upon you the degree of Doctor of Philosophy in course. Your writings are marked by originality of thought, keen historic penetration and the courage to battle valiantly for the truth as you see it.

Your combined knowledge to an extraordinary degree of rabbinic, hellenistic and patristic literature has established for you a world-wide reputation as the leading authority on the Second Jewish Commonwealth covering a portentous period in the evolution of the religious forces of Judaism and Christianity.

By a unanimous vote of the Faculty of this College, approved by a unanimous vote of the Board of Governors, we gladly admit you to the Degree of Doctor of Laws, honoris causa, and declare that you are entitled to all the Honors, Rights and Privileges to that Degree appertaining. In token whereof, I hand you this diploma.

May 22, 1957

ABRAHAM A. NEUMAN
President

HEBREW UNION COLLEGE

=JEWISH INSTITUTE OF RELIGION

Solomon Zeitlin

Scholar, teacher and editor - whose many writings have splendidly covered the highways and byways of our past - whose sense of method and spirited interpretation guided many of his students to creative scholarship - whose vigor and convictions shine in each issue of the learned journal he so effectively edits.

By virtue of the authority vested in me as President of the Hebrew Union College-Jewish Institute of Religion I confer upon you the Degree of

DOCTOR OF HEBREW LETTERS, Honoris Causa

New York, New York
June 7, 1964

Nelson Glueck
President

YESHIVA UNIVERSITY

Citation

by

DR. SAMUEL BELKIN

President

in

conferring the honorary degree of

DOCTOR OF HUMANE LETTERS

upon

DR. SOLOMON ZEITLIN

34th Annual Commencement Exercises

Tuesday, June 15, 1965

YOU ARE MASTER OF THE COMPLETE RANGE OF SACRED AND SECULAR JEWISH LITERATURE. AS THE AUTHOR OF MONUMENTAL WORKS ON THE HISTORY OF THE SECOND JEWISH COMMONWEALTH, YOU HAVE STIMULATED RESEARCH THROUGHOUT THE GLOBE. AS AN INSPIRING TEACHER, YOU ARE BELOVED BY YOUR DISCIPLES. FOR YOUR INTELLECTUAL HONESTY AND FOR YOUR DEVOTION TO BASIC RESEARCH, YOU ARE ADMIRED BY YOUR COLLEAGUES. WE ARE PROUD THAT MANY OF YOUR FORMER STUDENTS OCCUPY IMPORTANT ACADEMIC POSITIONS AT OUR UNIVERSITY.

IN APPRECIATION FOR YOUR GREAT CONTRIBUTIONS TO JEWISH SCHOLARSHIP, WE DEEM IT A PRIVILEGE TO CONFER UPON YOU THE DEGREE OF DOCTOR OF HUMANE LETTERS, HONORIS CAUSA.

IN TOKEN THEREOF, I CAUSE TO BE PLACED OVER YOUR SHOULDERS THE VISIBLE SYMBOL OF OUR HIGH REGARD FOR YOU, AND I HAND YOU THIS DIPLOMA.

INDEX OF SUBJECTS

INDEX OF SUBJECTS

(*Numbers denote the bibliographical item.*)

H

I

ADDENDA

SELECTED LIST OF HEBREW EXPRESSIONS

(*Numbers denote the bibliographical item.*)

ת

SELECTED LIST OF GREEK AND LATIN EXPRESSIONS

(Numbers denote the bibliographical item.)

SELECTED LIST OF TEXTS DISCUSSED

(Numbers denote the bibliographical item.)

SELECTED LIST OF MODERN AUTHORS NOTED

(Numbers denote the bibliographical item.)